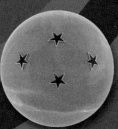

# The Overstreet® Guide to
# COLLECTING VIDEO GAMES

## BY CARRIE WOOD

RAE CARRA
KURT KALATA
ZANNE NILSSON
ROBERT M. OVERSTREET
CONTRIBUTING WRITERS

MARK HUESMAN
LAYOUT & DESIGN

MARK HUESMAN
AMANDA SHERIFF
J.C. VAUGHN
CARRIE WOOD
EDITORS

TOM GAREY, KATHY WEAVER
BRETT CANBY, ANGELA PHILLIPS-MILLS
ACCOUNTING SERVICES

SPECIAL THANKS TO
DIAMOND INTERNATIONAL GALLERIES,
HAKE'S AMERICANA AND COLLECTIBLES, ERIK HOLNIKER,
JAY JACKSONRAO, DENIZ KAHN, JAKE MARINO, BRETT MARTIN,
RE:GEN, THE VIDEO GAME MEMORABILIA MUSEUM,
AND HUCK RAJ TALWAR

GEMSTONE PUBLISHING • TIMONIUM, MARYLAND
WWW.GEMSTONEPUB.COM

If you're a longtime Overstreet fan, *The Overstreet Guide To Collecting Video Games* might not be the first thing that would pop into your mind. That could well change after you read this book. The market for collectible vintage video games may only be in its infancy, but it's growing rapidly, is getting organized, and has many passionate, devoted, serious fans. As they are coming together, it reminds me of the early days of comic book collecting that spawned *The Overstreet Comic Book Price Guide*.

There are still many to whom collecting video games might seem odd, but for the most part they just haven't stopped to consider how long video games have been around. Not only have the games and game systems themselves become highly sought after, but so have various related items as well. As it has been in just about every field, nostalgia may be the first impulse that makes older material collectible, but markets rarely develop solely from nostalgia. Our old friends supply and demand seem to always get into the mix as well. We've had video games for decades now. It's really only natural that things have evolved to the point where this book was a must.

Carrie Wood, our assistant editor and the driving force behind this volume, was also one of the guiding lights behind *The Overstreet Guide To Cosplay*. While she is versed in many different areas of collecting, her understanding of the video game market, the collectors, and the games themselves made her a nearly perfect candidate to do this book.

What she and her team of writers and our team at Gemstone Publishing have done is nothing short of amazing. They've showcased the developers, the systems, the games and more in a way that makes the hobby incredibly accessible. They've also managed to do this in a way that might well make experienced gamers and collectors think about things differently.

As always, let us know what you think.

Robert M. Overstreet
Publisher

**GEMSTONE PUBLISHING**

**STEPHEN A. GEPPI**
PRESIDENT AND
CHIEF EXECUTIVE OFFICER

**ROBERT M. OVERSTREET**
PUBLISHER

**J.C. VAUGHN**
VICE-PRESIDENT
OF PUBLISHING

**MARK HUESMAN**
CREATIVE DIRECTOR

**AMANDA SHERIFF**
ASSOCIATE EDITOR

**CARRIE WOOD**
ASSISTANT EDITOR

**BRAELYNN BOWERSOX**
STAFF WRITER

WWW.GEMSTONEPUB.COM

**GEPPI'S ENTERTAINMENT MUSEUM**

**STEPHEN A. GEPPI**
FOUNDER AND
CHIEF EXECUTIVE OFFICER

**MELISSA BOWERSOX**
PRESIDENT

WWW.GEPPISMUSEUM.COM

THE OVERSTREET GUIDE TO COLLECTING VIDEO GAMES. JANUARY 2017.
ISBN: 978-1-60360-200-6
PUBLISHED BY GEMSTONE PUBLISHING, INC., 1940 GREENSPRING DRIVE, SUITE I, TIMONIUM, MD 21093.

# TABLE OF CONTENTS

# INTRODUCTION

Video games have been a part of my life for as long as my memory can reach. As a small kid, I got to play on my mother's old Atari 2600 and had a tendency to negotiate for an extra half-hour's worth of play time on games like *Frogger* and *Breakout*.

Many of my childhood friends had consoles that I didn't: the girls across the street who had a Sega Genesis, who I'd play *Sonic the Hedgehog 2* with; the girls around the corner with the Super Nintendo who would let me have a go at *Kirby Super Star*; the brother and sister in the house behind us with a Nintendo 64 who I vainly attempted to defeat at *Super Smash Bros.*; the boy down the street with the PlayStation who took turns with me as we tried to finish *Spyro the Dragon* together.

Though my parents never bought me a more contemporary home console for fear that I'd never leave the house again (and they were probably right), they caved and compromised on a handheld when *Pokémon* came out and I wouldn't shut up about it. I have a very distinct memory of my mother taking me to the department store, getting to pick out my Game Boy Color and *Pokémon Red*, and playing it that night until I could barely keep my eyes open anymore.

What my parents originally believed to be a phase or a fad – or perhaps simply hoped against hope that it would be – has been a major part of my life since then. From my first handheld *Legend of Zelda* quest, to daydreaming of *Golden Sun* in middle school, to exploring the vast clouds in *Skies of Arcadia*, to diving into the deepest dungeons of *Skyrim*, gaming has been interwoven in my everyday life for nearly 20 years now. And clearly the same holds true for millions of other people around the world.

I believed that this book was a necessary addition to Gemstone's overall "How-To" line of books because of how video games have so obviously grown from a niche market to a form of everyday multimedia. Video games and their related merchandise are as collectible as comic books, movie memorabilia or sports collectibles. And the people who do so are just as passionate about their collections as anyone else in any other collecting hobby. Though video games are relatively young compared to comic books or the sort, that fact alone doesn't make gaming collections any less legitimate.

This book examines not just the history of video games, but also three major types of collecting in this hobby: by franchise, by console, and by developer. We also have some wildly informative interviews on arcade cabinets and pinball machines, and on game-related merchandise and how to avoid fakes. On top of that, we've got a really great report on some of the most valuable games on the market right now. It is my sincere hope that this guide will aid seasoned collectors as much as it helps newcomers to game collecting.

I must express my gratitude towards our Vice-President of Publishing J.C. Vaughn, who believed that this project was a good idea from the start. This book is also the result of the efforts of everyone involved, including my cohorts at Gemstone Publishing, Mark Huesman (Creative Director) and Amanda Sheriff (Associate Editor). I also want to thank my contributing writers – Rae Carra, Kurt Kalata, and Zanne Nilsson – who did an incredible amount of work in researching and reporting for this project.

And finally, I want to thank my parents, who – even though they might not have understood everything – at least supported my interest, whether by driving me to the store or outright buying me a new game for the holidays. (Or, in my mom's case, suffering through the second *Pokémon* film in theaters for my sake.)

I hope that those of you who have picked up this book find it useful, engaging and informative. It's been an absolute joy and privilege to get to work on this, and I hope to expand the knowledge from this edition with further volumes.

Game on!

*- Carrie Wood*

# VIDEO GAME HISTORY

To really understand the value of video games today, you have to put them in perspective. This chapter provides a look at the history of this popular hobby, which has gone from a small, nerdy niche hobby to one of the most widespread, popular and financially profitable forms of mass media today.

But the history of gaming might go much further back than you may realize.

Gaming didn't start with the arrival of Pong or with the Golden Age of video arcades, nor did it begin with the first home consoles. You may be surprised to learn that the earliest examples of what we would certainly classify as a "video game" started as far back as World War II.

The latest technology advances seem to be coming and going faster than ever before, which has certainly taken things to a whole new level. But while we may be excited for powerful processors and the first steps into virtual reality, it's important to look back and see where this wonderful hobby got started.

# The Early History of Gaming

## By Carrie Wood

Though common knowledge might place the beginning of video gaming in the 1980s arcade scene, or with the first *Pong* home editions, the history of video games actually goes back much farther than that. The technical definition of the term "video game" would require the game to have a video signal transmitted through a cathode ray tube – though the current interpretation is more along the lines of "anything on electronic hardware that contains an element of interactivity," or something along those lines. Using this broad definition, the first video games actually surfaced in the 1950s, using technology created during World War II.

The earliest known written computer game was a chess simulation, developed by none other than Alan Turing (the man behind the cracking of the Enigma Machine and the Turing Test) and

**Alan Turing**

David Champernowne (a mathematician and economist at the University of Oxford and later at Cambridge). The game was called *Turochamp* and the pair completed it in 1948, but it never actually made it to a proper computer.

As far as games that were actually implemented, the earliest one was *Bertie the Brain*, a tic-tac-toe machine built by Josef Kates for the 1950 Canadian National Exhibition; and *Nimrod*, built in 1951 by Ferranti for that year's Festival of Britain, which played the game of Nim. Both *Bertie* and *Nimrod* allowed people who attended their respective events to play their games against an artificial intelligence (AI). They were created not so much for the purpose of entertainment, but rather for the purpose of showing off the AI programs that the developers had created.

*Tennis for Two*, devel-

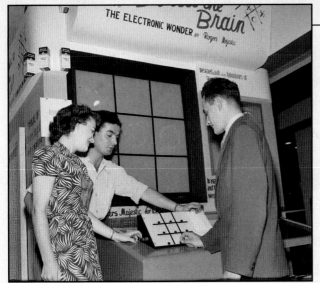

ers at the Massachusetts Institute of Technology. *Spacewar!* pits two players against each other in spaceships as they attempt to destroy one another while also navigating within the gravity well of a star. Each ship has a limited number of missiles as well as limited fuel, and must shoot at the other ship without getting sucked into the star. The first operational version of the game was finished in 1962, but the game wasn't truly complete until April of that year. The game proved popular in the 1960s and was recreated on other computer systems; it would be ported to many other consoles throughout the 1970s and 1980s.

oped at the Brookhaven National Laboratory in 1958, was the first game created for entertainment purposes. It used an analog computer and an oscilloscope to play the game, and was therefore one of the first games to have a proper graphic display. It debuted at an open house on October 18, 1958, and was brought out just once more after that before it was dismantled. It's generally considered the predecessor to *Pong*.

A few years later, *Spacewar!* was programmed by Steve Russell and others at his fictional "Hingham Institute" with the goal of implementing it on comput-

By the early 1970s, computing had evolved to the point where it was slowly becoming more affordable for companies – though still significantly too expensive for home use, it was at the point where coin-operated video game machines were becoming a reality. When Nolan Bushnell, an engineering graduate from Utah, saw *Spacewar!*, he sought to create a coin-operated version for the public. Working with fellow engineer Ted Dabney, they

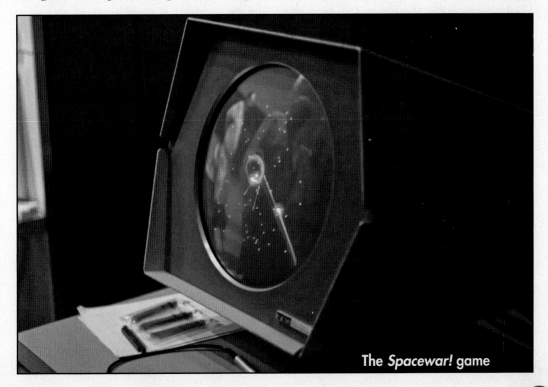

The *Spacewar!* game

## The Magnavox Odyssey console

created *Computer Space* in 1971. *Computer Space* varied the *Spacewar!* gameplay by pitting a single player against two AI flying saucers. Though it was a commercial failure, *Computer Space* marks the first commercially-released video game.

Meanwhile, Ralph Baer – who had spent years as an engineer for multiple defense contractors – had been plugging away at a video game system that would operate with a standard television set since the mid-1960s. Baer had been working on technology (diode-transistor logic circuits, mainly) that would generate images on screen that could be controlled by the person playing. By 1971, he had finished work on what would become the Magnavox Odyssey, the very first home video gaming console.

The Magnavox Odyssey released in September of 1972, though it was harshly limited game-wise by its limited processing power, which could only render three dots and a line at any given time. The graphics were actually defined by plastic screens attached to the television itself. Though the console (similar to *Computer Space* before it) didn't perform well, it managed to influence the birth of the arcade industry, with Baer's design ideas crossing paths with Bushnell's business ideas.

Bushnell and Dabney also founded Atari in '72, and after seeing the Magnavox console, struck out in an attempt to emulate its design. Al Alcorn had been hired that year, and the company charged him with recreating the Magnavox's games. The result was *Pong*,

computing systems were on the rise, and they gained their own unique games throughout the 1970s. However, many computers were using teletypes rather than monitors, and even other types of terminals were only able to render character-based graphics. Because of this, most computer games of the period were strategy or puzzle-based. The most significant game of this era was probably *Colossal Cave Adventure*, released in 1976. The game, also known colloquially as just *Adventure*, borrowed many elements from the then-newly-released *Dungeons and Dragons*, and is considered the most notable precursor to the entire role-playing game genre of video games.

Computer games would become significantly more popular with the arrival of the Commodore 64 in 1982, which had rather advanced graphical and audio capabilities for its time. It also allowed for people to use their Atari 2600 controllers with the system, helping it to become the most popular home computer of its era (and the best-selling single computer model of all time). Apple's Macintosh also came out, and while it lacked the color of the popular Apple II, it attracted developers due to the better operating system support. Other popular models around this time included the Atari ST and the Commodore Amiga.

which reached the mass market in March of 1973 and absolutely ignited the coin-operated game industry. The year it released, it sold about 70,000 units.

For the rest of the 1970s, the coin-operated gaming industry was somewhat up and down. Market saturation impacted sales, and though some companies attempted "cocktail table" variants of the machines, those never really took off. That said, there were some early arcade hits, including *Tank* and *Gran Track 10* from Atari; Midway also emerged during this decade with games like *Gun Fight* and *Wheels*.

The rise in popularity of video games – as well as of solid-state pinball machines – helped to solidify arcades as a trendy spot, which in turn increased the number of arcades. The growth of shopping malls during this period of time also included the growth of arcades; parents would often leave their children in the arcade areas while they went elsewhere to shop in the malls. Arcades were a mainstay of the mall scene by the end of the '70s.

Console-wise, as mentioned, the Magnavox Odyssey didn't catch on in the mass market, primarily due to its primitive technology. However, by the middle of the '70s, Atari had created a home version of *Pong*. They released the system through Sears in 1975, and later published it themselves the following year. By 1977 the dedicated *Pong* systems (and clones of it by other companies) had sold close to 6 million units in the United States.

In the arcades and at home, fast-paced action was the norm, and most popular games involved target shooting or racing of some sort. Meanwhile, home

**The Commodore 64**

The video game scene in the United States was aided greatly by the rise of arcade technology in Japan at this time. *Breakout* was a huge hit in Japan, and the company Taito helped create tabletop units, which became popular in restaurants and snack bars. Taito was also responsible for *Space Invaders* (which would be distributed in North America by Midway), a game that helped introduce many basic gaming concepts such as a "life" system, gaining extra lives through points scored, and high score tracking. *Space Invaders* was also the first game to have background music of any kind, though it was a simple four notes. In Japan, more than 200,000 *Space Invader*-like games (including knockoffs) were in arcades by the middle of '79, and in America, 60,000 cabinets were moved. The American arcade scene was also helped with the arrival of Atari's *Asteroids* in 1979, which alone moved another 70,000 cabinets.

The competitive nature of high score systems helped draw players away from pinball machines and onto the video game cabinets, and the period of time between 1978 and 1982 is retroactively considered the "Golden Age" of arcades for this reason. Most of the biggest arcade hits were released during this time, such as *Defender* (1980), *Missile Command* (1980), *Galaga* (1981), *Tempest* (1981), *Donkey Kong* (1981), and *Q*bert* (1982). By far and wide the single biggest hit was 1980's *Pac-Man*, which sold 96,000 units alone; *Pac-Man* also

was the first of many games to feature an identifiable mascot character, which helped spur many *Pac-Man* related toys outside the gaming realm.

Revenue jumped spectacularly in the arcades during these four years. In 1978, coin-operated video game revenue was $308 million – by 1982, it was a $8.9 billion dollar industry. The number of arcades in the U.S. also more than doubled, from about 10,000 in '81 to over 25,000 in '83.

Though Atari released their Atari 2600 console in 1977, they didn't really take off in the home console market until the early 1980s. Their breakthrough was when they released a home version of *Space Invaders* in 1980, which helped their sales explode in '80 and '81. The company further released home versions of other popular arcade hits such as *Missile Command*, *Asteroids* and *Defender*. By 1981, Atari held a commanding 65 percent share of the home video game market – other companies, such as Mattel, Magnavox and Fairchild, fell far behind. Though Atari released an advanced version of their console, the Atari 5200, in '82, it failed to perform as well as the 2600. Coleco also released their ColecoVision by the 1982 holiday season, but soon found themselves in a market that would prove unsustainable.

Activision also got started around this time. A group of four Atari programmers sought greater recognition for their games, and struck out in 1979 to form what would be the first third-party game development company. They had a string of hits in the early 1980s that included *Kaboom!, River Raid* and *Pitfall* that helped establish them as a game development force despite not creating any hardware of their own.

Handheld gaming was also available for the first time by the early 1980s, thanks to Milton Bradley's Microvision and Nintendo's Game and Watch. The Game and Watch ended up being more successful (and influential) due to more reliable games and better battery life.

However, things came to a screeching halt for video gaming in 1983 when the industry completely crashed in North America. Many companies went bankrupt, while others, such as Magnavox and Coleco, just abandoned the gaming industry entirely. Activision managed to survive thanks to their developing games for the surviving home computer market while game consoles flopped.

There were many factors that caused the industry crash. The rising competition from the home computer market meant that many consumers were simply not interested in making a home console purchase anymore.

The console market itself was also completely oversaturated. At the time of the crash in late '83, consoles available included: the Atari 2600, the Atari 5200, the Bally Astrocade, the ColecoVision, the Coleco Gemini, the Fairchild Channel F System II, the Magnavox Odyssey 2, the Mattel Intellivision and Intellivision II, the various Sears Tele-Games systems, and the Vectrex. The fact that most of these systems had incredibly poor titles – some of them high-profile, such as the 2600 port of *Pac-Man* and the notoriously bad *E.T. The Extra-Terrestrial* – only added to the problem.

Immediate fallout of the crash included the infamous burial by Atari of many of their over-produced games and consoles in a New Mexico landfill in 1983. Sales also plummeted during this period;

home console sales dropped from about $3 billion in '82 to roughly $100 million in 1985.

However, all was not lost. Japan's gaming industry was more than stable during this period – it was thriving. Companies such as Nintendo and Sega, both run out of Japan with major success in the arcade and console scenes there, suddenly had plenty of room to move into the North American market. And did they ever. Nintendo released their Family Computer system in the United States as the Nintendo Entertainment System in October of 1985 and helped restart the floundering American console market.

By the end of the 1980s, Nintendo sold more than 35 million NES units in the United States, completely dominating the market. The home console market in general reached annual sales figures close to $5 billion, completely exceeding its previous high point in the early '80s. Most importantly, Nintendo did everything they could to prevent another crash. They implemented a strict overseeing of third-party development, which helped to avoid the many low-quality console titles that killed the market in the first place.

The 8-bit generation was truly underway at this time. As the 1990s got started, it was a time of incredibly fast technical advancement, which continued throughout the decade.

Nintendo's NES system

# Into the 1990s

### By Carrie Wood

The 1980s came to a close with Nintendo having a total stranglehold on the home gaming console market, thanks to the 35 million Nintendo Entertainment System/Famicom units they had moved worldwide by the end of the decade. The tail-end of the '80s also featured the introduction of the company's *Nintendo Power* magazine, as well as their first handheld system, the legendary grey-brick Game Boy.

The 8-bit era of gaming – called as such because of the 8-bit processors in the machines – also included machines such as the Sega Master System (also known as the Sega Mark III), the ZX Spectrum, and the Commodore 64. Notable games released in this time period were Nintendo's *Legend of Zelda*, Enix's *Dragon Quest*, Square's *Final Fantasy*, and Konami's *Metal Gear*. All of these have since become significant franchises in the three-plus decades since their original launch.

As technology continued to improve worldwide, it was reflected in improvements in gaming consoles. The 16-bit era of gaming technically kicked off in 1987 with the TurboGrafx-16's release in Japan; the system released in limited quantities in America in 1990. The TurboGrafx came about because Hudson Soft, part of the manufacturing team, had wanted to sell advanced graphics cards to Nintendo and failed at doing so; they instead partnered with NEC to create the console. It was notable for being the first gaming console to have a CD-ROM peripheral as well as having the first portable counterpart with identical hardware to the console version. It was successful in Japan, at one point becoming the top-selling system in the nation, but failed to make a splash in overseas markets.

The first worldwide success for 16-bit machines arrived with the release of the Sega Genesis, also known as the Sega Mega Drive. The system launched in Japan in

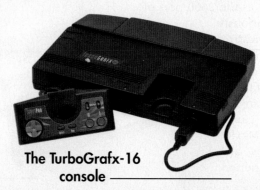

The TurboGrafx-16 console —

October of '88 before arriving in North America in August of the following year. The system's sales were driven by the popularity of the Sega-exclusive title, *Sonic the Hedgehog*, a series which would rival Nintendo's *Super Mario* in many ways for years to come and essentially beginning the first "console war" between the companies.

The rivalry between Sega and Nintendo truly got started when the latter released the Super Nintendo Entertainment System, or SNES, in November 1990 in Japan and in North America in August 1991. Sega was actually able to outsell Nintendo for four holiday seasons in a row, actually outselling the SNES two-to-one during the '91 holiday rush, thanks to the popularity of *Sonic*, which was packed in with the Genesis. Another "killer app" title for the system was the first *John Madden Football*; by January of 1992 Sega had a 65 percent share of the 16-bit console market, marking the first time that Nintendo was not the console leader in the market since the NES's launch.

Sega's advertising also contributed to its success during this period, with a "cooler" approach echoing the pop culture of the time, and now-legendary slogans such as "Genesis Does What Nintendon't" used frequently in television and print ads.

Sega also introduced their own handheld device, the Game Gear, in the early 1990s, releasing in Japan in 1990 and in the west in 1991. The Game Gear shared much of its hardware with the Sega Master System and because of that, was able to render full-color graphics and was far technologically superior to Nintendo's Game Boy. However, despite being several years ahead of Nintendo's handheld in terms of pure tech, it suffered from poor battery life and an overall lack of support in terms of

**Sega's Game Gear**

software. The Game Boy wouldn't go full-color until 1998, but the original black-and-white 8-bit edition outpaced any and all of its colorful competition for the majority of the decade.

As far as Nintendo consoles during the early 1990s, the NES continued to sell over its 16-bit counterparts, though the SNES eventually overtook the market by the middle of the decade. Nintendo was in no rush to get another console to the market, seeing as their first one still performed so well against its technologically-superior competition; it wasn't until Sega's systems took off that Nintendo opted to come into the 16-bit market. Neither the Genesis nor the SNES maintained any sort of huge lead for any significant length of time – it wasn't until the release of *Donkey Kong Country* in 1994 that the Super Nintendo took over the market. The SNES also came packed with the popular *Super Mario World*, drawing people away from other potential purchases.

The Super Nintendo console featured a number of peripheral devices, some more successful than others. One of these was the Super Game Boy, an adapter cartridge that allowed for gamers to play their Game Boy titles through the SNES. Beyond the advantages of a significantly larger screen to see the games on, the Super Game Boy also allowed players to substitute

**Super Game Boy adapter cartridge**

the in-game palettes and customize the look of the screen border.

Plus, the SNES's hardware was built as to not become obsolete within just a few years; it was easy for software developers to interface a special chip within the cartridge to display graphics that were supposedly beyond the system's capabilities. The Super FX chip, as it came to be called, provided advanced graphics to the point that 3D structures could be rendered. Its most notable usage was in *Star Fox*, the first game to use polygonal graphics.

Because of this capability, the 16-bit Super Nintendo was able to hold its own even as competitors moved on into 32-bit processing. The SNES became the best-selling console of its era, moving more than 49 million units worldwide during its lifetime. Meanwhile, Sega continued to move forward with new technology, with mixed success.

The Sega Saturn console released around the world between the fall of '94 and summer of '95. Though the company had found worldwide success with the Genesis – thanks to *Sonic the Hedgehog* and the head start on Nintendo – the 32-bit Saturn wouldn't be a repeat of that.

Though its initial launch was pretty successful, thanks to a near-perfect port of the popular arcade fighting game *Virtua Fighter* being a launch title for the system, and it sold out the initial shipment of 200,000 units on the first day. The system eventually exceeded a million sales within the first six months of release. However, interest rapidly declined after the holiday season thanks to stiff competition from both Nintendo and newcomer Sony.

The other big mistake Sega made with the Saturn was the North American release. The original plan was to launch it on "Saturnday," September 2, 1995; however, in a surprise move at the first Electronic Entertainment Expo on May 11 of that year, Sega of America announced that they had already shipped 30,000 units for immediate release at some major gaming retailers. The announcement upset retailers who weren't in on the release, including KB Toys, who responded to it by dropping Sega from their gaming lineup entirely. The Expo also proved disastrous for Sega in general, as after they announced the price of the Saturn at $399 (or $449 with a game), Sony unveiled the PlayStation's US price point. Then-president of Sony Computer Entertainment, Steve Race, famously got on stage, announced the $299 price point of the PlayStation, and walked off stage to applause.

Because of the surprise months-early Saturn launch, American retailers had no time to prepare for the system, its line of games, or to promote anything for it. The Saturn only had six games available for the West at launch as well. The Saturn was praised critically for its technological advancements over the previous generation, though gamers never quite warmed up to the bizarre controller layout it had; it only sold 9.26 million units worldwide, and was discontinued in the US by 1998.

As Sega faltered, a newcomer to the field arrived in the form of Sony and their PlayStation, which arrived worldwide between 1994 and 1995. The console actually came about, ironically enough, because of dealings between Sony and Nintendo. Nintendo had, at one point, approached Sony to develop a CD-ROM add-on for the Super Nintendo, tentatively titled the "Play Station." Sony during this time planned out a SNES-compatible Sony-branded gaming console as well. However, things quickly fell apart between the two companies, as Nintendo President Hiroshi Yamauchi cancelled the plans after he discovered the

**Sony's PlayStation**

contract was heavily in Sony's favor. Sony actually then took their plans to Sega, who shot them down.

Sony still wanted to develop a gaming console, so they moved forward with the PlayStation (now without the space) on their own. After they saw the positive reception to *Virtua Fighter*'s 3D graphics on the Sega Saturn, Sony made those graphics their focus on what they wanted out of their hardware. Thanks to the previously-mentioned successful E3 presentation, hype for the PlayStation was massive in anticipation of its release. The system was an instant success in Japan, moving more than 2 million consoles in the first six months.

The PlayStation was the first successful CD-ROM-based console and was largely responsible for putting cartridge-based systems to rest. CDs allowed for developers to push their games past what would be

console war of the 64-bit era was between the PlayStation and the Nintendo 64. The N64 released in Japan in June of '96, in North America of September of that year, and elsewhere around the world in 1997. Though they largely had to play catch-up to Sony, who got the jump on them in the 64-bit era, Nintendo's popular first-party titles helped to make the system a success.

The Nintendo 64 arrived at a price of just $199 – matching the price of the PlayStation and the Saturn, both of which had already spent time on the market – and was in incredible demand at launch; it outsold both Sony and Sega in 1997, moving more than 3.6 million consoles in its first full year. Nintendo's sales jumped by more than 150 percent during this time. The fact that Nintendo had already dominated the console market meant that, despite the strong showing from newcomer Sony, gamers were largely brand-loyal during this period of time.

allowed by a cartridge, and they were also significantly less costly to produce than cartridges. The appeal of developing on a CD drew major third-party developers away from Nintendo, who maintained cartridges through the 64-bit era, including Square, Enix, and Konami. Major third-party releases on the PlayStation included *Metal Gear Solid* and *Final Fantasy VII*.

As the Saturn struggled, the biggest

The Nintendo 64 was also able to see wild early success thanks to in-house "killer app" titles such as *Super Mario 64, Donkey Kong 64, Super Smash Bros.* and

The Nintendo 64

*The Legend of Zelda: Ocarina of Time* – the last of which is still considered to be one of the single greatest games ever made. However, sales declined as the end of the decade approached, as developers were drawn away from the cartridge-based system of the N64 to the CD capabilities of the PlayStation. The system's total lifetime sales were roughly 33 million – a respectable number, far ahead of Sega, but trailing significantly behind Sony.

**Game Boy Color**

Nintendo's successor to the Game Boy, the Game Boy Color, also arrived during this time, in the fall of 1998. As you can tell by the name, it was their first full-color handheld system and the true sequel to the original grey brick Game Boy (the Game Boy Pocket, a slimmer version of the Game Boy, released in 1996). Though the Game Boy Color had just three launch titles of its own – *Tetris DX, Wario Land II,* and *Pocket Bomberman* – it was bolstered by the fact that it was backwards-compatible with any other previous Game Boy title. The wild popularity of the first *Pokémon* titles played also into the early success of the Game Boy Color, as they were among games that could have a limited color palette displayed on a GBC.

PC gaming during the 1990s also remained strong as computers became faster and more powerful. Many PC titles during the early half of the decade were distributed on floppy discs, giving rise to shareware distribution; companies would put a trial or demo portion of their game on a floppy for just a few dollars so people could try the game before buying it. This practice later gave rise to "demo discs" given away for free in gaming magazines as floppys became less of a viable option for game distribution.

New PC technology included affordable 3D accelerator cards, allowing for more detailed 3D graphics on computers. As genres evolved on consoles, they did the same on PC. Text-based adventures gave rise to graphic-based adventures, such as *Myst,* which also included puzzle elements. Real-time strategy was also popular, and titles such as *Warcraft* and *Starcraft* helped to introduce the world to easy online gaming through the genre. *Quake* was one of the early pioneers of online play in the first-person shooter genre. Meanwhile, coding in general advanced, and browser plug-ins such as Java and Flash gave rise to browser-based gaming.

As the world neared the end of the century, it was a time of incredibly rapid technological advancement that would be reflected in gaming consoles, handhelds, and personal computers.

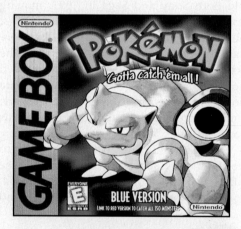

BY CARRIE WOOD

# THE NEXT GENERATION & BEYOND

As the 21st century dawned, the rapid technological advancements kept up their brisk pace and led to tougher competition in the video game market than ever before. And with the entry of a new major company on the market, the console wars were harder fought as more quality options for home consoles became available.

The follow-up to the Saturn, the Sega Dreamcast, started this generation of consoles when it released in 1998 in Japan, and elsewhere the next year. Though it got a significant head-start on Sony and Nintendo, the reputation damage that Sega suffered from the failures of the Saturn meant that it was essentially doomed from the start. The Dreamcast did make significant advancements in terms of technology, and is notably the first home console to include a built-in modem for online play and other internet support.

Sales for the Dreamcast were mediocre, as it moved just a touch more than 9 million units, but the system has since become somewhat of a cult favorite among gamers thanks to the software lineup, which includ-

ed such hits as *Shenmue, Space Channel 9,* and *Jet Set Radio.* Sega discontinued the Dreamcast completely on March 31, 2001, and shifted to becoming a third-party software developer instead, marking the end of their run at the home console market after 18 years.

Sony's second console, the PlayStation 2, arrived in 2000. The system was the first true "complete" home entertainment system, with the ability to play DVDs and CDs in addition to its game lineup. Though it

**The PlayStation 2**

**The Sega Dreamcast**

did not originally include a focus on online play, Sony later added that functionality to the system. The PS2 was also backwards compatible for the original PlayStation's controller as well as its game lineup. With the cutting-edge technology for the time, plus significant third-party support from companies like Square-Enix (who exclusively released big titles such as *Final Fantasy X* on the system), the PlayStation 2 proved to be the biggest success of its generation. Selling well even after the release of its successor, the PS2 became the most popular and best-selling console of all time, moving more than 155 million units worldwide.

Nintendo made the move to disc-based gaming with the release of the GameCube, which arrived in 2001. However, unlike the regularly-sized DVD discs used in other consoles of its time, the GameCube used smaller optical discs that were similar to miniDVDs. This format was just a third of the PS2's disc size, meaning that games that could be single-disc on a PS2 release ended up as a multi-disc release for the

GameCube. The fact that the GameCube lacked the backwards compatibility of the PS2 (as well as any ability to play any CDs or DVDs) also led even some Nintendo faithful to jump to other systems.

While the GameCube certainly maintained a solid foothold in the market, ultimately selling almost 22 million systems, it strengthened the market reputation of Nintendo being a company that only made systems and games for children, while the other console options were seen comparatively as more mature. Even the design of the hardware – with a somewhat cutesy, colorful box as a console and the large multicolored buttons on the controller – fed into this preconception of Nintendo.

Though their dominance of the console market slipped, Nintendo maintained a chokehold on the handheld market, with the release of the Game Boy Advance in 2001. The 16-bit processor allowed for a number of ports of popular SNES games, and the screen's full-color display was a hit with gamers. The GBA received a couple of redesigns in its lifespan, the most popular of which was the Game Boy Advance SP,

**Game Boy Advance**

which introduced a clamshell design that would be echoed by its successor. The GBA line in total sold more than 81.5 million units around the world, and crushed the competition from the likes of the WonderSwan, the Neo Geo Pocket Color, and the infamous N-Gage.

The biggest surprise of this console generation was the introduction of Microsoft to

**The GameCube**

the home console market with the release of the original Xbox system. The Xbox was actually originally short for "DirectX Box" as the console itself was based on DirectX graphics technology and largely developed by Microsoft's DirectX team.

**The original Xbox**

The Xbox released in November 2001 in North America and in 2002 elsewhere around the world. With the fact that it had been largely produced with PC technology of the time, the Xbox proved to be a platform for games that had previously only been available on PCs. With their killer app *Halo: Combat Evolved*, Microsoft was able to establish itself as a legitimate contender in the home console market. Though it didn't catch up to Sony's absolute dominance during this period, it did end up toe-to-toe with Nintendo, moving about 24 million units worldwide. Worth noting, however, is that almost all of these sales happened in the North American market; Microsoft still has yet to succeed in Asian territories.

This generation of gaming in general saw rise to three major trends: online gaming, the modding of games, and the advent of mobile gaming.

Online gaming took off largely due to how affordable internet connectivity was becoming around the world, allowing for the introduction of massively multiplayer online role-playing games into the PC market. Even in the console market, MMOs such as *Phantasy Star Online* for the Dreamcast and *Final Fantasy XI* for the PS2

proved to be popular. And Microsoft introduced their own online gaming service to the console arena with the arrival of Xbox Live, allowing for online competitive play for widely popular titles such as *Halo*.

Though the modding of PC titles had been around since the mid-1990s, things really took off as the tools required to create mods became more available, and the addition of the internet to the mix allowed people to share their mods more quickly and to a wider audience. The most famous mod of this time was *Counter-Strike*, which released in 1999; though it is largely its own

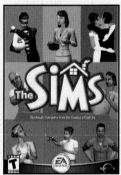

game today, it began as a mod for *Half-Life*. Other popular games for modders were *Unreal Tournament* and *The Sims*.

Mobile gaming wouldn't truly take off in America until the arrival of smartphones later in the decade, but in the early 2000s the idea started to get rolling in Japan. Japanese phones started to see a number of puzzle and virtual pet titles that quickly grew in popularity. Nokia's N-Gage system arrived in 2003, and blended a phone with a handheld gaming unit. Though the system was a failure (and its taco-like design was a butt of many jokes), it introduced the idea of having a phone act as a gaming system to the American market.

The following generation for video gaming got started on the handheld market in 2004, when the Nintendo DS and the PlayStation Portable released within a month of each other at the end of that year. The PSP was Sony's first entry into the handheld market, and boasted powerful hardware that could run more technologically-advanced titles. The DS – which stands for "Dual Screen" – went a more novelty-focused route, with two screens in which the bottom one was a touchpad. The DS also carried over the clamshell-like, foldable design from the GBA SP.

The Nintendo DS

While the PSP proved to be popular in Japan, it never quite attracted the attention of American gamers in the same way that Nintendo was able to. A large part of this had to do with the available software lineup, which was heavily weighted with JRPGs and visual novels – two genres that have never seen consistent widespread popularity in the U.S. The fact that Nintendo already had 15 years' worth of support from the Game Boy line meant that they had a significant brand-loyal built-in audience for the release of the DS. The touch-pad of the DS also drew a wider audience. While the PSP sold a respectable approximate 82 million units, the DS ran away with the handheld duel with more than 154 million devices sold worldwide.

Though Microsoft was a little late to the party in the previous generation, they got a strong head start in this next generation of console wars with the release of the Xbox 360 in November 2005. Featuring high-definition graphics and HDMI support in a con-

The Xbox 360

sole for the first time, it was a solid option for the most hardcore gamers.

Despite the system's initial popularity, its reputation was marred with system failures, the most notorious being the "Red Ring of Death." The RROD name came from the three red lights on the 360's power indicator, which would show in the event of a general system error. The frequency in which this error occurred in the original models of the 360 necessitated that Microsoft extend warranties far past their original expiration date. Further 360 models, including the redesigned Xbox 360 S, largely solved this issue; the 360 line of consoles sold 84 million units worldwide.

The direct competitor to the 360 was Sony's PlayStation 3, which arrived in 2006.

The PlayStation 3

Though it boasted superior technology, including the introduction of Blu-Ray technology (which allowed the PS3 to also act as a Blu-Ray DVD player), the fact that it cost $200 more than the 360 at launch caused it to get off to a slow start. The market dominance that Sony had enjoyed since their original PlayStation launched largely stalled out until the release of slimmer, more cost-friendly PS3 units later on. The system eventually somewhat caught up to the 360, and the PS3 family sold about 80 million units around the world.

Nintendo made a bold move in this home console generation, opting to change the way that games were played instead of simply upgrading the platform they were played on. With the Wii console, Nintendo introduced motion technology to the world of gaming; while the Wii was technically not much of an upgrade from the GameCube (and didn't really come close to the system specs of the 360 or PS3), it far outsold its competitors, with more than 100 million Wii consoles sold worldwide.

**The Wii**

By emphasizing the motion-based gameplay, even small tech demos like *Wii Sports* became huge hits for Nintendo. The change in gameplay (while remaining as family-friendly as Nintendo always had been) also drew in a much wider, more casual gaming audience compared to the hardcore mature gaming crowd of Sony and Microsoft. However, while the Wii sold gangbusters – and was later imitated by

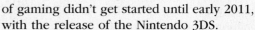

Sony's PlayStation Move and Microsoft's Kinect peripherals – Nintendo couldn't escape their reputation as being the "kiddie" alternative to the serious consoles on the market.

As the decade ended, things largely stayed the same for a few years. While the consoles and handhelds all received various upgrades and remodels, the console generation at large was the longest ever. The current generation of gaming didn't get started until early 2011, with the release of the Nintendo 3DS.

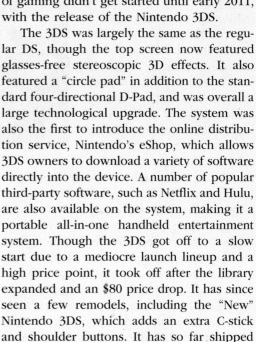

The 3DS was largely the same as the regular DS, though the top screen now featured glasses-free stereoscopic 3D effects. It also featured a "circle pad" in addition to the standard four-directional D-Pad, and was overall a large technological upgrade. The system was also the first to introduce the online distribution service, Nintendo's eShop, which allows 3DS owners to download a variety of software directly into the device. A number of popular third-party software, such as Netflix and Hulu, are also available on the system, making it a portable all-in-one handheld entertainment system. Though the 3DS got off to a slow start due to a mediocre launch lineup and a high price point, it took off after the library expanded and an $80 price drop. It has since seen a few remodels, including the "New" Nintendo 3DS, which adds an extra C-stick and shoulder buttons. It has so far shipped more than 61 million units worldwide.

Sony countered Nintendo with their own handheld, the PlayStation Vita, which released between late 2011 and early 2012. Featuring touchscreen technology on the front and back, as well as a double-joystick button layout, the Vita was marketed as a much more powerful and mature alternative to the 3DS. While it initially saw some success, it failed to attract many western companies to develop for the platform, leading the library to end up heavily weighted with Japanese-style games that really only have a niche audience in the U.S. It has been somewhat recently ignored by Sony, who left it completely out of most of their major 2016 presentations. Exact sales figures have not been released, but it has been estimated to have sold roughly 10 million units.

On the home console front, however, Sony has continued to succeed; the PlayStation 4 launched in November 2013 and has largely run away with the current generation so far. The PS4 was designed with more social gaming in mind, with the ability to stream gameplay online added via a "share" button on the controller. The system received a slim build that released in September 2016; a Pro edition, with emphasis on 4K gaming, released at the end of the year as well. So far, Sony has taken control of the console market sales-wise, with more than 40 million consoles sold so far.

The PlayStation 4's main rival is the Xbox One, the latest console from Microsoft; both released within a week of each other. The Xbox One has been promoted by Microsoft as an all-in-one entertainment console, with the ability to split-screen multiple applications and an emphasis on various other non-gaming uses for the system. The Xbox One originally shipped with an upgraded version of the Kinect sensor, but was eventually ditched after interest died off. The introductory price on the system was $499, making it $100 more than the PS4 at launch, and with how Microsoft has continued to gain any interest from the Asian market, the Xbox One has only sold approximately 10 million consoles so far. A slim version was released in 2016, and a total hardware upgrade currently known as "Project Scorpio" is rumored for a 2017 launch.

While the Wii was a runaway success for Nintendo, the follow-up of the Wii U has largely been a flop. With a GamePad controller that featured a large touch-screen, the two-screen home console was somewhat alienating to many customers who couldn't quite figure out what to make of it. The Wii U launched in November 2012, giving it a year's head-start on Sony and Microsoft, but has failed to make much of an impression. Though certain games, such as *Mario Kart* and *Super Smash Bros.*, helped to drive console sales to an extent, the Wii U not only lost most of its casual audience of the Wii, but continued to lack any appeal for a more mature audience; it has only sold roughly 13 million units.

At the end of 2016 Nintendo announced their new system, a hybrid between home console and handheld, called the Nintendo Switch. Players will be able to insert the "Joy-Con" controller units onto either side of the console itself, which includes a screen on one side, and take their console gaming on the go. As of this book's publication, not much is yet known about the system. It is scheduled for a March 2017 release.

Video gaming has certainly come a long way since the days of *Pong* and *Pac-Man*. Players have gone from standing side-by-side at arcade cabinets to connecting with each other around the world via online services. Systems have gone from blocky 8-bit sprites to fully three-dimensional, high-definition, photo-realistic graphics. Companies have come and gone. And though first thought of as a fad or a passing trend, the future of video games is as bright as it's ever been.

The PlayStation 4

The Nintendo Switch

# COLLECTING BY CONSOLE

Console collecting is definitely one of the more expensive areas to get into, seeing as how much more pricey gaming hardware is when compared to software. Consoles also take up significantly more space than games, and are overall generally more difficult to maintain. However, with how many gamers have been brand-loyal over the years, the fact that people have entire collections dedicated to the likes of Sega, Sony, Nintendo and Microsoft should come as no surprise.

These companies are of course hardly the only console producers out there, and plenty of people have collections that involve the likes of Atari, Coleco, 3DO, Magnavox, Philips, SNK and more. But since including each of these likely would have resulted in needing a separate book to do all of them justice, we opted to focus on the four that have experienced the greatest longevity in the industry.

Console collecting can make for a truly great collection display, especially with cases of people who want all of the various special edition or different color consoles that have been made available with many systems over the years. While some may consider it excessive to have every different color of Nintendo 64 or PlayStation 2, it's a marvel to see all of them lined up.

This chapter provides a look at Microsoft, Nintendo, Sega and Sony, and at the history of each of them – and maybe will give some insight into why people continue to be so passionate about and loyal to each of them.

# SEGA

## By Carrie Wood

Though today they're primarily known as the company that plays home to Sonic the Hedgehog, Sega's history began much earlier than the 1990s. The company was actually founded in 1940 in Hawaii as Standard Games; their primary business was in coin-operated machines such as slot machines, which they sent to military bases as a way for the men to pass their time.

Following the war, they relocated to Tokyo, as the U.S. had started to outlaw slot machines. In 1952 the company changed its name to Service Games of Japan, and they started marketing more to the general public. By 1960, they had changed their name again to Sega – derived from **Se**rvice **Ga**mes – and by the middle of the decade had merged with their main competitor, Rosen Enterprises. Their first manufactured arcade game was a submarine simulation called *Periscope*, which would become the first arcade game in the U.S. that cost just a quarter per play.

## ARCADE SUCCESS AND THE MASTER SYSTEM

Sega was able to take advantage of the booming arcade scene of the late '70s and early '80s, and by 1982 was taking in a yearly revenue of more than $214 million. Games that Sega produced for arcades included *Zaxxon* (the first game with isometric graphics), *SubRoc 3D* (the first game with stereoscopic 3D graphics), as well as *Head On, Turbo, Astro Blaster, Monaco GP* and many others. Several of these would be licensed to the Coleco company for their ColecoVision console.

Like many companies involved in video games, Sega was impacted severely by the industry crash of 1983, causing a revenue loss of nearly $100 million that year. The company did, however, release their first home console in '83, the SG-1000. As their first entry into the home console market, the SG-1000 released exclusively in Japan and didn't see much in the way of success; much of this had to do with Nintendo's Famicom simply proving to be more popular (though Nintendo also sported better hardware). The CSK Holdings Corporation bought out Sega during this period of time, and Isao Okawa became the company's Chairman.

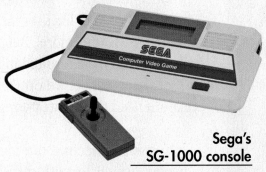

Sega's
SG-1000 console

The SG-1000 saw a few different models that weren't successful, but the company finally nailed the home console model with the Sega Mark III – known in the west as the Sega Master System. The Master System was meant to be a direct competitor to the Famicom/Nintendo Entertainment System,

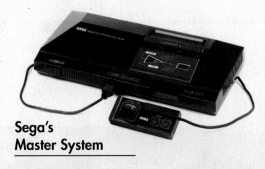

Sega's
Master System

and featured better hardware than Nintendo did by this point. Released in Japan in 1985 and in North America the following year, it sold decently, beating out Atari, but failed to match Nintendo's worldwide success.

Master System games that proved popular included *Psycho Fox, Phantasy Star*, as well as the *Alex Kidd* games. Alex Kidd himself ended up acting as Sega's primary mascot until a certain blue hedgehog game along a few years alter. *Phantasy Star* also became a long-running franchise for Sega across their systems.

## THE GENESIS AND THE HANDHELD MARKET

Sega's 16-bit console, the Sega Genesis, first arrived in Japan in October 1988 as the Mega Drive before making the trip to North America in '89. The system was backwards-compatible with Master System games and helped to drive a feud between Sega and Nintendo that would last throughout the 1990s.

### The Sega Genesis console

Part of the marketing campaign for the Genesis' western release was the slogan that simply said: "Genesis Does What Nintendon't." The re-branding of the company focusing on the Genesis as an edgier, "cooler" console to have over the NES helped to drive Sega to end up with a 65 percent share of the home console market in the U.S. for a brief period of time in the '90s. That was also helped along by the company's new mascot, Sonic the Hedgehog.

*Sonic the Hedgehog* arrived on the Genesis in 1991 and differentiated itself from Nintendo's *Super Mario* series by focusing on high-speed running and action, achieved by using what Sega referred to as "blast processing" in the marketing (but what has since been revealed to be a fairly simple coding trick). Sonic quickly overtook

Alex Kidd as the company's mascot of choice – since Alex Kidd was perceived as being too close to Mario – and it helped that his game was well-received. *Sonic the Hedgehog* was praised widely for its lively characters and colorful scenery, and the game would help the Genesis out-sell the Super Nintendo at a two-to-one pace during the 1991 holiday season.

Meanwhile, Sega was in the process of working their way into the handheld market as well. Their portable gaming device, the Game Gear, released in Japan in October of 1990 and in North America the following spring.

The handheld was essentially a portable version of

the Sega Master System and featured a significantly more powerful processor than Nintendo's Game Boy as well as a full-color screen (the Game Boy wouldn't go full-color until 1998). However, the powerful technology came at the cost of battery life; the Game Boy required four AA batteries and would run for about 30 hours, but the Game Gear required six AA's and would burn through them in about five hours.

The Game Gear experienced a strong initial launch, thanks in part to Sega's marketing plan that made it seem like a more "mature" option to the Game Boy (as well as by directly comparing the graphic capabilities of the two) in a similar fashion that they took to promoting the Sega Genesis. However, the Game Gear experienced a pretty quick decline due to the fact that the battery life was so shoddy and that Sega had refocused their efforts into the successor to the Genesis, the Sega Saturn. Though

it sold 11 million units, it was never able to catch up to the Game Boy, and the Game Boy Pocket's release in 1996 was the final nail in the coffin for the Game Gear. Popular Sega titles released across both the Genesis and the Game Gear during this time included *Ecco the Dolphin, Shinobi, NBA Jam, Earthworm Jim, Prince of Persia*, and, of course, various *Sonic the Hedgehog* games.

## THE SATURN CONSOLE AND SEGA'S DOWNTURN

On November 22, 1994, Sega released the successor to the Genesis, the Sega Saturn. It was the first gaming console to use CD-ROM format for its games, preceding Sony's PlayStation. The initial launch of the system in Japan was great; the initial shipment sold out in the first day, and the near-perfect port of the arcade hit *Virtua Fighter* sold at a nearly one-to-one ratio with the console. Within six months, Sega had sold more than a million Saturn consoles.

**The Sega Saturn console**

However, things quickly went awry when Sega moved to release the console in the West. Though Sega of America CEO Tom Kalinske had originally announced that the Saturn would be released in the US on September 2, 1995, Sega of Japan ordered that there be an early launch to try and give the company an edge over the PlayStation. This led to the surprise announcement at the first Electronic Entertainment Expo on May 11 of that year that Sega had already shipped 30,000 Saturns to various retail-

ers in the US for immediate release. The retailers themselves had no time to prepare for the launch and were upset with Sega because of this, leading to KB Toys dropping Sega entirely.

Sony in particular immediately overtook Sega, selling more PlayStation units in two days of that console's launch compared to five months' worth of sales for the Sega Saturn. By 1996, the PlayStation was outselling the Saturn two-to-one. Sony's easy development tools for the PlayStation also took third-party support away from Sega. In fact, the first *Tomb Raider* game was being developed with the Saturn in mind, but was moved to the PlayStation. Lara Croft ended up as one of the PlayStation's most popular characters, to the point where she was considered an unofficial mascot by many.

By March of 1998, Sega reported that they had taken a loss of $309 million on the Saturn, and they began focusing on their next console, the Dreamcast. The Saturn was not without its crop of popular exclusives, though, which included *Panzer Dragoon Saga, Dragon Force, Nights into Dreams,* and *Guardian Heroes.* The Saturn did not get a *Sonic the Hedgehog* game that was exclusive to it, however, and that is considered part of the reason for its failure to thrive in the market.

## SEGA'S FINAL CONSOLE: THE DREAMCAST

Rumors of a new piece of Sega hardware started swirling as early as 1995, though the original thought by many was that it would be an add-on piece to the Saturn. The Dreamcast's development involved a collaboration between several different teams, including people from IBM; the console was known under various codenames such as "Blackbelt," "Whitebelt," and "Dural."

A leading factor in the Saturn's commercial failure was that it was expensive to produce, so Sega opted for a much different approach. They built the machine based on hardware that was in line with most computers of the time, which ended up reducing the cost to produce the Dreamcast. Sega was also convinced by economist (and future CEO of Sega.com) Brad Huang to include a modem, a feature that would prove somewhat revolutionary at the time.

both came on strong (plus Microsoft entering the market later in that console generation), the Dreamcast quickly entered a state of decline. Isao Okawa took over as president of the company in May of 2000; he had previously advocated that the company abandon the console business entirely and instead focus on software.

On January 31, 2001, Sega made the announcement that they would completely discontinue the Dreamcast and no longer make any home console hardware in the video game industry. The system ended production on March 31, 2001, and would eventually be cleared out of stores at the abysmally low price of just $49.95.

## The Sega Dreamcast console

Sega was confident in their Dreamcast at launch, and the system ended up drawing much of the public's interest – thanks largely in part to the promotion of *Sonic Adventure*, a game that would launch shortly after the console itself. The Dreamcast launched in Japan on November 27, 1998, and the company had hoped that the system would move at least a million units in its first three months in order to gain a hold on the market before the new Sony and Nintendo consoles launched. However, less than 900,000 moved in that time period.

In North America, the system launched on September 9, 1999 (the 9/9/99 date was heavily hyped by marketing) for $199. More than 225,000 units moved in the first 24 hours – a sales record at the time – and by that holiday season Sega held a solid 31 percent share of the video game market in North America.

This initial wave of interest didn't last, though. Between the lackluster Japanese sales and the fact that Sony and Nintendo

The Dreamcast's failure is largely credited to hype for the PlayStation 2, as well as a lack of support from major third-party developers such as Electronic Arts. However, the system maintains a significant following even today, and has been listed as one of the greatest consoles ever by publications such as IGN. The fact that it was the first to break into online gaming for consoles and the first to introduce now-commonplace features like second-screen technology and voice chat has helped maintain its status.

Popular games for the Dreamcast included *Sonic Adventure*, *Jet Set Radio*, *Shenmue*, *Space Channel 5*, and *Crazy Taxi*. Most of these have seen ports to other systems over the years.

## SUCCESSFUL TRANSITION TO SOFTWARE DEVELOPMENT

Since the discontinuation of the Dreamcast, Sega has worked exclusively as a third-party developer to create titles for many of its former industry rivals – even Nintendo. Their very first game as a third party was *ChuChu Rocket!* for the Game Boy Advance. The company had been in early talks to be potentially merged into Microsoft's Xbox division, but those ultimately failed.

Sega has also acquired a number of other development studios over the years. Since 2005, they have acquired Creative Assembly (known for *Total War*), Sports Interactive (known for *Football Manager*), and Relic Entertainment (known for *Company of Heroes*). They've also collaborated with a wide variety of studios over the years on a multitude of projects, and maintain a sizable presence in arcades as well.

The *Sonic the Hedgehog* series continues to be Sega's most recognizable product, and the blue blur has appeared on Nintendo, Microsoft and Sony consoles. Their mascot has also been seen alongside Nintendo's Mario in titles such as *Super Smash Bros.* and *Mario and Sonic at the Olympic Games*, the latter of which has been a series since 2007.

Sega might have flopped out of the home console market, but it's fairly evident to see that, over the last decade-plus of software development, they'll continue to adapt and survive. Their continued success as developers and the continued presence of many of their most popular characters has just gone to show that they're still largely a force to be reckoned with in the gaming industry.

# SONY PlayStation

By Carrie Wood

Ever since bursting onto the scene more than 20 years ago, the PlayStation line has been one of the heaviest hitters in the video game industry. Between the four iterations of their home console, their handheld market entries and their new virtual reality headset, Sony has proven over and over again that their video game hardware will always be on the cutting edge of technology.

## ORIGINS

The PlayStation's origins go back to 1988, when it was conceived as a joint project between Sony and Nintendo in order to create a CD-ROM attachment for the Super Famicom console. By 1991, Sony had unveiled a Super Famicom with a built-in CD-ROM drive, called the "Play Station," at the Consumer Electronics Show. Just a day after the CES announcement, Nintendo severed ties with Sony and opted to partner with the Philips company on the same tech; the split was primarily caused by disagreements on how the two companies would share revenue generated by the project.

Enraged by the slight, Sony President Norio Ohga gave Ken Kutaragi (an executive who had previously managed one of Sony's hardware engineering divisions) the task of developing the PlayStation in order to go directly head-to-head with Nintendo in the console market. Sony eventually founded their Sony Computer Entertainment division in 1993, which is where the PlayStation was pushed forward into full development.

The first PlayStation arrived in Japan in December 1994 before arriving in the west the following year. Surrounded by industry hype after a series of tech demos, the console proved to be an immediate success around the world, featuring launch titles that included *Air Combat, Ridge Racer* and *Rayman*. The system differentiated itself from both Nintendo and Sega's systems by focusing more on third-party developers, while the other two were very first-party focused.

### The PlayStation

Though the industry at the time was dominated by Nintendo and Sega, Sony was able to edge their way in by appealing to older gamers that were not being served by the other companies; the PlayStation was marketed as a more mature option than the other offerings in the industry. By the late 1990s, Sony was just as well-regarded of a console brand as Nintendo or Sega. The considerable success of the PlayStation's disc format is regarded as a leading factor in the industry switch away from cartridge-based software.

The original PlayStation received a slimmed-down, redesigned edition called the PSone, which released in July 2000. Both versions combined have sold more than 120 million units worldwide.

### The PSone

## MASSIVE SUCCESS AND FURTHER GENERATIONS

The PlayStation 2 arrived in 2000, a little more than a year after Sega's Dreamcast and about a year before Microsoft's Xbox and Nintendo's GameCube. The latter two proved to be the biggest competition for Sony during this time (with Sega discontinuing the Dreamcast in 2001), and the year head-start was valuable. The PS2 brought in $250 million on the first day of release, and after the Dreamcast's demise it was the only console of its generation on the market for a full six months.

The PlayStation 2

The PS2 offered backwards compatibility for both its predecessor's games and controllers. It also functioned as a DVD player, giving it an edge on its competition. Though online functionality wasn't originally a focus for Sony in this generation, after Xbox debuted its popular Xbox Live service, it was added into the PS2.

The PlayStation 3

Like the original PlayStation, the PS2 received a slimmed-down model, called the Slimline, beginning in 2004. The PS2 console became the best-selling video game console in history, with more than 155 million consoles sold. More than 3,800 different software titles were developed for the system, with more than 1.5 billion games sold. Even after the PS3 debuted, the PS2 remained popular; the console wouldn't be discontinued completely until 2013, after 13 years of production, which is one of the longest runs on a video game console ever.

The PlayStation 3 was officially announced in 2005 at E3, and was released at the end of the following year. It made a number of improvements upon the PS2 that helped it stand out from its competition, not the least of which was the inclusion of Blu-Ray technology. The choice to include such advanced technology (for the time) caused the price of the system to be incredibly high. The original PS3 models were priced at $499 or $599 depending on the hard drive included – and even then, the consoles were selling at a huge loss for Sony due to the astronomical production costs (estimated by various sources to have been in the $800 area).

On top of that, the PS3 was in competition with the Xbox 360, which had a head start in the market and gained popular titles that had previously been exclusive to Sony consoles (such as *Grand Theft Auto*), and

The PS 3 Slim

The PS 3 Super Slim

the Nintendo Wii, which ran away with things sales-wise by appealing to a wider, more casual audience. These factors led to Sony taking a massive loss of $1.97 billion during the 2007 fiscal year. Fortunately, things turned around in the following few years as the technology involved to produce the PS3 became cheaper, and the console was able to turn a profit.

Two redesigned models were made for the PS3 – the Slim, and the Super Slim. The former released in 2009, and was positively received on top of selling well. The massive hard drive upgrade on top of a smaller size, reduced noise and lower risk of overheating made it a popular choice. The Super Slim arrived at the end of 2012, and was much smaller and quieter than either of its predecessors; however, the changed disc loader to a slide-top was a source of irritation for many. In total, the various models of the PlayStation 3 sold more than 80 million units worldwide. The PS3 era also introduced the PlayStation Network, an online service aimed at competing with Xbox Live.

The PlayStation 4

Most recently for Sony has been the advent of the PlayStation 4, which was announced in 2013 and released in November of that year. A technically advanced system, it contains an Accelerated Processing Unit that AMD has called their most powerful to date. The PS4 has expanded its appeal to independent developers – and Sony has supported them – in the way that it appeals to big third-party development companies.

In September 2016, Sony announced two different PS4 models – the PS4 Slim, and the PS4 Pro. The former released on September 15, 2016, and is 40 percent smaller than the original model. The Pro, on the other hand, features significantly upgraded hardware that allows certain games in the PS4 library to be played at 4K on compatible televisions. The PlayStation 4 family of consoles has taken a strong lead in the current generation's console wars, having sold 40 million units worldwide (against the Wii U's 12 million and the Xbox One's 20 million).

## HANDHELD ENTRIES

Though it's not the one people are most familiar with, Sony's first handheld gaming device was the PocketStation, released exclusively in Japan in January 1999. The device was somewhat of a combination of a memory card and a digital assistant. PocketStation software was usually distributed as a tie-in to a PlayStation title. While it sold well in Japan, it was never released elsewhere despite initial plans to take it to Europe and North America.

The first real handheld system for Sony was the PlayStation Portable, released in Japan in December 2004 and in America in March 2005. Created to be a competitor with the Nintendo DS, it featured a much larger screen and more powerful software than Nintendo's handheld. It was marketed as a more mature handheld gaming option than the DS, with the ability to browse the web and play movies on top of just games. The original PSP was followed by two slim models, the PSP-2000 and PSP-3000.

The original PSP

When the PSP launched, it was $100 more expensive than the DS, and the nature of the software – produced on Universal Media Discs (UMDs) – required additional memory cards to be purchased in order to save games, which was another additional cost. Launch titles such as *Dynasty*

*Warriors* and *Metal Gear Acid* helped to drive initial sales, and overall the PSP line did well, moving more than 82 million units around the world; however, the line never was able to catch the DS's success.

Another redesigned model, the PSP Go, released at the end of 2009. It removed the UMD drive and replaced it with internal flash memory to directly download software into the system. It also switched the overall design of the system to a slide mechanic. Reception was largely mixed, as the lack of a UMD port alienated previous PSP customers who would have had to buy those games a second time to play them on the PSP Go.

### The PSP Go

The PSP was succeeded properly by the PlayStation Vita, which arrived in Japan at the end of 2011 and in North America early the next year. Featuring touchscreen technology on the front and back of the system on top of a remarkably powerful processor for a handheld, it (like the PSP before it) was marketed as the more mature option to Nintendo's newest handheld, the 3DS. It also attempted to appeal to people who were getting into mobile gaming on their phones.

### The PS Vita

Though the Vita was initially well-received critically, it was once again far more expensive than its main competition, and sales stalled out. A lack of support from developers meant that the game library became very limited, and Sony all but ceased support completely for the device by the end of 2016; the Vita was notably absent from the company's E3 presentation and other major press conferences that year. It's been estimated that only about 10 million units have sold so far.

## OTHER PLAYSTATION PRODUCTS

The PlayStation TV, a "microconsole," was released around the world between 2013 and 2014. It is compatible with a number of PS Vita titles, but the "remote play" function has been more popular. It allows gamers to stream PlayStation 4 titles to another television that is connected to a PSTV. Though it was critically received well – and favorably compared to similar devices like Apple TV and Google Chromecast – Sony stopped shipping the device in early 2016.

As the idea of virtual reality has become an actual reality, Sony entered the field with the PlayStation VR in 2016. The headset device released on October 13, 2016, and is fully functional with the PlayStation 4. Launch games included *Batman: Arkham VR, Driveclub VR,* and *Battlezone.* Though it is still far too soon to say how the PSVR will fare in this emerging market against competition like the Oculus Rift, early reception has been favorable.

Over the last two decades or so, Sony went from an upstart gaming company trying to make the best of a fallout with Nintendo to one of the biggest names in the industry around the world. Clearly willing to take the risks necessary to put out what they believe to be the best product and remain on the forefront of new tech, Sony has been able to establish themselves as the company to beat over the last few console generations.

### The PlayStation VR

# MICROSOFT XBOX

BY ZANNE NILSSON

Microsoft's video game division has become rather, well, *divisive*, with some praising their products while others criticize their decisions, especially when it comes to studio closures. But one thing everyone can agree on is that the video game industry would look very different without Microsoft in it.

**The original Xbox**

## ORIGINS

As its name might imply, Microsoft Studios' origins lie in Microsoft itself, which was founded by Bill Gates and Paul Allen on April 4, 1975. Over the following years its software products came to dominate the personal computing industry. The company began dabbling in computer games in the 1980s and 1990s, releasing *Microsoft Flight Simulator 1.00* (1982) as well as game collections like the *Microsoft Entertainment Pack* (1990) to appeal to casual computer gamers such as bored office workers. The goal for the *Microsoft Entertainment Pack* was to make the Windows operating system more attractive to consumers that weren't large businesses.

**The "Duke" Controller**

While the company began releasing more and more games for their systems in the mid-to-late 1990s, Microsoft Studios – then known as Microsoft Game Division or Microsoft Games – didn't really take off until the arrival of Microsoft's first home game console, the Xbox.

## XBOX

On November 15, 2001, Microsoft released its Xbox console. The Xbox – short for "DirectX Box," referring to Microsoft's DirectX collection of multimedia application programming interfaces – was designed to compete with the Dreamcast, PlayStation2, and GameCube. It became a massive success which sold more than 24 million units overall. These sales were partially driven by the Xbox's "killer app," the first-person shooter *Halo*. Microsoft released dozens more games for their new console, including *MechAssault*, *Fable*, and *Halo 2*.

The Microsoft Game Studios label was officially unveiled in June 2002, and in November of that year the company launched its online gaming service known as Xbox Live. In spite of being a broadband-only subscription service in an era when broadband internet hadn't been widely adopted yet, Xbox Live proved to be popular and gained 23 million members by the beginning of 2010. But the road ahead wasn't without its bumps: in January 2004 Xbox team leader Ed Fries left the company, and later that year Microsoft Game Studios cancelled two upcoming massive multiplayer online role-playing games: *Mythica* and *True Fantasy Live Online*.

The following year, however, three well-known Japanese developers joined the studios: Tetsuya Mizuguchi, Yoshiki Okamoto, and Hironobu Sakaguchi – the latter best known as the creator of the *Final Fantasy* games. And the next console generation was just on the horizon.

## XBOX 360

The Xbox 360 was released in North America on November 22, 2005, followed by launches in 35 other countries in the year that followed. Like the original Xbox, the Xbox 360 was a big success, selling 80 million units worldwide by the end of 2013 – in spite of its hardware failure problems, which were indicated by the infamous "red ring of death" in the lights around the console's power button. An optional motion-sensing device known as the Kinect was released for the console in November 2010 to help the Xbox 360 compete with rival consoles' motion-sensing capabilities. The company published a massive amount of new titles for the Xbox 360, including *Gears of War*, *Halo 3*, *Mass Effect*, and *Fable II*.

A few days after the release of *Halo 3* on September 25, 2007, the *Halo* trilogy's developer Bungie announced that they would be parting ways with Microsoft to become an independent developer. The following year, Microsoft began building 343 Industries to make new *Halo* games, but didn't officially reveal them as the studio taking the reins of the *Halo* series until the middle of 2009.

During this same timeframe however, the company made the controversial decision to close or disband some of its

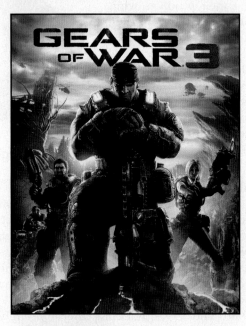

**The Xbox 360**

**The Xbox 360 Slim**

studios – including Aces Studio and Ensemble Studio – as an attempt to restructure to cope with the aftermath of the 2008 financial crisis. Afterwards, the company began expanding its remaining studios and even opening new ones. The division officially renamed itself Microsoft Studios in 2011 and began gearing up for the release of its next console.

## XBOX ONE

On November 22, 2013 – exactly eight years after the Xbox 360 first hit store shelves – Microsoft launched the Xbox One. The console, intended as an "all-in-one entertainment system," was not as wildly successful as its predecessors. The last official sales number given was in November 2014, when the system had shipped 10 million units worldwide, but its hardware was considered more reliable than the Xbox 360 had been.

In 2014, Microsoft Studios acquired the rights to the *Gears of War* and *Rise of Nations* franchises, as well as acquiring Mojang, the developer behind *Minecraft*. Microsoft Studios has published a good number of games for the Xbox One, including *Forza Motorsport 5*, *Killer Instinct*, *Halo 5: Guardians*, *Minecraft: Xbox One Edition*, *Ori and the Blind Forest* and *Gears of War: Ultimate Edition*.

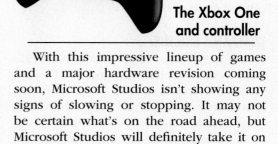

The Xbox One
and controller

With this impressive lineup of games and a major hardware revision coming soon, Microsoft Studios isn't showing any signs of slowing or stopping. It may not be certain what's on the road ahead, but Microsoft Studios will definitely take it on with all they've got.

# Nintendo®

BY CARRIE WOOD

Nintendo has been a name synonymous with video gaming for decades, thanks to the success of their home consoles as well as their various long-running franchises like *Super Mario, Metroid, Star Fox, The Legend of Zelda*, and *Pokémon*, among many others. Though the Nintendo that people are most familiar with has specialized in video games, their history goes much farther back than the first appearance of their red-capped mascot.

## COMPANY ORIGINS

On September 23, 1889, Nintendo Koppai was founded in Kyoto by Fusajiro Yamauchi. This Nintendo was a card shop specializing in Hanafuda cards. Hanafuda (translated literally as "flower cards") differ from other cards in that they use illustrations, rather than numbers, to differentiate between them. The style of game combines traditional Japanese games with Western-style playing cards. Yamauchi's Hanafuda cards in particular became popular, as they were hand-painted on mulberry tree bark.

For years, Nintendo Koppai specialized in playing cards. It wasn't until the 1960s that they started to branch out into other ventures. Fusajiro Yamauchi's grandson, Hiroshi Yamauchi, renamed the company to simply "Nintendo" in 1963, and experimented with a variety of different businesses, including a taxi company, a television network, and an instant rice company, among others.

In 1966, Nintendo started developing toys, including the Ultra Hand, Ultra Machine, and the Love Tester. The Ultra Hand was an extendable arm, the Ultra Machine was a launcher that lobbed soft balls for someone to hit with a bat, and the Love Tester tested how much two people really loved each other by having one person each hold a sensor. These three in particular continue to make small cameo

appearances in popular games today, such as the *Animal Crossing* and *WarioWare* series.

Nintendo started to develop electronic games in the 1970s. A young man named Shigeru Miyamoto was hired by the company during this period, and he started designing a little arcade game called *Donkey Kong*. This game also introduced a character known as Jumpman, who would eventually become Mario. The massive success of *Donkey Kong* propelled the company forward, allowing them to license the game for a variety of home consoles such as the Atari 2600 and the ColecoVision; they eventually developed their own home gaming console system, the Family Computer, or Famicom, better known in the United States as the Nintendo Entertainment System.

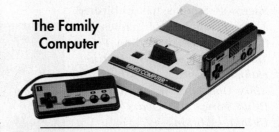

The Family Computer

## HOME CONSOLE DOMINANCE

The NES, as the Famicom, experienced massive early success in Japan thanks to successful ports of Nintendo's arcade games, including the popular *Donkey Kong* and *Donkey Kong Jr.* The company then turned their sights on the American market, and had originally planned to enter it via a partnership with Atari – which quickly dissolved by the end of 1983.

Nintendo went through a few different iterations of the American version of their home console, originally calling it the Nintendo Advanced Video System, and later referring to it as the Advanced Video Entertainment System. Meanwhile, the American video game market was in the middle of an industry-wide crash, and many gaming magazines believed that nothing Nintendo did would prove to be successful.

The Nintendo Entertainment System arrived in the U.S. in 1986 (following a brief test run in certain markets in '85) and included launch titles like *Duck Hunt, Excitebike, Ice Climber, Wrecking Crew* and of course *Super Mario Bros*. The NES helped to rebuild the fractured video game market in the states, and Nintendo's stringent policy of product approval and licensing helped regain consumer confidence. By 1989, the Famicom was present in 37 percent of Japanese households, and by 1990, 30 percent of American households had an NES. The brand's slogan – "It Can't Be Beaten" – held up even as competition arrived in the early '90s, such as Sega's Genesis system. The NES sold an unbelievable 61.9 million units around the world.

### The Nintendo Entertainment System

The successor to the NES, the Super Nintendo Entertainment System, arrived first as the Super Famicom in Japan in 1990 before coming to the west in 1991. Nintendo had been in no rush to make a 16-bit console, as the 8-bit NES was holding strong in the market. Eventually, they were forced to reconsider. The Super Famicom proved to be an instant success in Japan, moving so many units so quickly that it had actually attracted attention from the Yakuza, and precautions became necessary to prevent systems from being stolen. The new system quickly outsold Nintendo's rivals, and the company reestablished itself as the one to beat.

### The Super Famicom

### The Super Nintendo Entertainment System

The SNES released in the U.S. on September 9, 1991, and came bundled with *Super Mario World*, leading to early success. The console faced stiff competition in America from the Sega Genesis; though the Genesis saw a head-start on the market, and had a much larger selection of games, it never was able to consistently maintain a lead on the SNES. The early competition between the SNES and the Genesis saw the first true "console war" between Sega and Nintendo.

Even as other companies entered the 32-bit era, such as Sega with the Saturn, Nintendo was able to hold strong with their 16-bit system with games such as *Donkey Kong Country*. The game used such advanced graphics that it rivaled many 32-bit titles on other systems, and created the image that 32-bit systems weren't offering much more than what was already on the SNES. This helped extend the life of the SNES, which didn't cease production until 1999. A second, slimmer version of both the Super Famicom and the SNES were produced in the late 1990s as well. In total, more than 49 million SNES units sold worldwide, making it the best-selling console of its era.

Gamers first got to decide whether to "Get N or Get Out" with the release of the Nintendo 64. The system arrived in Japan on June 23, 1996, and would arrive in North America that September. Despite the SNES being a success, Nintendo suffered losses from the Japanese recession of the time, and competition from Sega also drove the company to start developing a 64-bit console in the early 1990s. The console was originally called the Ultra 64, and was publicly shown off in 1994 for the first time – though it did not have a controller yet. It was shown off again in its finished form a year later, now being called simply the Nintendo 64. Though it was originally slated for a Holiday 1995 release, only to be pushed back to the following year.

The fact that the console had been delayed drove hype for its eventual release, where it launched at a $199 price tag to best compete with Sega and Sony's systems. The system launched with just two games – *Pilotwings 64* and *Super Mario 64* – though Nintendo emphasized the overall quality of both games as selling points.

## The Nintendo 64

The Nintendo 64 was widely praised upon its release, with the choice to stick with cartridges (despite Sony's PlayStation already using CD-ROMs) called a smart one due to the lack of loading times when compared to PlayStation games. *Time* magazine went on to dub it their 1996 Machine of the Year, saying it had "done to video gaming what the 707 did to air travel" and also claiming it had revitalized the game market as a whole. Sales-wise, it was a significant success, having moved nearly 33 million units worldwide during its lifespan. It ended up being a better success in America than in Japan; this was credited by some Japanese developers to the fact that the N64 lacked roleplaying games. The Nintendo 64 did have some games that would go on to become legendary in their respective genres – *Super Mario 64, The Legend of Zelda: Ocarina of Time*, and *GoldenEye 007* are all considered to be some of the most influential games of all time.

## HEAVY COMPETITION AND REVOLUTIONIZING HOME GAMING

By the time the 21st century rolled around, the video game market was hitting an incredible pace, and Nintendo kept up when they released the GameCube on September 14, 2001. The system was Nintendo's first piece of hardware to use discs instead of cartridges, and though it struggled to compete at times with the PlayStation 2 and Xbox, it carved out its own niche thanks to strong software titles during its lifespan.

The GameCube was developed out of a partnership between Nintendo and ArtX, a graphics hardware design company. ArtX worked on designing the graphics processor starting in 1998, and the following year the system was first publicly unveiled as "Project Dolphin." In August 2000, the console was officially announced as the Nintendo GameCube, and at E3 2001 the launch lineup was shown off, including titles such as *Luigi's Mansion*.

## The GameCube

One of the standout features of the system was its controller, which was largely influenced by the PlayStation's DualShock series. Taking into consideration feedback (both positive and negative) from the Nintendo 64's three-pronged controller, the design for the GameCube's controller instead featured more of a handlebar design and now featured two analog sticks. In 2002, Nintendo launched the WaveBird version of the controller – the very first wireless controller developed by a first-party publisher.

By the time the GameCube's lifespan ended in 2007, more than 600 games had released for the system; these included significant first-party Nintendo releases such as *Pikmin, The Legend of Zelda: The Wind Waker,* and *Super Mario Sunshine* as well as third-party favorites such as *Resident Evil 4* and *Crazy Taxi*. The system never took the majority share of the market, but sold a respectable 21.7 million units worldwide.

The Wii arrived as the GameCube's successor in 2006. Originally codenamed "Revolution," the Wii introduced motion control gaming and was primarily focused on different kinds of player interaction rather than pure technical processing power. By taking that approach, the Wii was able to target a much wider demographic and entice more casual gamers to purchase it.

The Wii was also backwards-compatible with GameCube discs, instantly expanding the system's available game library.

**The Wii**

At launch, the Wii was in such high demand that it was frustratingly impossible to purchase despite claims from company representatives that they were producing nearly 2 million consoles every month. In total, it sold nearly 102 million consoles worldwide – by far and away the best-selling Nintendo console, and the best-selling console of its generation. However, the motion-focused gameplay alienated many hardcore gamers, and a lack of third-party support made it even less appealing to that crowd.

**The Wii U**

The sequel to the Wii, called the Wii U, arrived at the end of 2012. Combining the motion control of the Wii with a large touchscreen in the GamePad controller, it also continued the practice of backwards compatibility. The Wii U received lukewarm critical reception, with many people being confused as to how the touch screen would be used in innovative ways, and a lack of blockbuster titles (plus virtually no third-party support) made people reluctant to purchase it as well. Though the Wii U came out about a year before the Microsoft and Sony next-gen consoles, its head start

did it no favors, and it has so far only sold about 13 million consoles.

On October 20, 2016, Nintendo announced their latest home console, the Nintendo Switch. Previously referred to as the "NX," the Switch will be a hybrid home console and handheld, involving a small screen that can be taken on the go. It is scheduled to arrive in March 2017.

**The Nintendo Switch**

## HANDHELD HISTORY

Besides home consoles played through televisions, Nintendo has been able to maintain a strong hold on the portable game market since the release of the Game Boy in 1989. Created by Gunpei Yokoi – who had previously worked on the simple but portable Game & Watch series – the Game Boy proved to be an immediate success around the world.

There were a number of other handhelds on the market around the same time, including full-color efforts like the Sega GameGear and the Atari Lynx. Thanks to a solid lineup of popular games such as *Tetris*, *Super Mario Land* and *The Legend of Zelda: Link's Awakening*, the little black-and-white Game Boy was able to hold up against the competition. A slimmer version of the system arrived in 1996, called the Game Boy Pocket.

Perhaps the biggest software impact for the Game Boy were the original *Pokémon* games, which released in 1996 – well into

**Game Boy**

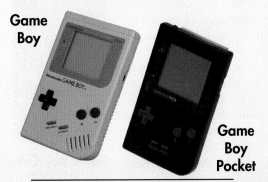

**Game Boy Pocket**

the Game Boy's life cycle. The first generation of *Pokémon* games became the best-selling RPG on the system, selling almost 24 million copies around the world, in turn helping to drive Game Boy sales in a serious manner.

A bizarre spinoff of the Game Boy arrived in the form of the infamous Virtual Boy in 1995. The device was a 32-bit table-top 3D console marketed as being the first "portable" console to display "true 3D graphics" right out of the box.

**Virtual Boy**

The system was an objective commercial failure for Nintendo, and they discontinued it less than a year later in 1996, for a number of reasons. One, the system was simply uncomfortable to play – it required that the person playing have the system on their face the whole time, leading to people being hunched over for the entirety of their gaming. Some even complained about dizziness, nausea and headaches. The graphics were also underwhelming, as they were simply red-on-black, monochromatic images, and did not produce the true immersive experience that Nintendo had touted it would. It sold only about 770,000 units – but is considered somewhat of a collector's item by hardcore Nintendo fans.

A true successor to the original Game Boy arrived in 1998 with the release of the Game Boy Color. The GBC was slightly larger than the Game Boy

**Game Boy Color**

Pocket, but featured a full-color screen. It was also backwards-compatible with the entire Game Boy library, a first for any handheld system on the market. The Game Boy and GBC combined to sell more than 118.6 million units around the world.

The last entry in the Game Boy line, the Game Boy Advance, released in Japan on March 21, 2001, followed by a western release the following June. The system first surfaced in the late 1990s under the name "Project Atlantis." Though the GBC was developed around that time, Project Atlantis' system specifications, including a 32-bit processor, didn't show up until the GBA arrived. When it did debut in 2001, it marked a significant difference in basic design, as it went with a landscape/horizontal design rather than the previous generations' portrait-style design; it put the screen in the middle with buttons on either side rather than at the top with the buttons below it.

**Game Boy Advance**

**Game Boy Advance SP**

The original GBA was a hit, but the system in general got better as it aged, too. A second GBA model, called the GBA SP, released in early 2003, featuring a clamshell design and back-lighting. In 2005, a second variation was released, called the Game Boy Micro. It went back to the horizontal orientation of the original, but is significantly smaller. Despite heavy competition, a strong catalog of games helped the GBA to sell more than 81.5 million units around the world by the time it was discontinued.

The successor to the Game Boy line came in 2004, with the release of the Nintendo DS. The system made use of two screens that worked together (DS actually stood for Dual Screen) and introduced wireless connectivity to the handheld line. Sporting a clamshell design and backlighting, similar to the GBA SP, it also included backwards compatibility with the entire GBA library via a second cartridge port in the bottom of the system.

The Nintendo DS

The DS received a few revisions during its lifespan. First, a slimmed-down version of the system was released, called the DS Lite. About two ounces lighter than the original model, the Lite also featured a brighter screen. Two more models were released – the DSi and the DSi XL. The standard DSi was about the same size and weight of the Lite, but added in digital cameras and allowed players to access an online shop to download games. The XL model had the same capabilities but was, obviously, much larger. Notably, the DSi models lacked the GBA port, meaning they were no longer backwards-compatible.

The DS line as a whole combined to sell more than 154 million units worldwide, making it the second best-selling video game console of all time.

The Nintendo 3DS arrived in early 2011 as the successor to the DS. Maintaining an overall similar look, the 3DS added a circle-pad in addition to the D-pad; the top screen now also could display stereoscopic 3D effects without the use of glasses or any other peripheral. The 3DS got off to

a slow start, largely due to a weak launch lineup and a high price point ($250). Six months after it launched, Nintendo severely dropped the price by $80, down to $169 – and that paid off, as the 3DS has since taken off sales-wise.

The Nintendo 3DS

Like the DS, the 3DS has had a number of models available to it. First was an XL model, simply a larger model of the same system. The Nintendo 2DS was also released; it plays all of the 3DS's games without any 3D display available (thus the 2D part of the name), and is in more of a slate-like design instead of a foldable clam-

The "New" Nintendo 3DS XL

shell. Most recently, the "New" Nintendo 3DS (that is indeed the name) released in both regular and XL forms in 2014 and adds a second analog stick and extra shoulder buttons, which add functionality to certain games. The 3DS family has gone on to sell roughly 60 million units around the world.

Though Nintendo has certainly had its ups and downs over its nearly 130-year history, it's pretty clear that they're here to stay. Through continuing innovations, this company's longevity is a testament to the video game industry as a whole.

# COLLECTING BY FRANCHISE

Every game has its most hardcore and devoted fans – even the smallest series and one-off games have people who have dedicated entire collections to them. But some franchises clearly stand above the rest in regards to popularity and longevity; many series have gone from simple game franchises into massive multimedia entities.

The series featured here consist of some of the most influential game franchises of all time. Games such as *Super Mario* and *Final Fantasy* have influenced entire genres of video games and continue to do so even today. *Pokémon* and *Sonic* have been cartoon series and comic books for nearly as long as they've been video games. These franchises are some of the most widespread into other media to the point where collecting that media is just as intensive as collecting the games themselves.

And obviously, these are not the only ones. We easily could have gone on about the likes of *Resident Evil*, *Tomb Raider*, *Castlevania*, and many others. But this chapter should provide a look into why so many people are so passionate about these series in particular, and includes checklists on the key games in these long-running franchises.

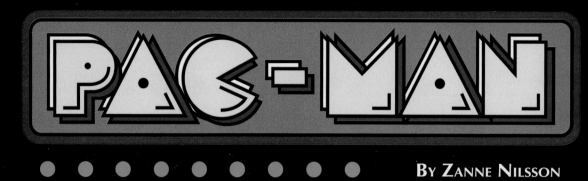

# PAC-MAN

BY ZANNE NILSSON

Sometimes, the simplest games are the best, and *Pac-Man* is a perfect example of that. A yellow guy eats dots and avoids ghosts – that's the whole game. But that yellow circle with a mouth would go on to become one of the first A-listers in the gaming industry and has established himself as a recognizable mascot in the years since he first ate his way through arcades in 1980.

*Pac-Man*'s popular origin story – according to its creator, Toru Iwatani, as quoted in Steven L. Kent's *The Ultimate History of Video Games* – is that in April 1979 Iwatani set out to create "a game for the female gaming enthusiast" based around the concept of eating, and that the appearance of the Pac-Man character himself came to Iwatani while he was having pizza for lunch. Whether this is true or not is up for debate; some sources, including previous interviews with Iwatani himself, contradict this account.

But whatever his precise origins, there's no denying that Pac-Man has become one of the most enduring and recognizable video game characters in history. From the original blockbuster arcade game *Pac-Man,* released by Namco (and distributed in the USA by Bally/Midway) in 1980, to the recent *Pac-Man and the Ghostly Adventures* games, Pac-Man has gobbled his way into the hearts of millions of gamers.

## THE ARCADE ERA

*Pac-Man* has a simple concept: the player, as Pac-Man, travels through a maze eating pac-dots while four colorful ghosts – known as Blinky, Pinky, Inky and Clyde – pursue him. Touching the ghosts kills Pac-Man, but if he eats one of the four large power pellets situated near the corners of the maze, Pac-Man can temporarily eat the ghosts for extra points. The player also receives bonus points for eating bonus items which are most commonly different kinds of fruit, but keys, bells, and even a boss from *Galaxian* appear as bonus items.

*Pac-Man* became a massive hit, and in the U.S. it notably brought women to arcades in droves. So it's unsurprising that Bally/Midway's 1981 sequel *Ms. Pac-Man* – created not by Iwatani but by nine

American college students led by Kevin Curran and Doug Macrae – featured a female spin on the character, complete with lipstick and a little red hair bow. *Ms. Pac-Man* included gameplay enhancements such as a variety of mazes and bonus items which wander around the maze instead of staying in one place. *Ms. Pac-Man* also proved to be a hit, and outsold even the original *Pac-Man* machines by more than 10,000 units.

Other Bally/Midway-made arcade sequels soon followed, including *Pac-Man Plus*, *Baby Pac-Man*, *Professor Pac-Man*, and *Jr. Pac-Man*. However, Namco hadn't authorized any of Bally/Midway's sequels, causing Namco to cancel its licensing agreement with Bally/Midway. Namco did eventually adopt *Ms. Pac-Man* as an official *Pac-Man* title and produced their own arcade sequels throughout the 1980s, including *Pac & Pal*, *Pac-Land* and *Pac-Mania*. Production of *Pac-Man* arcade games has continued into the present day; the most recent release was *Pac-Man Chomp Mania* in 2013.

## PAC-MAN COMES HOME

It wasn't long before *Pac-Man* games began appearing in home versions, including table-top mini-arcade machines and ports for the Atari 2600 and 5200, Apple II, Commodore 64, Intellivision, Nintendo Entertainment System, and MSX. Due to hardware and development limitations, the highly-anticipated Atari 2600 version didn't much resemble the original, and it's frequently cited in popular gaming mythology as being a contributing factor in the North American video game industry crash of 1983. However, the 2600 port only represented one of a whole host of issues plaguing the industry at the time.

Starting in 1993, Namco began creating exclusive new *Pac-Man* games for home consoles and computers, including (but not limited to) such titles as *Pac-Attack*, *Pac-Man 2: The New Adventures*, *Pac-In-Time*, *Pac-Man World*, *Ms. Pac-Man: Quest for the Golden Maze*, *Pac-Man Vs.*, *Pac 'n Roll*, *Pac-Man Party*, *Pac-Man and the Ghostly Adventures* and *Pac-Man 256*. Some of these games removed Pac-Man from the maze environment and instead featured him as the hero in side-scrolling or 3D adventures. *Pac-Man* games are also featured in multiple game compilations in both arcade and home releases, as well as being available on mobile devices and as plug-and-play games.

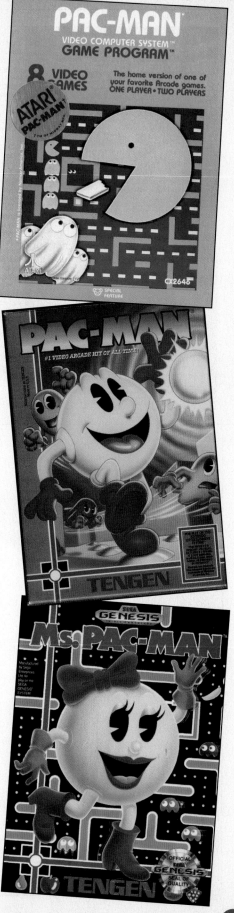

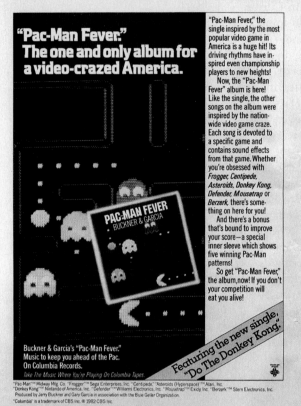

## PAC-MAN FEVER

Even outside the video game world, Pac-Man has become a cultural icon. And like all cultural icons, Pac-Man has appeared everywhere in almost every conceivable form. Most visible is the wide variety of *Pac-Man* merchandise. During the first wave of Pac-Mania, fans could wake up in their bed with Pac-Man sheets and eat Pac-Man cereal while wearing a Pac-Man T-shirt and hat then head out into the world in a car with a Pac-Man license plate.

Today, nostalgia-fueled products include a remote-controlled plastic Pac-Man (complete with sound effects), Pac-Man plush toys, and Pac-Man candy in a tin shaped like a miniature Pac-Man arcade machine. Even Nintendo got the rights to manufacture a Pac-Man amiibo figure which

"Pac-Man" TM Midway Mfg. Co. ©1980 Midway Mfg. Co.

**BUCKNER & GARCIA**
**Pac-Man Fever**

Columbia
8202

can be used with some Nintendo games. Speaking of which, you can now pit Pac-Man against other video game icons like Mario and Sonic the Hedgehog in the latest *Super Smash Bros.* fighting games from Nintendo on the 3DS and Wii U systems.

*Pac-Man* made its mark in the music world as well. In late 1981, songwriters Jerry Buckner and Gary Garcia wrote and released a song about the original game, called "Pac-Man Fever." The catchy little tune, like the game that inspired it, became a huge hit, selling over a million copies and peaking at number 9 on the Billboard Hot 100 list. It was quickly followed by an album of the same name exclusively featuring songs written about video games, including tunes about such classics as *Donkey Kong*, *Centipede* and *Frogger*. While the album didn't do as well as the "Pac-Man Fever" single, it still marked an important milestone as being one of the earliest concept albums based solely on video games, paving the way for later video-game-themed musicians and bands. Such is the popularity of the song that an updated version of "Pac-Man Fever" called "Pac-Man Fever (Eat 'Em Up)" was released in 2015.

The *Pac-Man* series also managed to spawn not one but two animated TV shows. The first, known as *Pac-Man* or *Pac-Man: The Animated Series* was on air from 1982 to 1984. It chronicles the adventures of Pac-Man as he fights to protect Pac-Land and his family – Pepper (or Ms. Pac-Man) and Baby Pac – from the Ghost Monsters, led by the evil Mezmeron. Basically: ghosts attack, Pac-Man eats a power pellet, goodbye ghosts. A few of the arcade and home games were either inspired or influenced by this series.

On the opposite end of the complexity scale there's the currently-running show, *Pac-Man and the Ghostly Adventures*, the backstory of which involves the Pac-World president's younger brother being stripped of his corporeal form as punishment for leading an attempted military coup, prompting him to try and take over Pac-World using an army of ghosts. In this universe, Pac-Man (or "Pac" as he's commonly known) is a high-schooler and the last of the yellow Pac-People in Pac-World – even his parents are gone. Pac's recently-discovered destiny is to defeat the ghosts and send their leader back to the Nether-World forever. He's aided by his high school friends Cylindria and Spiralton, and four ghosts secretly working to help him: Blinky, Pinky, Inky, and Clyde. The series has directly spawned two video games so far and could influence other *Pac-Man* games in the future.

It's safe to say that *Pac-Man*, once thought of as just another video game fad, is here to stay. The game and character have thoroughly pervaded not only pop culture but "high culture" as well; the original game was added to the collections of both the Smithsonian Institution and the Museum of Modern Art, helping to ensure that the game and its iconic characters are preserved for future generations. Not bad for a game about a yellow circle that eats things.

## KEY GAMES:

- ☐ **Pac-Man**
- ☐ **Ms. Pac-Man**
- ☐ **Pac-Land**
- ☐ **Pac-Mania**
- ☐ **Pac-Attack**
- ☐ **Pac-In-Time**
- ☐ **Pac-Man World**
- ☐ **Ms. Pac-Man Maze Madness**
- ☐ **Pac-Man: Adventures in Time**
- ☐ **Pac-Man World 2**
- ☐ **Pac-Man and the Ghostly Adventures**

# HALO

BY ZANNE NILSSON

The *Halo* series has become one of the most influential first-person shooters in video game history, known for innovative game mechanics and complex plots that prove that a fun action game can be just as epic and story-driven as a good role-playing game. But when the first game of the franchise started development, it wasn't envisioned as being the beginning of a series of games – or even as an FPS.

## THE ORIGINAL TRILOGY

Though *Halo* is now almost synonymous with Microsoft, the first game in the series was first publically announced at Apple's Macworld Conference & Expo in 1999. At the time the game's developer, Bungie, was creating *Halo* as a real-time strategy game; it became a third-person action game by the time the first trailer for the game was released at E3 2000.

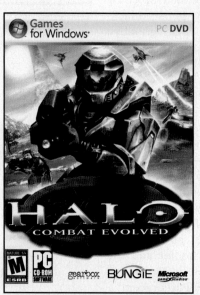

In June 2000, Microsoft acquired Bungie and announced that *Halo* would now be an exclusive game for its upcoming console, the Xbox. *Halo* was changed into an FPS and the planned online multiplayer aspect of it was scrapped because the Xbox's online service, Xbox Live, wouldn't be ready in time for the game's release. The game, renamed *Halo: Combat Evolved*, launched on the same day as the Xbox: November 15, 2001.

*Halo: Combat Evolved* takes place in the 26th century, when humanity has colonized other planets. The player takes on the role of Master Chief Petty Officer John-117 (or simply "Master Chief"), a "supersoldier" developed as part of the SPARTAN-II project on the human-colonized planet Reach. Master Chief is one of the few survivors of an attack on Reach by the Covenant, a group of advanced alien races dedicated to wiping out all of humanity for religious reasons. After his fleeing ship crashes on a mysterious ring-shaped structure the Covenant calls "Halo," Master Chief – accompanied by a group of Marines and the AI construct Cortana – must battle against the Covenant, a parasitic alien race known as the Flood, and robotic drone Sentinels to save his ship's captured captain, stop the Flood, and destroy the Halo.

While *Halo: Combat Evolved* adhered to many of the gameplay conventions of other FPS games, it also featured some innovative mechanics, including a regenerating energy shield, a limited inventory of unique weapons, and the ability to perform melee attacks while a gun is equipped. These innovations were a source of praise amongst players and critics, as was the AI in the game. *Halo: Combat Evolved* also included very well-received local multiplayer modes which could support up to 16 players via LAN – a first for a console game. *Halo: Combat Evolved* sold millions of copies and became a major selling point for the Xbox system itself.

When development on *Halo 2* began, Bungie was determined to include online multiplayer, a goal which negatively impacted other areas of development – including the story, which alternates the player between playing as Master Chief and a Covenant commander known as Thel 'Vadam. During the course of the game the humans must defend Earth against a Covenant attack, civil war starts in the Covenant, and both humans and Covenant forces must fight the Flood. In spite of the game's unsatisfying cliffhanger ending, *Halo 2* went on to sell several more millions of copies and was highly praised by critics, especially for its well-executed online multiplayer modes.

Development on *Halo 3* started while many members of Bungie's staff were still working on *Halo 2*. Because the game was being developed for Microsoft's new console, the Xbox 360, many improvements were planned, including better graphics – though the game couldn't render in true HD resolution like other Xbox 360 games. New features in *Halo 3* included high-powered but unwieldly "support weapons," a map-editing tool called Forge, and the ability to save gameplay films.

In *Halo 3*, Covenant and human forces

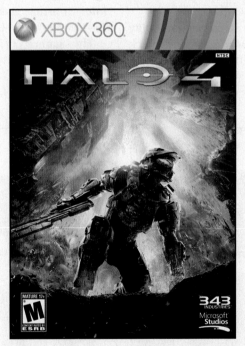

are transported to a massive structure outside the Milky Way galaxy called the Ark. The Flood arrive and begin to infest the Ark, and Master Chief and his allies must work to stop the Flood and save the galaxy. *Halo 3*, released on September 25, 2007, went on to sell 14.5 million copies around the world, making it the best-selling Xbox 360-exclusive title of all time.

## THE RECLAIMER SAGA

However, the partnership between Bungie and Microsoft wasn't destined to last. After finishing *Halo 3*, Bungie left Microsoft to become an independent company. Microsoft retained the rights to the *Halo* franchise and created their own new division to handle the series: 343 Industries. The group quickly started work on their first project, *Halo 4*.

One of 343 Industries' goals in developing *Halo 4* was to tie together all the different *Halo*-related media, which impacted the new game's plot and visual design. *Halo 4*'s story was also partially shaped by a desire to explore the relationship between Master Chief and Cortana as she experiences a form of AI mental decline known as "rampancy" – a subplot which was informed by Creative Director Josh Holmes' experiences watching his mother struggle with dementia.

*Halo 4*'s story, which begins four years after the end of *Halo 3*, pits Master Chief against an ancient warrior known as the Didact, who tries to access and use a device which can combat the Flood. The device – called the Composer – digitizes living organisms, destroying their physical forms to render them immune to Flood infection. *Halo 4* introduced new enemies known as Prometheans, and its multiplayer mode included the competitive War Games section and the ten-episode story mode Spartan Ops, which could also be played solo. The game grossed $220 million at launch, setting a new record for the *Halo* franchise.

Development soon began on the next game in the series, *Halo 5: Guardians*, which tried to broaden the scope of the *Halo* universe, partly by introducing new major characters as part of a group called Fireteam Osiris. The game's story, which picks up where *Halo 4*'s Spartan Ops campaign leaves off, begins with Fireteam Osiris being sent to retrieve Doctor Catherine Halsey – creator of the SPARTAN-II project – from a Covenant-controlled planet. Shortly afterwards, Fireteam Osiris is dispatched to capture Blue Team which, led by Master Chief, has gone rogue to find Cortana.

One of the most striking gameplay changes in *Halo 5: Guardians* is its lack of offline capabilities outside of the single-player campaign mode. But this controversial development decision didn't stop

*Halo 5: Guardians* from being a commercial success, as it grossed $400 million worldwide in the first week following its release. *Guardians* was supported by a slew of post-release downloadable content updates well into 2016, and a free version of the game's map editing tool was released in September 2016.

## SPINOFFS, ARGS, AND OTHER MEDIA

The massive success of the *Halo* franchise led to a number of spinoffs from the main series: a real-time strategy game called *Halo Wars* (2009); two FPS games, *Halo 3: ODST* (2009) and *Halo: Reach* (2010); and two twin-stick shooters, called *Halo: Spartan Assault* (2013) and *Halo: Spartan Strike* (2015).

The games of the first trilogy were marketed before their releases using three different alternate reality games. The ARG for *Halo 2*, called *I Love Bees*, was the most

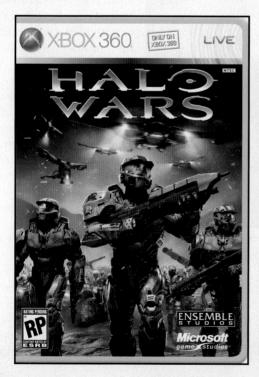

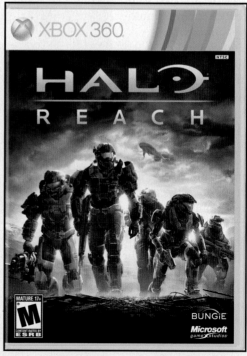

successful and influential one and is cited as being one of the major ARGs to help legitimize the form as a viable marketing tactic.

The *Halo* series also expanded into other media, including novels, comic books, anime shorts, and web series. Numerous in-canon books have been released, including *Halo: First Strike*, *Halo: The Fall of Reach*, and *Halo: The Flood*, among many others. The universe of *Halo* was also expanded with graphic novels and comics books that have been penned by some of the industry's top talent. These have included the Marvel-published *Halo: Uprising*, and written by Brian Michael Bendis, and *Halo: Helljumper*, written by Peter David. More recent comic books, such as *Halo: Escalation*, have been published by Dark Horse.

The franchise has also entered the live-action realm, with *Halo 4: Forward Unto Dawn* and *Halo: Nightfall*. *Forward Unto Dawn* originally released as a web-series consisting of 15-minute episodes and looked at the early days of the Human-Covenant War. *Nightfall* provided a closer look at the origin of Agent Jameson Locke, portrayed in the film by Mike Colter; it featured Ridley Scott as an executive producer.

An anime series, *Halo Legends*, released in 2010. It was a collaboration between five Japanese animation houses – Bones, Production I.G., Casio Entertainment, Studio 4-C, and Toei Animation – and was directed by Shinji Aramaki. Six of the stories were in-canon, while Toei's contribution was made as a parody. The series was distributed by Warner Bros.

## IMPACT AND LEGACY

*Halo*'s cultural impact can't be underestimated. The series has become one of the most iconic video game franchises of all time, and Master Chief has become almost as recognizable as Mario or Sonic the Hedgehog. The series helped turn the Xbox and its successors into some of the biggest gaming consoles in the world, making Microsoft a major competitor in the home console market. And the main games of the *Halo* series have helped shape the way FPS games are made to this day. No matter where the franchise goes from here, *Halo* is guaranteed to have a lasting legacy.

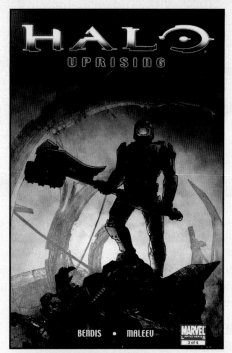

## KEY GAMES:

☐ **Halo: Combat Evolved**

☐ **Halo 2**

☐ **Halo 3**

☐ **Halo 3: ODST**

☐ **Halo: Reach**

☐ **Halo 4**

☐ **Halo 5: Guardians**

## POKÉMON

BY CARRIE WOOD

For more than two decades, trainers of all ages around the world have strived to "be the very best, like no one ever was." What was initially thought of as a fad has secured its legacy in gaming, animation and elsewhere.

### THE ORIGINS OF GAME FREAK AND POKÉMON

The *Pokémon* series is the brainchild of Satoshi Tajiri, who began development on the games shortly after founding his development company, Game Freak, in 1989. The company evolved from an arcade-focused gaming fanzine of the same name that Tajiri wrote and edited in the early 1980s. He was joined by Ken Sugimori (who later became the illustrator on *Pokémon*) in the magazine effort, and when they found games of the era lacking, their solution was simply to develop their own games. Early Game Freak titles included *Quinty*,

an arcade game published by Namco. Tajiri thought of the *Pokémon* concept after seeing the Game Boy's capacity to communicate between two systems via a link cable.

Tajiri was also inspired by his childhood hobby of insect collecting and wanted to create a game containing insect-like creatures, which he called Pocket Monsters (which is where the shortened "Pokémon" derives from). He also wanted to make sure that Pokémon never die in battle, instead simply getting knocked out, in an attempt to prevent "pointless violence" from filling his games.

Tajiri received help from Shigeru Miyamoto after successfully pitching the *Pokémon* concept to Nintendo. The development of the first *Pokémon* series took a full six years – the longest ever for any game in the series – and nearly bankrupted Game Freak entirely. Tajiri himself never took home a paycheck during this period.

Creatures, Inc., a subsidiary of Nintendo, invested in Game Freak to help get them through the development (they maintain a one-third share of any *Pokémon*-related franchise rights today).

The original Game Boy releases of *Pokémon Red* and *Pokémon Green* hit Japan on February 27, 1996, and kick-started what has become a massive media franchise.

The two *Pokémon* titles followed the same plot: the player begins in Pallet Town in the Kanto region where they start their journey to become a Pokémon Master. In order to become the Champion, they must defeat the eight regional Gym Leaders, fight their way through Victory Road, and defeat the Elite Four at the Indigo Plateau. Along the way, they will encounter their rival several times, and fight against the villainous Team Rocket – a group of evil trainers who use Pokémon as tools to complete their crimes. The difference between the games were the Pokémon included on the cartridge – several creatures are exclusive to each version, meaning that in order to "catch 'em all," players must trade with others via the Game Boy Link Cable to get the other version's exclusive Pokémon.

After *Pokémon Red* and *Green* took off in popularity, an enhanced version called *Pokémon Blue* was also released in Japan. It was the Japanese version of *Pokémon Blue* that was ported to other regions as *Pokémon Red* and *Blue* versions. The major differences from *Red/Green* and *Blue* were the sprite designs, though minor tweaks in-game were also made. When the games were being translated to English, the American staff actually wanted to change the sprites further to make them more "beefed up," though that idea was shot down.

## POKÉMANIA

Though the Japanese staff had reservations about the game's North American release, it proved to be a huge success, selling 9.85 million units in the U.S. on top of more than 10 million already sold in Japan. The success spurred Nintendo and Game Freak to create another enhanced remake, *Pokémon Yellow*, also known as the "Special Pikachu Edition," which released in 1998 and aimed to make better use of the color palette available on the Game Boy Color.

*Pokémon Yellow* also featured slight story changes that aligned it better with the *Pokémon* anime series: the player always starts with Pikachu (instead of choosing one of three potential starter Pokémon), and anime-exclusive characters like Jessie, James, Nurse Joy and Officer Jenny all appear. Sprites were also upgraded again to better match the anime designs. *Pokémon Yellow*'s release coincided with the first *Pokémon* film in Japan. Despite being essentially the same game as *Red, Blue* and *Green*, it sold incredibly well and was actually the fastest-selling handheld title ever at the time of its launch. It also helped boost Game Boy console sales around the time period, from 3.5 million in '98 to 8 million in '99.

Between the games, the anime, and a popular card game on top of that, *Pokémon* had sufficiently taken over the world by the close of the 20th century. But this was only the beginning for the series, which would soon see a huge influx of new creatures to collect.

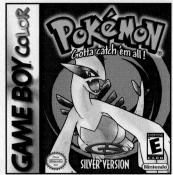

## FURTHER GENERATIONS AND CONTINUING POPULARITY

The second generation of the *Pokémon* games began in 1999 in Japan, and the following year elsewhere, with the release of *Pokémon Gold* and *Pokémon Silver* for the Game Boy Color. The games introduced players to a new region, Johto, with 100 new monsters and eight new badges to collect. Those who finished the Johto challenge were then able to revisit Kanto, seeing how things have changed in the three years between *Red/Blue* and *Gold/Silver*.

*Pokémon Gold* and *Silver* continued the massive success of their predecessors and helped the *Pokémon* franchise go from a multi-million dollar franchise into a multi-billion dollar one. The second generation of games was also critically acclaimed, with the variety of improvements made, such as the day/night system that ran off an in-game clock, particularly praised. Similarly to how *Red/Blue* were followed up with *Yellow*, *Gold/Silver* also received a third version – though this one made significantly greater leaps than the previous generation did.

*Pokémon Crystal* was released for the Game Boy Color around the world between 2000 and 2001. It marked the first time that the player was able to choose the gender of their character with the introduction of a female playable character, and the plot focused heavily on the legendary Pokémon Suicune (featured as *Crystal*'s cover mascot) and the mystery of the Unown. *Crystal* was also the first time that the battle sprites were animated, a feature that really pushed the GBC to its limits.

As technology evolved, so too did *Pokémon*, with the third generation of games arriving for the Game Boy Advance in 2002 – *Pokémon Ruby* and *Sapphire*. This generation introduced 135 new Pokémon, and was set in Hoenn, an area inspired by Japan's Kyushu region. Though the games continued to sell well, they were criticized for removing some of the features that had been present in *Gold/Silver/Crystal*, such as the day/night cycle and the animated sprites. The GBA would later see *Pokémon Emerald*, the follow-up to *Ruby/Sapphire*, but would also be the first home to a set of remakes: *Pokémon FireRed* and *LeafGreen*, enhanced remakes of *Red/Green*. This was the first time that a main series *Pokémon* title was ported to a more contemporary system, and would set a standard followed in later generations.

The Nintendo DS would play home to two generations – the fourth, with *Pokémon Diamond*, *Pearl* and *Platinum*, and the

fifth, with *Pokémon Black, White, Black 2* and *White 2*.

The fourth generation, starting with *Diamond/Pearl* in 2006, introduced 107 more Pokémon to the Pokédex, It also introduced a number of features that are now standards for the series, such as online battling and trading via Wi-Fi. *Pokémon Platinum* was released in 2008, with a slightly altered plotline focusing on the mysterious Pokémon Giratina. In 2009, remakes of *Gold* and *Silver* released as *HeartGold* and *SoulSilver*; they rank among the highest-rated DS games of all time and were also some of the best-selling on the system.

*Pokémon Black* and *White* arrived in September 2010, and were set in the region of Unova, which was based on New York City – the first time that the game's region was based on a place outside of Japan. The games featured graphical upgrades even when compared to the previous generation (which was also on the DS) and introduced greater internet and wireless features, plus another 156 new Pokémon. Even though the Nintendo 3DS had been released already, *Pokémon Black 2* and *White 2* released in 2011, marking the first (and so far only) time that there were numbered sequels within the main series of *Pokémon* games.

*Pokémon* finally arrived on the 3DS system in 2013 with the release of *Pokémon X* and *Y*, which were the first main *Pokémon* games rendered in 3D. Set in the France-influenced Kalos region, *X/Y* introduced just 72 new Pokémon but did bring a massive new battle feature, called Mega Evolution, plus the new Fairy-type classification. In 2014, remakes of the third generation games, called *Pokémon Omega Ruby* and *Alpha Sapphire*, also released; they ran off of the same game engine as *X/Y* and were a huge leap from the GBA versions of the game. Notably, there was not a direct follow-up in the form of a third game or a numbered sequel for *X/Y*, and the series instead continued on into the current generation.

*Pokémon Sun* and *Moon* mark the seventh generation of games, and released during the 20th anniversary year for the franchise, in November 2016. *Sun* and *Moon* are set in the tropical, Hawaii-

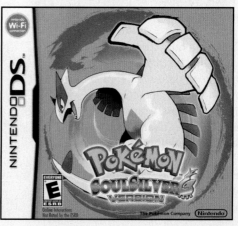

inspired Alola region, and are the first to feature "regional variants" of Pokémon from past generations.

## SPINOFFS AND SIDE STORIES

Outside of the main series of games, there have also been a number of spinoff titles. Some of these have been more successful than others, and have managed to turn into long-running series on their own.

For the Game Boy and Game Boy Color, fans could pick up *Pokémon Pinball,* a fairly straightforward pinball simulation with Pokémon appearances; *Pokémon Trading Card Game*, an RPG similar to the main series in many ways that replaced Pokémon battles with trading card matches; and *Pokémon Puzzle Challenge,* which was a *Tetris Attack*-style game with Pokémon elements.

The Nintendo 64 was also home to some of the most popular spinoffs, such as *Pokémon Stadium* and *Stadium 2,* which focused exclusively on battles in a 3D environment; *Pokémon Snap,* a photography simulator where the player completed tasks for Professor Oak by taking pictures of various Pokémon; *Pokémon Puzzle League,* a puzzle-battle game with appearances from Pokémon anime characters; and *Hey You Pikachu,* where the player takes care of a pet Pikachu. Pikachu and Jigglypuff also appeared as playable characters in the first *Super Smash Bros.*

Spinoff series have included the *Pokémon Mystery Dungeon* series, which now includes seven

games on its own. The *Mystery Dungeon* games all feature the player character as a human who was suddenly turned into a Pokémon and classic roguelike gameplay. Another major spinoff series is *Pokémon Ranger,* which has three games and is more of a traditional RPG.

Various other spinoffs have included *Pokémon Trozei!, Pokémon Picross, Pokémon Rumble, Pokémon Channel, Pokémon Conquest, Pokémon Dash, Pokémon Art Academy, Pokken Tournament,* and many more. The spinoff games severely outnumber the main series games at this point, but have generally helped to fill in the gaps between main line releases.

Perhaps the most notable spinoff title as of late has been *Pokémon Go,* a mobile title for smartphones that allows players to catch Pokémon in the real world via the use of GPS and AR technology. The app, developed in a partnership between Nintendo and Niantic, quickly became one of the most downloaded ever.

## POKÉMON IN OTHER MEDIA

The easiest to speak of is the *Pokémon* anime series, which has been around nearly as long with the same level of popularity of the games themselves. The anime debuted on April 1, 1997, introducing the world to Ash and Pikachu as they're joined by Misty and Brock on their own adventure. (Incidentally, the Japanese names of Ash and his rival, Gary, are Satoshi and Shigeru, named after Satoshi Tajiri and Shigeru

Miyamoto.) Ash, Pikachu and their pals have now been featured in more than 900 episodes in the still-ongoing series, plus 18 full-length feature films.

The anime series had originally been planned to run about a year and a half, about as long as it would have taken to finish the first story arc (the Kanto region story). However, due to the incredible popularity of the show, they extended the run, and as it continues with new episodes today, it's now one of the longest-running anime series ever.

And what is a media franchise without a comic book tie-in, anyway? There have been several different *Pokémon* manga series, including *Magical Pokémon Journey* and *Pokémon: The Electric Tale of Pikachu*, but the longest-running has been *Pokémon Adventures* (known as *Pokémon Special* in Japan), which began serialization in March 1997 and has been ongoing ever since; it's so far been collected into 52 volumes. The story of *Pokémon Adventures* is closer to the games, following the trainer Red as he seeks to take down Team Rocket, collect eight gym badges, and become a Pokémon Master. In fact, Satoshi Tajiri once said in an interview that he believed *Pokémon Adventures* to be "the comic that most resembles the world I was trying to convey."

To look at *Pokémon* by the numbers, so far it's been: 900-plus anime episodes, 18 films, nine television specials, 25 main series video games, more than 40 spin-off games, 64 card game sets, 52 manga volumes, and (so far) 802 total Pokémon to collect. But the most important number is 20 – 20 full years of the *Pokémon* franchise. If anything says "this is hardly a fad," it's that. *Pokémon* is not merely a kids' cartoon or a silly video game; for many, it's a hobby and a beloved series that they've followed into adulthood. Here's to 20 more years (and maybe another 800 or so new creatures)!

## KEY GAMES:

**MAIN SERIES:**
- Red/Blue/Yellow
- Ruby/Sapphire/Emerald
- FireRed/LeafGreen
- Diamond/Pearl/Platinum
- HeartGold/SoulSilver
- Black/White
- Black 2/White 2
- X/Y
- Omega Ruby/Alpha Sapphire
- Sun/Moon

**SPINOFFS:**
- Stadium series
- Mystery Dungeon series
- Ranger series
- Pokémon Snap
- Pokémon Trading Card Game
- Pokken Tournament

# SONIC THE HEDGEHOG

BY CARRIE WOOD

Though his heyday of the 1990s is now behind him, Sonic the Hedgehog remains one of gaming's most recognizable characters. Thanks to his more than 25 years' worth of history, Sega's Blue Blur has been a popular choice for collectors around the world to focus on.

Sonic himself was created when Sega decided they needed a mascot character that could truly compete with Nintendo's Super Mario. A variety of concepts were conceived, and the hedgehog – originally called "Mr. Needlemouse" by the creative team – was settled on. After a couple of small changes, including making him blue to match Sega's logo, Sonic was born. Known for his quick feet and easy-going attitude, Sonic was marketed heavily as a "cooler" alternative to Mario. He actually first appeared as a cameo in the game *Rad Mobile*, an arcade racing title developed by Sega, in the form of an air freshener that can be seen hanging off the rear mirror.

## SPEEDING ONTO THE GENESIS AND EARLY SUCCESS

*Sonic the Hedgehog* arrived on the Sega Genesis on June 23, 1991, and was an imme-

diate success. The game followed Sonic as he faced off against Dr. Ivo "Eggman" Robotnik, who has trapped the various animals who live on South Island and enslaved them to power his robot army. Sonic must rescue the animals as well as collect the powerful Chaos Emeralds before Robotnik can. A side-scrolling platforming title, *Sonic the Hedgehog* distanced itself from its competition by focusing on high-speed action.

The game proved to be incredibly popular, with critics praising the lively look of the graphics in addition to the smooth gameplay. The reception to *Sonic* propelled sales of the Genesis and resulted in a sequel, *Sonic the Hedgehog 2*, to enter development almost instantaneously; it debuted in November 1992 and introduced Sonic's friend and sidekick, Tails. It also introduced one of Sonic's signature moves, the Spin Dash. *Sonic 2* became the second best-selling Genesis game ever (behind its predecessor) and propelled the series forward.

Another direct sequel, *Sonic the Hedgehog 3*, arrived in 1994, adding another main character to the franchise – Knuckles the Echidna, who would become one of Sonic's rivals as well as an ally. Knuckles served as an antagonist alongside Robotnik, but eventually became a playable hero in *Sonic & Knuckles*, which arrived later in 1994. *Sonic 3* and *Sonic & Knuckles* had originally been designed to be a single game, but due to technology limitations of the time had to be split between two cartridges. The *Sonic & Knuckles* cartridge used "lock-on technology" which allowed it to connect to and access data from *Sonic 3*, as well as *Sonic 2*, in order to play as Knuckles in either title.

The Sega CD was a CD-ROM attachment to the larger Genesis console, and ended up with its own *Sonic* title when *Sonic CD* arrived in late 1993. Two more main characters made their debut in the title – Amy Rose and Metal Sonic – and the story followed Sonic as he traveled through time in an effort to save Amy. Though not as much of a best-seller as earlier titles (largely due to the fact that the Sega CD itself wasn't terribly popular), *Sonic CD* was widely acclaimed and is considered one of the best entries in the franchise to date. The game was ported to a number of different consoles and also received a mobile phone port, helping it to reach a wider audience in the years since it first released.

Outside of the main series, a spin-off title called *Sonic Spinball* was also released, in 1993. The game was a pinball title that featured Sonic himself as the ball. *Spinball* was developed because *Sonic 3* wasn't coming along in a timely fashion, and thanks to the popularity of the Casino Zone stage in the earlier titles, it was figured by the creative team that a spinoff focusing on that stage would be successful. Despite critically mixed reviews, it sold decently and was later ported to the Game Gear. It's also notable for being one of the few games in the franchise to include characters from the *Sonic the Hedgehog* and *Adventures of Sonic* cartoon shows.

Other spinoffs released during the first few years of *Sonic*'s history included the puzzle-platformer *Sonic Labyrinth*, the kart racers *Sonic Drift* and *Sonic Drift 2*, and the Tails-centric *Tails Adventure* and *Tails' Skypatrol*.

## SHIFT TO THE SATURN AND STRUGGLES AT SEGA

The Sega Saturn arrived around the world between 1994 and 1995 and was almost immediately marred with issues due to bizarre marketing choices by Sega themselves. During its lifespan, a handful of *Sonic* titles arrived, though few of them managed to stand out. *Sonic 3D Blast* was one of the first on the system, though it had been developed with the Genesis in mind and was sent to the Saturn really just for the sake of having any *Sonic* title on the new console.

*3D Blast*, unlike the typical side-scrolling platforming of other *Sonic* titles, shifted to an isometric top-down environment that included three-dimensional sprites. The Saturn version of the game did feature enhanced graphics but generally plays the same as the Genesis edition. *Sonic 3D Blast* managed to be ported to the Saturn in just four months.

The big reason why *Sonic 3D Blast* ended up on the Saturn is that Sega had concerns that another title in development, *Sonic X-Treme*, would end up canceled. They were right: *Sonic X-Treme* never arrived. The game started development in 1994, following the release of *Sonic & Knuckles*, and the intention was to create a *Sonic* game that featured full three-dimensional graphics. However, the game design kept changing, and the game engine changed as well, leading the *X-Treme* project to end up stuck in development hell.

A visit from Sega of Japan representatives, including CEO Hayao Nakayama, didn't help things, as they were staunchly unimpressed by the game's progress. Eventually, *Sonic X-Treme* was cancelled in early 1997. The debacle over *Sonic X-Treme* – which led the Saturn to be left without a new main-entry *Sonic* title – is credited as being a leading factor in the Saturn's untimely demise.

Two spinoffs did make their way to the doomed console, however: *Sonic R* and *Sonic Jam*. *Sonic R* was another racing game that featured the main characters of the series, while *Sonic Jam* was a compilation disc containing *Sonic the Hedgehog, Sonic 2, Sonic 3* and *Sonic & Knuckles*.

## AN ADVENTURE ON THE DREAMCAST

When Sega was getting ready to launch their Dreamcast console, they were also developing what would become the first fully three-dimensional *Sonic* title, *Sonic Adventure*. The game became a launch title for the Dreamcast and was released alongside the console in 1998 and 1999 as the Dreamcast rolled out in Japan and elsewhere.

With the transition to 3D gaming, Sonic himself gained a new look, becoming overall much taller and lankier with longer spines as well. The idea was to redesign him so that he would look better in 3D, as the original short-and-stout Sonic had been designed to be seen from the side for the 2D platforming generation.

*Sonic Adventure* became the best-selling title on the Dreamcast and propelled the sales of the system itself. A sequel, *Sonic Adventure 2*, arrived in 2001, introducing the fan-favorite characters Shadow and Rouge. Though it received positive reviews, it didn't sell as well as its predecessor, and

couldn't help the Dreamcast's declining sales; the Dreamcast itself was discontinued in March 2001. The only other *Sonic* title on the Dreamcast was *Sonic Shuffle*, a board game-inspired spinoff.

*Sonic Adventure 2* received some additional attention on the Nintendo GameCube, becoming the first game in the series to release on a Nintendo platform. *Sonic Adventure 2: Battle* had a variety of minor upgrades and proved to be popular, helping to extend the lifespan of the title at large.

## RUNNING INTO VARIED SUCCESS ON OTHER CONSOLES

The Dreamcast – though very much a critical darling – was a commercial failure, and Sega ceased the production of new console hardware following its discontinuation. However, the company was able to refocus its efforts into strengthening their software, and became a third-party developer for other consoles. This effectively has allowed the *Sonic* franchise to live on, and it's continued to appear on a wide variety of platforms in the years since the Dreamcast's demise.

Outside of successful ports of *Sonic Adventure* and *Adventure 2*, the series saw original games become popular on different systems. The first of these was *Sonic Advance* for the Game Boy Advance in 2001, which returned to the classic speedy 2D platforming while retaining some elements seen in the 3D titles. It received two sequels in '03 and '04.

*Sonic Heroes* served as the follow-up to the *Adventure* titles, and was released on the GameCube, PlayStation 2 and Xbox simultaneously. While it featured overall similar gameplay, players now controlled a team of three characters rather than just one at a time. Early spinoff titles on other consoles included *Shadow the Hedgehog,*

*Sonic Riders* and *Sonic Rivals*.

Moving further into the aughts, Sonic did have some stumbles, starting with the notorious *Sonic the Hedgehog* in 2006 (commonly referred to as just *Sonic '06*). The game was an outright failure on multiple fronts given its rushed development cycle – which led to a number of messy glitches in-game – and its bizarre romantic sub-plot, which turned off longtime fans. Other games that failed to catch popular positive opinions included *Sonic and the Secret Rings, Sonic and the Black Knight, Sonic Unleashed*, and *Sonic Boom*.

However, there have been some standouts, including *Sonic Colors* and *Sonic Generations*, the latter of which celebrated the series' 20th anniversary in 2011 by highlighting both the old-school and new-school Sonics with stages in both two and three dimensions. Sonic has also teamed up with his longtime rival, Mario, in the *Mario and Sonic at the Olympic Games* series, a sports game collection focusing on the various Olympic events. He also joined the *Super Smash Bros.* lineup starting with *Brawl*.

It's become obvious that *Sonic the Hedgehog* won't be going anywhere, as Sega will be producing *Sonic Mania* – a game celebrating the character's 25th anniversary – for a 2017 release. The game will go back to the basics, echoing the look and feel of the classic Genesis titles.

## SONIC IN OTHER MEDIA

Essentially from the get-go, Sonic and the crew started showing up in other media, not the least of which has been various cartoon series. DiC Entertainment was the first out of the gate with *Adventures of Sonic the Hedgehog*, broadcast starting in 1993 in syndication for a total of 65 episodes. The second series by DiC, called just *Sonic the Hedgehog*, also started in '93 but featured a slightly darker tone. *Sonic Underground* was the final DiC Sonic-related cartoon, produced in 1999, and introduced a separate canon outside of the series of games. *Underground* featured Sonic's two siblings, Sonia and Manic, as they seek to liberate the planet from Dr. Robotnik. The Hedgehog trio also played instruments that could be used as weapons.

Two anime series have been produced: a *Sonic the Hedgehog* two-episode OVA series based on *Sonic CD*, and *Sonic X*. *Sonic X* was mixed in regards to its critical reception but proved to be popular around the world, as it would end up being shown on the Fox Saturday morning block in America. Most recently, a CGI cartoon series based on *Sonic Boom* has aired, featuring the new redesigns of the main characters. Though the *Sonic Boom* games haven't been popular, the series itself has been praised as being a fun depiction of the classic *Sonic* cast.

The *Sonic the Hedgehog* comic book has been published, ongoing, since 1993 by Archie Comics. Archie has also been home to a number of other related comic books, including *Sonic Universe, Sonic X, Sonic Boom* and *Knuckles the Echidna*. The books all generally feature their own storylines separate from the games (with the exception of *Sonic Boom*, based on the games and cartoon) and have on occasion crossed over with Archie's *Mega Man* comic books.

Between the games, comic books, cartoon shows and a number of other merchandise, there's no shortage of *Sonic the Hedgehog* to collect – and the Blue Blur clearly hasn't shown any signs of slowing down after more than two and a half decades.

## KEY GAMES:

☐ **Sonic the Hedgehog**
☐ **Sonic the Hedgehog 2**
☐ **Sonic the Hedgehog 3**
☐ **Sonic CD**
☐ **Sonic 3D Blast**
☐ **Sonic Adventure**
☐ **Sonic Adventure 2**
☐ **Sonic the Hedgehog (2006)**
☐ **Sonic Unleashed**
☐ **Sonic Colors**
☐ **Sonic Generations**
☐ **Sonic Boom**

SUPER MARIO

The mustached plumber with the red cap has become video gaming's number-one icon since his first appearance in *Donkey Kong* in 1981. Shigeru Miyamoto's greatest creation, Super Mario, has leapt his way into the hearts of many around the world over the last three and a half decades. With more than 200 games in the overall *Mario* franchise, it would take its own book for a full discussion of each of them; this instead hopes to serve as a more general look at this legendary franchise.

## MARIO'S ORIGINS

Miyamoto had been tasked with creating an arcade hit that would bring Nintendo back from the financial straits it endured after the commercial failure of *Radar Scope*. The resulting game was *Donkey Kong*, where a character simply named "Jumpman" had to rescue his damsel in distress, Pauline, from the antagonistic ape for which the game was named.

An early example of the platforming genre as a whole, *Donkey Kong* proved to be a massive hit, selling more than 60,000 cabinets by the end of June 1982. Home versions of the game were made, helping to continue *Donkey Kong*'s popularity and spur a number of arcade sequels, such as *Donkey Kong Jr.*; *Donkey Kong* of course would also turn into its own successful franchise with console darlings like *Donkey Kong Country*.

Jumpman was later renamed Mario, after Nintendo's office landlord, Mario Segale. As the story goes, Nintendo was behind on their payments, and after Segale burst into the office demanding rent and

exchanged some testy words, Nintendo of America President Minoru Arakawa decided to name their mascot after him.

The *Mario* branding itself was first used for 1983's *Mario Bros.*, which also introduced Mario's younger brother, Luigi. In this title, the two must work together to defeat the various creatures that have been invading the sewers beneath New York City. Creatures were defeated by one of the brothers flipping them over and then kicking them away. Though not nearly as successful as *Donkey Kong*, *Mario Bros.* was a respectable success in the arcades.

## GOING SUPER

The series took a turn for the fantastical with the release of *Super Mario Bros.* in 1985. Taking place in the Mushroom Kingdom, Mario and Luigi must rescue Princess Toadstool (who would later be named Princess Peach) from the evil Bowser. Helping to popularize side-scrolling platformers, the game truly kicked off Mario's reign with genuinely fun gameplay coupled with colorful graphics. As a pack-in title for the Nintendo Entertainment System, it helped to fuel sales for the system as well.

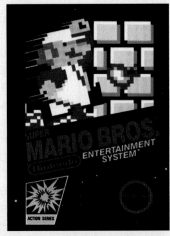

*Super Mario Bros. 2* is interesting, as Japan and America got entirely different games. Japan's *Super Mario Bros. 2* used the game engine from the first title but added significantly more complex elements (such as weather) to it, resulting in more complex levels and an overall higher difficulty. This *Super Mario Bros. 2* was restricted to Japan because Nintendo believed that a *Mario* game that was too difficult would alienate the American audience the company had fought so hard to get. It was later released in North America as *Super Mario Bros: The Lost Levels*.

Instead, the U.S. version of *Super Mario Bros. 2* was actually a reskinned version of the Japanese game *Doki Doki Panic*. Interestingly enough, *Doki Doki Panic* was originally based on a discarded prototype for a *Mario* game, making it basically a *Mario* game that was turned into *Doki Doki Panic* and then reconverted back into a *Mario* game. The game marked the first time that Princess Peach and Toad were available as playable characters in addition to Mario and Luigi. This *Super Mario Bros. 2* went back to Japan as *Super Mario USA*.

*Super Mario Bros. 3* released in Japan in 1988 before coming to the west in 1990. Once again, the Princess has been kidnapped by Bowser, and it's up to Mario and Luigi to save the day. This game remains a fan favorite for a number of reasons – a world map, the appearance of Bowser's seven children (the Koopalings), the various power-ups (such as the Tanooki Suit and the Frog Suit), among other things. *Super Mario Bros. 3* was a massive commercial success, becoming one of the best-selling games of its time (moving 17 million copies), and is considered one of the greatest games ever.

Mario went portable in *Super Mario Land* for the Game Boy in 1989. The game was the first handheld appearance for the franchise besides Game & Watch ports of earlier titles. Continuing the sidescrolling platformer tradition, Mario leapt his way

into Sarasaland in order to save Princess Daisy (who has since become a supporting character in the series) from the evil Tatanga. This was followed up with a sequel, *Super Mario Land 2: 6 Golden Coins*, in 1992; the sequel introduced Mario's rival, Wario.

Two original titles were released for the SNES: *Super Mario World*, a fairly straightforward platformer that introduced some new power-ups, as well as the ability to ride Yoshi for the first time; and *Super Mario World 2: Yoshi's Island*. While *Yoshi's Island* is technically part of the *Super Mario* series, it has since been spun off into its own series. The game is a prequel to the *Super Mario* franchise as a whole, and focuses on Yoshi, who must protect Baby Mario from being kidnapped as they seek Luigi.

## A THIRD DIMENSION

Serving as a launch title for the Nintendo 64, *Super Mario 64* arrived in 1996. The game was the first three-dimensional platformer in the series, introducing an open world based around Peach's castle. Bowser has trapped Peach, and Mario must save her by collecting the Power Stars hidden throughout the levels. The game helped the sales of the N64 (which otherwise did not have much in the way of other games at launch) and is considered one of the most influential titles ever.

*Super Mario Sunshine*, the second 3D adventure, released for the GameCube in 2002. Mario must take on an evil doppelganger who has vandalized Isle Delfino. The game borrowed many elements from *Super Mario 64* while adding a whole

other gameplay mechanic with the FLUDD water-squirting backpack that Mario uses. A critical success, *Sunshine* moved more than 5.5 million copies.

Two 3D *Mario* games released for the Wii: *Super Mario Galaxy* and *Super Mario Galaxy 2*. Taking the series to outer space, Mario must travel between galaxies to collect Power Stars as he seeks to once again rescue Peach, whose entire castle has been taken to space by Bowser. *Super Mario Galaxy* is one of the best-reviewed games of all time, and its sequel was no slouch in that department either.

The *Super Mario* series maintained its three-dimensional platforming with *Super Mario 3D Land* for the 3DS in 2011, and *Super Mario 3D World* for the Wii U in 2013. Both games were critically acclaimed; *3D World* also brought back Peach and Toad as playable characters for the first time in the main series since *Super Mario Bros. 2*.

## RETRO REVIVAL

A subseries of the franchise came about in 2006 on the DS with the arrival of *New Super Mario Bros.*, a game that sought to reboot the two-dimensional sidescrolling platforming gameplay of yesteryear. By placing 3D objects on a 2D plane, it resulted in a 2.5D effect; bringing back classic power-ups like the Fire Flower gave it the retro feel that Nintendo aimed for. Mario and Luigi were playable in the game, which released to wide critical acclaim and sold more than 30 million copies worldwide. The game received a direct sequel, *New Super Mario Bros. 2*, on the 3DS in 2012. While the Mario Brothers must save Princess Peach, they must also collect 1 million gold coins.

Two more *"New"* games released – *New Super Mario Bros. Wii* and *New Super Mario Bros. U*, for the Wii and Wii U, respectively. Both featured cooperative gameplay, and made use of their respective system's controllers in unique ways. *New Super Mario Bros. Wii* was a critical and commercial success, selling nearly 30 million copies around the world. *New Super Mario Bros. U* was praised for its creativity and for using the GamePad controller in unique ways, and though it is the second best-selling title on its console, lackluster Wii U console sales mean the game only has sold about 5.5 million copies.

## MARIO'S MANY OTHER ADVENTURES

Besides the main *Super Mario* series, Mario has starred in a number of other tie-in and side series that have become behemoths in their own right. One of the most popular of these is the *Mario Kart* franchise, which began in 1992 with the release of *Super Mario Kart*. The go-kart racer pits Mario, Luigi, Peach and the rest of the Mushroom Kingdom crew against each other in races that feature tricky courses and familiar power-ups.

The *Mario Kart* series has released five games for home consoles, three portable titles, plus a handful of arcade-only titles that have been co-developed by Namco. The most recent entry in the series is *Mario Kart 8*, which introduced high-definition graphics to the franchise and anti-gravity racing, plus a variety of downloadable content. The *Mario Kart* franchise as a whole is the most successful and longest-running kart racing series ever, and has in total moved more than 100 million copies worldwide.

Mario apparently got his doctorate somewhere along the way, leading to the *Dr. Mario* series of puzzle games. Beginning in 1990 on the NES and Game Boy, the player is tasked with getting rid of viruses by dropping capsules in the correct way to eradicate them. Further games in the series have included *Dr. Mario 64, Dr. Mario Express,* and *Dr. Luigi.* The *Mario's Picross* series of games has also come along as a Mario-focused puzzle series.

The role-playing genre has also played home to Mario and his pals, beginning with *Super Mario RPG* in 1996, which was developed by Square (of *Final Fantasy* fame). Though there have been no direct sequels to the SNES fan favorite, a number of other RPG games have featured Mario, and are divided into the *Paper Mario* and *Mario & Luigi* series.

*Paper Mario* first released for the N64 in 2000 to wide critical and commercial success. The graphics, which combined the flat paper Mario with a fully 3D world, immediately grabbed the attention of gamers around the world. The series was followed up with *The Thousand-Year Door, Super Paper Mario, Sticker Star,* and *Color Splash.* The *Mario & Luigi* series began in 2003 on the GBA with *Superstar Saga,* which was followed by *Partners in Time, Bowser's Inside Story,* and *Dream Team.* A crossover between the two franchises occurred with *Mario & Luigi: Paper Jam* in 2015 for the 3DS.

The first *Mario Party* title released in '99 for the N64, and has been followed up by nine numbered sequels in addition to a handful of spinoffs, such as *Mario Party Advance, Mario Party DS, Mario Party Island Tour,* and *Mario Party Star Rush.* The games all feature four-player competitive action in which the players try to win a board game by going head-to-head in a variety of minigames. The *Party* franchise has sold about 40 million copies worldwide.

And of course, the entire *Super Mario* crew has competed against each other in a variety of sports titles, including the *Mario Tennis, Mario Golf, Mario Strikers,* and *Mario Baseball* series, plus one-off titles like *Mario Hoops 3-on-3* and *Mario Sports Mix.* Mario has also taken on his longtime rival Sonic the Hedgehog in the now ongoing series of *Mario and Sonic at the Olympic Games.*

## MARIO IN OTHER MEDIA

A number of cartoon series have been produced over the years, beginning with *Saturday Supercade* in 1983; the series ran for two seasons and featured Mario, Donkey Kong and Pauline from *Donkey Kong* as well as other arcade mascots like Frogger and Q*Bert. Further cartoon series based just on the *Mario* games have included *The Adventures of Super Mario Bros. 3*, which aired in 1990, and *Super Mario World*, which aired in 1991-1992.

The best-known television show featuring the characters, though, was *The Super Mario Bros. Super Show!* which broadcast in first-run syndication between September 4 and December 1, 1989. It combined live-action segments with cartoon ones, and featured Captain Lou Albano as Mario, with Danny Wells as Luigi. The show (and its silly ending theme), though goofy, is warmly remembered by many fans and has received multiple home video releases.

A number of *Super Mario* comics have been produced over the years. In Japan, the *Super Mario-Kun* manga series has been serialized in *CoroCoro* since 1990, and follows Mario through the various game plotlines. Another manga, *Super Mario Adventures,* ran in 1992 and was serialized in *Nintendo Power* magazine. In 2016, Viz Media released a collection of these comics, which had long been out of print.

In America, Valiant Comics produced the *Nintendo Comics System* books between 1990 and 1991. The comics primarily focus on Mario and the gang, but also introduced a number of characters not seen in the games. In 1991, Mario had two different books from Valiant – *Super Mario Bros.* and *Adventures of the Super Mario Bros.*

And in regards to the big screen, there's the infamous *Super Mario Bros.* film, released in 1993. Starring Bob Hoskins and John Leguizamo as Mario and Luigi, respectively, the brothers must take down King Koopa. It was the first live-action major motion picture to be based on a video game, but despite the enduring popularity of the game series, the film was a disaster – critically panned by the press, it only made $21 million against a $48 million budget.

Though many things have changed from the 8-bit arcades to the high-definition era of today, Mario hasn't done much of anything different. The optimistic plumber continues to hop on Goombas and join forces with his brother when necessary to take down the ever-lurking evil of Bowser and save Peach. Mascots have certainly come and gone over the years – especially in gaming – but Mario endures, and it's pretty unlikely he'll be leaving anytime soon.

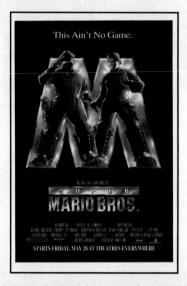

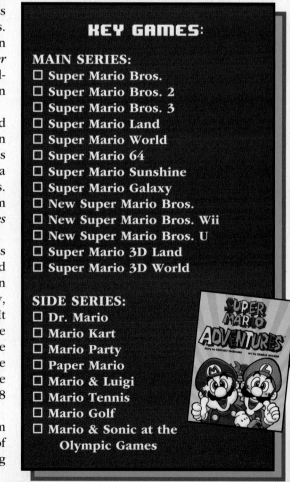

**KEY GAMES:**

**MAIN SERIES:**
- ☐ Super Mario Bros.
- ☐ Super Mario Bros. 2
- ☐ Super Mario Bros. 3
- ☐ Super Mario Land
- ☐ Super Mario World
- ☐ Super Mario 64
- ☐ Super Mario Sunshine
- ☐ Super Mario Galaxy
- ☐ New Super Mario Bros.
- ☐ New Super Mario Bros. Wii
- ☐ New Super Mario Bros. U
- ☐ Super Mario 3D Land
- ☐ Super Mario 3D World

**SIDE SERIES:**
- ☐ Dr. Mario
- ☐ Mario Kart
- ☐ Mario Party
- ☐ Paper Mario
- ☐ Mario & Luigi
- ☐ Mario Tennis
- ☐ Mario Golf
- ☐ Mario & Sonic at the Olympic Games

# THE LEGEND OF ZELDA

## BY CARRIE WOOD

Second only to *Super Mario*, *The Legend of Zelda* has stood as one of Nintendo's best-loved franchises for more than 30 years. Following the many adventures of Link as he seeks to rescue the Princess Zelda from the clutches of Ganon, *The Legend of Zelda* has set the bar for action-adventure games since it first released on February 21, 1986.

### EARLY SUCCESS ON THE NES

*The Legend of Zelda*'s plot was explained in the instruction booklet – the game itself doesn't lend itself much to storytelling. The story takes place in the land of Hyrule, which is in chaos after the Prince of Darkness, Ganon, leads his army to conquer it in his quest to obtain the Triforce of Wisdom. Hyrule's princess, Zelda, splits the Triforce into eight pieces and hides them away before she is kidnapped by Ganon. Before she's taken away, she tells her maid Impa to find someone with enough courage to save her and Hyrule. Impa later is rescued by Link and tasks him to become powerful enough to defeat Ganon and restore the Triforce.

When the game is beaten for the first time, the player is given access to the "Second Quest," which reconfigured the dungeons and item placements as well as provided stronger enemies to fight. Harder replays (often referred to as "New Game+")

weren't something that *Zelda* invented, but the game popularized the idea with the entirely different dungeon layouts it provided.

The game was developed by Shigeru Miyamoto and Takashi Tezuka; Miyamoto produced it while Tezuka came up with the story. *The Legend of Zelda* and *Super Mario Bros.* were actually developed by the same team of people, though the goal was to take the games in entirely different directions – *Mario* was intended to be linear, while *Zelda* wasn't. *The Legend of Zelda* became the first NES game to sell more than a million copies, and went on to sell 6.5 million total on the system.

The second game, *Zelda II: The Adventure of Link*, arrived on the Famicom in January 1987 and on the NES late the next year. It eschewed the top-down perspective of the first game for a side-scrolling adventure; it also introduced RPG elements such as experience points that weren't used before, nor were they ever used again in future games.

A direct sequel to the events of the inaugural title, *The Adventure of Link* focused on the titular character as he once again must revive Zelda, who has fallen to the effects of a sleeping spell. He must recombine the Triforce of Courage and keep its power away from Ganon's followers, who seek to revive Ganon after his death in the first game. Link's final challenge is a shadowy copy of himself, Dark Link, a character that would pop up again in future installments. Though not as much of a critical darling as the first title, *Zelda II* ultimately moved 4.38 million copies around the world, making it the fifth best-selling NES title overall.

## NARRATIVE FOCUS IN THE '90s

*The Legend of Zelda: A Link to the Past* arrived on the Super NES in 1991 and, despite being the third game overall, wasn't directly related to the story of either of the first games. Reverting to the overhead perspective of the first game, *A Link to the Past* follows Link as he seeks to rescue Hyrule from the clutches of Ganon.

Link begins the game by receiving a telepathic message from Princess Zelda, who is held captive in the castle dungeon by the wizard Agahnim; the wizard seeks to break the seal that holds Ganon in the Dark World and allow him to take over Hyrule. Link must travel throughout Hyrule and through the Dark World as well in order to rescue the descendants of the Seven Sages before they can be sacrificed to break the seal. After defeating Ganon once again, Link touches the Triforce and uses his wish to restore Hyrule to the way it was before Ganon and Agahnim took power.

*A Link to the Past* introduced many items and concepts that would become staples in future installments, such as the Master Sword, the ocarina, and the idea that there are parallel worlds. The game was a landmark title for the SNES, selling 4.61 million copies around the world, and is one of the most critically-acclaimed on the system.

The first handheld installment, *The Legend of Zelda: Link's Awakening*, first released in 1993 on the Game Boy (and would later be upgraded in full color and ported to the GBC as *Link's Awakening DX* in 1998). The first game set outside of Hyrule, *Link's Awakening* featured the hero as he explored the mysteries of Koholint Island and sought to wake the Wind Fish from his seemingly eternal slumber in an egg at the top of Mt. Tamaranch. Gathering the eight instruments of the Sirens, Link enters the Wind Fish's dream world and

conquers the Nightmare that plagues him. But as it turns out, waking the Wind Fish has some pretty far-reaching consequences.

Like its predecessors, *Link's Awakening* received critical acclaim, helping to boost the sales of the Game Boy by 13 percent the year it released. It sold more than 3.83 million copies, and the DX version sold another 2.22 million.

After five years, the next main installment in the franchise arrived with *Ocarina of Time* on the N64 in 1998. The first three-dimensional adventure for the series, it followed Link as he sought to end Ganondorf's reign of terror throughout Hyrule. Beginning the game as a child, Link first must gather three spiritual stones that are the keys to the Sacred Realm where the Triforce rests. Once claiming all three and entering the Temple of Time, Link grabs the Master Sword and opens the Sacred Realm, only to have Ganondorf claim the Triforce for himself. Frozen for seven years, Link awakens as an adult and is now tasked with reuniting the Seven Sages to seal Ganondorf away. After Ganondorf is defeated by Link, he turns into the monstrous boar-like Ganon using his Triforce of Power. Link and Zelda defeat him for good, and Ganondorf is sealed away in the Dark Realm.

*Ocarina of Time* was first shown off as a tech demo for the Nintendo 64 in 1995 and spent the next few years being developed alongside *Super Mario 64*. One of Miyamoto's original ideas for the game was to have it be in a first-person perspective, but that idea was scrapped in favor of having Link visible on-screen. The game received widespread critical acclaim, picking up a number of Game of the Year Awards from various publications, and sold 7.6 million copies around the world. It has since been called the Greatest Game of All Time by various outlets as well.

# INTO THE 2000s

The follow-up to *Ocarina of Time* was *The Legend of Zelda: Majora's Mask*, released in 2000. It follows Link as he explores the land of Termina, where the moon will crash into the town in three days. Link must use those three days – going back to the start via time-travel as many times as necessary – to prevent that event from happening. The vibe of the game was much darker than any other title up to that point, dealing with themes of death and loss; the time management factor also created a sense of perpetual impending doom that has not been seen before or since.

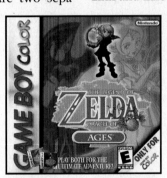

While *Ocarina* saw years of development, *Majora's Mask* was turned around relatively quickly, being finished by the development team in just a year. The game received heaps of praise upon release, with many people enjoying the inventiveness of the three-day system, but was far overshadowed by the success of *Ocarina*. *Majora's Mask* sold 3.36 million worldwide on the N64.

Two titles for the Game Boy Color, *Oracle of Ages* and *Oracle of Seasons*, simultaneously released in 2001. The games are two separate stories; *Seasons* takes place on Holodrum as Link seeks to rescue Din, the Oracle of Seasons, while *Ages* takes place in Labrynna where Link must defeat the sorceress possessing Nayru, the Oracle of Ages. The gameplay styles of the games were also different, with *Ages* being far more puzzle-based and *Seasons* concentrating more on battle and action.

Both *Oracle* games could be linked together with a password system, allowing one to be played as a sequel to the other. In the secret linked ending, the witch Twinrova kidnaps Zelda and tries to revive Ganon, but the Prince of Darkness comes back as a mindless beast and must be defeated. Originally, a third title had been planned to tie into the other two, but was scrapped due to the difficulty of coordinating three games at once. *Oracle of Ages* and *Oracle of Seasons* together moved about 8 million copies.

The next console entry proved to be somewhat controversial. A GameCube software demonstration in 2000 had shown off a realistically-rendered Link and Ganondorf, but Nintendo pivoted about as hard as possible away from that with the release of *The Wind Waker* – a cel-shaded romp through a flooded Hyrule.

In *The Wind Waker*, Link sets sail with the pirate Tetra in order to rescue his sister, who has been kidnapped by a large bird called the Helmaroc King. Along the way, the story of why Hyrule was flooded and where the missing Princess Zelda really went is explained. Though the game's initial release was polarizing among fans due to the cartoony graphics, *The Wind Waker* proved to be a critical and commercial success, moving more than 3 million copies around the world; fans have since warmed to the toon style as well.

That toon aesthetic would be carried into the next handheld title, *The Minish Cap*, released for the Game Boy Advance in 2004. In this game, Link could shrink down to a miniscule size using a talking cap named Ezlo; Link and Ezlo together work to defeat the sorcerer Vaati, who has petrified Princess Zelda. A somewhat quaint adventure compared to the scale of even other previous handheld releases, *The Minish Cap* was warmly received by the media and moved about a million copies within a year.

At the tail end of 2006, *The Legend of Zelda: Twilight Princess* released for the GameCube and for the Wii; it was designed with the GameCube in mind, but Nintendo opted to make it a Wii title as well as the GameCube was nearing the tail end of its life cycle. Introducing the more realistic style that fans had craved since that GameCube tech demo in 2000, *Twilight Princess* focused on an older Link who must prevent Hyrule from being taken over by the corrupted Twilight Realm. After being turned into a wolf, Link receives assistance from Midna; together they take down the King of the Twilight, Zant, and the man pulling all the strings – Ganondorf.

*Twilight Princess* received universal acclaim upon its launch, with the GameCube version scoring slightly higher; many people didn't care much for the "waggle" controls necessary for the Wii version. The game sold 8.85 million copies between both platforms, making it the best-selling installment in the franchise.

By the end of the decade, two titles for the Nintendo DS released – *Phantom Hourglass* and *Spirit Tracks*. Both featured the toon style established by *The Wind Waker*, and both acted as sequels to it as well. *Phantom Hourglass* released in 2007 and would sell 4.13 million copies; *Spirit Tracks* actually allowed players to play as Zelda herself (as her spirit inhabited the form of an armored Phantom) and sold about 2.6 million units.

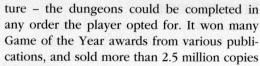

## ORIGINS AND REMAKES

In 2011, *The Legend of Zelda: Skyward Sword* released for the Wii. The game went back to the very beginning of the *Zelda* timeline and helped to further explain the origin of Hyrule as well as the conflict that plagues Link, Zelda and Ganon for generations to follow. Despite complaints from many players about the motion controls, *Skyward Sword* continued the trend of stellar reviews and strong sales, moving 3.41 million copies.

Since the release of *Skyward Sword,* there have been multiple remakes of older titles for newer systems. Both N64 titles, *Ocarina of Time* and *Majora's Mask*, were ported to the 3DS in 2011 and in 2015, respectively. *Wind Waker* received a graphical upgrade and rerelease for the Wii U in 2013, and *Twilight Princess* got the same treatment in 2016 for the game's 10th anniversary.

*The Legend of Zelda: A Link Between Worlds* was released for the 3DS at the end of 2013. Serving as a successor to *A Link to the Past*, the winding adventure took Link from Hyrule to the game's version of the Dark World, known as Lorule, in order to defeat the sorcerer Yuga before he can resurrect Ganon. Unlike many other *Zelda* titles, *A Link Between Worlds* was a non-linear adven-

ture – the dungeons could be completed in any order the player opted for. It won many Game of the Year awards from various publications, and sold more than 2.5 million copies worldwide.

A smaller *Zelda* adventure for the 3DS, *Tri Force Heroes*, arrived in 2015. The game has a focus on cooperative multiplayer, and players must work together in a team of three different-colored Links to solve puzzles and complete challenges. The reception was lukewarm, as the single-player mode was said to be lacking, but it sold a respectable 1.14 million copies.

The next major installment in the series will be *The Legend of Zelda: Breath of the Wild*, which is to receive a release on both the Wii U and the Nintendo Switch console in 2017. The game was officially announced in 2013 and has dealt with a series of delays, but trailers showed off a massive open world for this version of Link to explore after he awakens from a long slumber.

## SPINOFFS AND CAMEOS

A number of spinoff titles, large and small, have been released for the *Zelda* franchise. A handful of games concerning the side-character Tingle have launched for the DS, including *Freshly-Picked Tingle's Rosy Rupeeland*, *Tingle's Balloon Fight*, and *Color Changing Tingle's Love Balloon Trip*; the puzzle games have mostly been limited to Japan, and reception has been mostly mixed.

*Link's Crossbow Training* came out for the Wii in 2007. It used graphics from *Twilight Princess* and made use of the Wii Zapper controller, being bundled with the controller itself. Though reviews were mixed, it sold well.

A *Dynasty Warriors* crossover title, *Hyrule Warriors*, released for the Wii U in 2014 and the 3DS in 2016. The hack-n-slash allows players to play not just as Link, but as Zelda, Impa, Skull Kid, and even Ganondorf himself. The game was positively received, even if it didn't sell particularly well.

Perhaps the most notorious *Zelda*-related games were those made for the Philips CD-i system in the early 1990s, resulting from a brief collaboration between Nintendo and Philips. The games, *Zelda's Adventure, Link: the Faces of Evil* and *Zelda: The Wand of Gamelon*, are easily the worst games in the franchise due to poor controls and infamously gross-looking graphics, plus the awkward voice acting. Nintendo has refused to acknowledge them as being in-canon, and they're the butt of more than a few jokes – but can be considered an addition to any *Zelda* collection.

Link has also made cameo appearances in a number of other games, including appearing as a playable fighter in the *Super Smash Bros.* series and in the GameCube version of *Soulcalibur II*. He was also added as a playable racer via downloadable content for *Mario Kart 8* on the Wii U.

## THE LEGEND OF ZELDA IN OTHER MEDIA

In 1989, a 13-episode cartoon series titled simply *The Legend of Zelda* was made by DiC for American audiences. The show loosely followed the events of the two NES *Zelda* titles, and created Link's "Well *excuuuuuse me*, Princess!" catchphrase. The show has been released on DVD multiple times.

The Hyrule crew were no stranger to print media either. Valiant Comics actually released a short series mostly based on the cartoon as part of their *Nintendo Comics System* line between 1990 and 1991; the line also included other properties like *Metroid, Punch-Out!!* and *Captain N*. The *Zelda* comics produced by Valiant appeared to fit story-wise between the events of the first two games, and were released on a monthly basis from February to August of 1990.

But the longer-running comics for the *Zelda* franchise have all come out of Japan. Manga series have run over the last three decades, based off of games such as *A Link to the Past, Majora's Mask, Ocarina of Time, The Minish Cap, Phantom Hourglass, Oracle of Ages* and *Oracle of Seasons*. The manga series themselves don't represent the game canon, and are more interpretations of the games' events.

The main team responsible for the *Zelda* manga series has been Akira Himekawa – a penname for a duo of women who have never revealed their real names. They have also worked on other properties such as *Astro*

*Boy* and *Nazaca*. The first adaptation they worked on was *Ocarina of Time*, published in 1999, and they've since done nine total adaptations (including both *Oracle* games as separate entries). Their most recent adaptation was that of *Twilight Princess*, which, though it came nearly a decade after the game released, coincided with the HD remake of the game on the Wii U.

The other notable *Zelda* manga was *A Link to the Past* by the late Shotaro Ishinomori. Ishinomori is best-known for his original work, *Cyborg 009*, which continues to have modern anime adaptations to this day; a character, Roam, modeled after Jet Link from *Cyborg 009*, appears in his *Zelda* work. His art was considered to be somewhat reminiscent of his mentor, Osamu Tezuka (*Astro Boy* creator), and his style as applied to *Zelda* made his adaptation a significant standout. The *Link to the Past* manga told an alternate version of the events of the game, and was actually created as a serial comic that ran in the *Nintendo Power* magazine. It wasn't until 2015 that this story was collected in a graphic novel format and rereleased.

*The Legend of Zelda* has become one of the most prolific and influential game series of all time. The dozens of games certainly stand in their own right, but the widespread multimedia has turned *Zelda* into more than just another video game series.

### KEY GAMES:

**MAIN SERIES:**
- ☐ The Legend of Zelda
- ☐ The Adventure of Link
- ☐ A Link to the Past
- ☐ Link's Awakening
- ☐ Ocarina of Time
- ☐ Majora's Mask
- ☐ Oracle of Ages/Seasons
- ☐ Wind Waker
- ☐ Minish Cap
- ☐ Twilight Princess
- ☐ Phantom Hourglass
- ☐ Spirit Tracks
- ☐ Skyward Sword
- ☐ Tri Force Heroes
- ☐ A Link Between Worlds
- ☐ Breath of the Wild

# FINAL FANTASY

## BY CARRIE WOOD

There are some franchises out there that become a standard by which all others in that genre are held to. *Final Fantasy* has certainly become that for role-playing games, particularly those out of Japan. The series has since expanded beyond the mainline games to include a number of spinoffs – many of which have dabbled in different types of gameplay – plus has entered a variety of different media, such as films, television, and comics.

### SERIES DEBUT AND THE NINTENDO ERA

The first *Final Fantasy* arrived on December 18, 1987 for the Nintendo Entertainment System. Created by Hironobu Sakaguchi, it was titled as a "final" game for him and potentially for Square as a company. As the story goes, Square was in dire straits financially after several unsuccessful game releases. Had *Final Fantasy* not done well, it may have led to Square going bankrupt as well as Sakaguchi leaving the industry and returning to

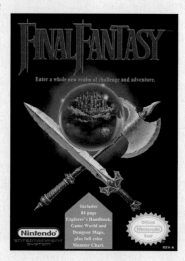

school. Fortunately for everyone, it was a success.

Though by today's standards the original *Final Fantasy* may seem very clichéd, it set a number of standards that the series has followed in the years since, such as the different party classes and many of the story elements. Musical motifs, particularly the "Victory Fanfare" and the title screen's "Prelude," have also continued to be used.

*Final Fantasy*'s success set in motion development for a sequel, *Final Fantasy II*, which arrived almost a year to the day later, on December 17, 1988. Similarly to the first game, the story focused on four kids who must save the world; *II* also introduced the chocobo creature to the franchise, as well as a character named Cid. It's now seen as a series tradition to have a "Cid" of some sort appear. It received positive reviews, but still doesn't have much of a fanbase outside of Japan – largely due to how it wasn't released in other regions until a PlayStation port of the game was made in the early 2000s.

*Final Fantasy III* debuted in 1990, again focusing on four youths who must save the world. The game introduced a more complex job/class system than the previous two entries, allowing for greater party customization throughout the game, with additional and more complex jobs becoming available later in the story. Like *FFII*, *III* didn't see an American release for many years; it took an enhanced remake for the Nintendo DS to be made in 2006 for any English-speaking audiences to get their hands on it.

With Nintendo's second major home console, the Super Nintendo, the *Final Fantasy* series was able to advance in many ways. *Final Fantasy IV* arrived in 1991 and was the first to feature a major focus on the narrative and on the characters' individual stories. It still maintained many of the elements seen in the first three, but it did introduce one major gameplay element: the Active

Time Battle system. ATB is a twist on the traditional turn-based combat, where characters can only act once their action meter is full again. It added a greater sense of urgency to the battles that had not been seen in the series before. *Final Fantasy IV* was released in the U.S. as *Final Fantasy II* (as the Japanese *II* and *III* hadn't made their way west), and was a massive hit worldwide. It is considered by many to be a landmark moment for the franchise due to its deep storyline and complex characters.

The series briefly returned to a Japan-only status with the release of *Final Fantasy V*, which focused on a hero named Bartz who must prevent the return of the evil sorcerer Exdeath. The game was later ported to the PlayStation in 1999.

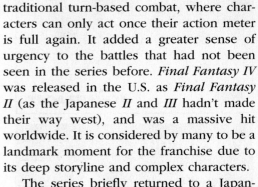

*Final Fantasy VI* (*Final Fantasy III* in the U.S.) released in 1994 to massive critical acclaim around the world. It was the first game in the franchise to be directed by someone other than Sakaguchi,

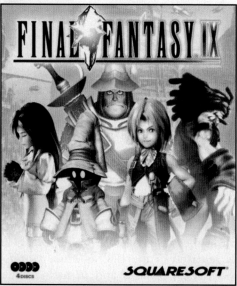

instead being helmed by Yoshinori Kitase. The story featured a total of 14 different playable characters – more than had ever been used before or since – and took place in a more steampunk, industrial environment, a first for the series. The game's villain, Kefka Palazzo, remains a fan favorite today. The deep and emotional storyline made *Final Fantasy VI* a standout in the franchise and the game is considered by many fans to be the best in the series – if not one of the best RPGs of all time.

## THE PLAYSTATION ERA AND MAINSTREAM SUCCESS

The release of *Final Fantasy VII* in 1997 was huge in many ways for the series, not the least of which had to do with the platform it was made for – the PlayStation. Though the game had originally been intended for the Nintendo 64 console, the N64's cartridge-based system was deemed to not have enough storage capacity for what the developers wanted to do, and instead *VII*'s development shifted to the CD-ROM- based PlayStation. *FFVII* also was the first game in the series to feature fully three-dimensional characters, rather than the 2D sprites that had been used on the Nintendo platforms.

The game focused on the story of Cloud Strife, a mercenary who joins up with others in order to stop the Shinra corporation from draining the life of the planet; along the way they must also put a stop to the villainous Sephiroth, who seeks to become a god by merging with the planet's lifestream. *FFVII*, helped by a huge marketing campaign before its release, was a massive commercial success and has since become the best-selling title in the franchise, having sold more than 11 million copies across multiple platforms.

Two more games in the main series were released for the PlayStation – *Final Fantasy VIII* and *Final Fantasy IX*. The former of the two would be the first game to use realistically-proportioned characters, rather than the cartoonish look of the previous entries; it also introduced a unique gameplay element known as the Junction System, which was used to improve various character statistics.

*FFIX*, on the other hand, made a brief return to the more cartoonish style while maintaining a serious plotline. It focused on the thief Zidane, who becomes involved in a political struggle as the mad Queen Brahne seeks to start a war. The true power behind Brahne's actions, a mysterious man named Kuja, as well as the nature of Zidane himself turn out to be far more deadly than first thought. *FFIX*, though it didn't sell nearly as well as the two that came before it, was however better received critically than any other game in the series.

When the PlayStation 2 came around, it too featured three main games – one of which was online. *Final Fantasy X* arrived in 2001, and was the first game in the series to feature fully 3D areas (rather than the flat pre-rendered scenes of the PS1 games), as well as introduce voice acting to the series. It would also be the first in the series to end up with a direct sequel.

*Final Fantasy XI* was a numbered entry, but was unlike any other that had come before, insomuch that it was a massively multiplayer online experience rather than a single-player RPG. Released in 2002, it featured real-time battles rather than turn-based and was actually the first MMORPG to feature cross-platform play, as it was published on the PS2, PC and the Xbox 360.

The series returned to its traditional single-player experience with the release of *Final Fantasy XII* in 2006. It wasn't without its own innovations, though; featuring an open world, a controllable camera and a number of changes to the battle system, *FFXII* was unlike any of the single-player games that had come before it. It too ended up with a direct sequel, plus spinoffs.

## THE NEW GENERATION OF FANTASY

With the shift into the PlayStation 3 and Xbox 360 by the end of the aughts, this franchise continued to evolve. The next numbered installation in the series, *Final Fantasy XIII*, released at the end of 2009 in Japan and early 2010 elsewhere.

The game had first been announced in 2006 and had actually been in development since 2004. Though it was criticized for its linear gameplay, *FFXIII* was praised for its graphics and became the fastest-selling entry in the series. It also became the flagship title for the "Fabula Nova Crystallis" collection of *Final Fantasy* games, which also included *XIII*'s two direct sequels plus spinoffs.

Another MMORPG, *Final Fantasy XIV*, released in 2010 for Windows computers and was not at all well-received. After years of fan backlash and criticism – to the point where many of the developers felt as though *FFXIV* had damaged the entire brand – the game was reworked and rereleased as *Final*

*Fantasy XIV: A Realm Reborn* for the PS3 and Windows in 2013, and released on the PS4 the next year.

The newest entry in the main series, *Final Fantasy XV*, was first announced as a spinoff of *FFXII – Final Fantasy Versus XIII* – at the 2006 Electronic Entertainment Expo. After spending years in development hell and fueling rumors that the project had been totally canceled, the game was rebranded and re-announced as *Final Fantasy XV* in 2013. It is due out at the end of 2016.

## SPINOFFS AND SEQUELS

Outside of the 15 mainline games, *Final Fantasy* is a series home to a wealth of spinoffs. Many of these are still traditional Japanese RPGs, including *The Final Fantasy Legend* and its two direct sequels – which, in actuality, are games out of the *SaGa* series that were rebranded for an American audience that was already familiar with the *Final Fantasy* brand. The entire *SaGa* series of games also started off as a *Final Fantasy* spinoff before turning into its own thing.

Then there's *Final Fantasy Mystic Quest*, a game designed with the American player in mind, for better or worse. The game was essentially a dumbed-down RPG as the Japanese developers at

Square didn't think that the American audience was good enough at the genre for a regular *Final Fantasy* title, and wanted to broaden the appeal of the brand by making an easier game. (This wasn't the first time a *Final Fantasy* title was made easier – the U.S. release of *FFIV* was also lightened up.) Though it did okay at the time, it didn't achieve Square's goal of making RPGs more popular in the west, and today it's considered by fans to be the single worst game in the series.

*Final Fantasy Tactics* is perhaps the most popular spinoff from the main series; released for the PS1 in 1997 (in America in '98), it was a tactical RPG that combined traditional *Final Fantasy* elements with a tactical gameplay style. It maintains a strong cult following today, and ended up with two spinoffs of its own: *Final Fantasy Tactics Advance* in 2003 for the Game Boy Advance, and *Final Fantasy Tactics A2: Grimoire of the Rift* in 2007 for the Nintendo DS.

One of the most recognizable mascots for the series is the Chocobo bird, and the character's ended up with more than a dozen spinoff games of its own. The *Chocobo* series has had mystery dungeon-style games, racing games, and minigame collections as well; many of these games have been Japan-exclusive, though just as many have made their way west.

*Final Fantasy* has also been home to a fighting game, *Dissidia Final Fantasy*, which features the main heroes and villains from the main series of games. It received a prequel, *Dissidia 012 Final Fantasy*, in 2011.

As far as sequels, the main series games have received several. *Final Fantasy X* was the first, with *Final Fantasy X-2*, which released in 2003 for the PS2 and focused on Yuna's quest to find Tidus after the events of *FFX*. *Final Fantasy XIII* received two direct sequels – *Final Fantasy XIII-2* and *Lightning Returns: Final Fantasy XIII* – continuing the story from the first game. *Final Fantasy IV* also received a sequel in 2008, *Final Fantasy IV: The After Years*, which took place 17 years after the events of the first game and revolves around the son of Cecil and Rosa.

With *FFVII* being the most popular game in the series, it's not surprising it's also played host to a number of spinoffs. Two prequels, *Before Crisis: Final Fantasy VII* and *Crisis Core: Final Fantasy VII*, have been made, focusing on some of the side characters from the main story before the events of the main game itself. *Dirge of Cerberus: Final Fantasy VII* was also made, releasing in 2006 and focusing on fan-favorite character Vincent Valentine.

## FINAL FANTASY IN OTHER MEDIA

With a franchise this large, it would be impossible to limit it to just video games. As early as 1994, the series started branching into other media with the original video animation, *Final Fantasy: Legend of the Crystals*. It took place in the same world as *FFV*, though the story was 200 years after

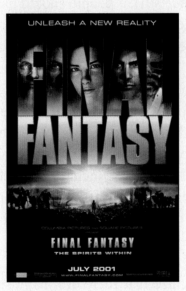

the events of the game.

Perhaps the most notorious example of the franchise in other media is the film *Final Fantasy: The Spirits Within*. Released in 2001, it marked the first film to try and portray photorealistic CGI humans on screen, and while it was hailed as a technical milestone, it was a box office bomb – making just $85.1 million against a budget of $137 million. The fact that it didn't bear any resemblance to any of the games was also a huge sticking point for many fans.

Two films have been made that are based directly on games – *Final Fantasy VII: Advent Children* in 2005 and *Kingsglaive: Final Fantasy XV* in 2016 – both of which are also CGI films, and both of which received favorable attention from fans. A 25-episode anime series, *Final Fantasy: Unlimited*, was produced in 2001 and contained many of the common elements from the games. Many games in the series have also been adapted into novels, beginning as early as *Final Fantasy II* in 1989, as well as manga and other books.

With 15 main series games, dozens of spinoffs, sequels and prequels, plus films and all sorts of other media and collectibles, one thing has been made absolutely clear since 1987: *Final Fantasy* is anything but "final."

# COLLECTING BY DEVELOPER

Similar to how people are brand loyal to their console producers, many gamers are just as loyal to developers and all of their products. That people should have shrines dedicated to the likes of Capcom's many series or to the blockbuster franchises of BioWare should come as no surprise.

This chapter serves to contextualize the history of these various developers – many of whom, like Activision and EA, have turned into more of a publisher than a developer, but still are important to include due to their impact on the industry overall. We've also included checklists of the most important series for each of these developers that someone looking to curate a developer-specific collection would want to include.

We do recognize that there are many significant developers who ended up left out, such as Konami, LucasArts, Rare, and others, who have contributed in large ways to the gaming industry and who are wildly popular subjects for collectors. Simply put – we ran out of space in this inaugural edition. We sincerely hope to shine a spotlight on these and many other important developers in further volumes.

# ACTIVISION®

BY CARRIE WOOD

Though third-party development has long been absolutely crucial to the growth of the video game industry, it didn't start off that way. One company in particular is responsible for the idea of third-party game development following a fallout with Atari – Activision.

## COMPANY ORIGINS

In the earliest days of home console entertainment, the idea of third-party development was completely foreign. Video games were published only by the companies who also made the systems; Atari of course was one of these, and was the only publisher of games for their 2600 console. This system irritated many of Atari's in-house developers, since Atari didn't give royalties or even credit to the people responsible for programming their titles.

Programmers David Crane, Larry Kaplan, Alan Miller, and Bob Whitehead met with Atari CEO Ray Kassar in 1979 and demanded better treatment from the company at large. Kassar scoffed at the idea, saying that "anyone can do a cartridge," leading the four programmers to leave Atari and begin Activision. The company's name was apparently derived from combining the words "active" and "television."

Activision went out of its way to credit and promote its game creators and developers, including giving every developer their own page in a game's instruction manual. By taking this approach, the company was able to attract some of the top talent in the business at the time. Atari, however, wasn't too pleased with how things played out – the four Activision founders' titles had made up more than half of Atari's software sales at the time, and legal action between Atari and Activision carried on into 1982.

The first smash hit for Activision was *Pitfall!*, released in 1982. The player controls Pitfall Harry as he races through a jungle in an attempt to get 32 different treasures in just 20 minutes, all the while avoiding various obstacles. The game was a technical marvel for the time, with colorful animated sprites rendered on the primitive 2600 hardware without any flickering or stuttering. *Pitfall!* ended up seeing a variety of ports to other consoles, selling 4 million copies in total, and cemented Activision as a proper development company.

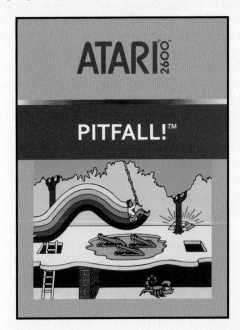

Later in the '80s, Activision purchased Infocom, a small developer primarily known for their text adventure games, and changed its overall corporate name to "Mediagenic." By the end of the decade, it was publishing games for the Nintendo Entertainment System, the Atari 7800, the Commodore 64, and the Sega Master System.

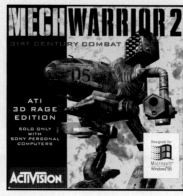

## FROM SMALL SUCCESS TO HUGE DISTRIBUTION

Mediagenic was taken over by an investor group led by Robert Kotick in December 1990, following a huge judgment on damages in a patent infringement suit against the company. The reorganization of the company involved a merger with The Disc Company; Kotick became CEO in 1991, and the company emerged from bankruptcy and changed its name back to Activision in 1992.

In 1989, the company had published a first-person mech pilot game, *MechWarrior*, based on the pen-and-paper game *BattleTech* from FASA. In 1995, following years of delays, *MechWarrior 2* released to critical acclaim – but FASA, displeased with how things had stalled in development, didn't renew their contract with Activision. A number of games were released under the *MechWarrior 2* name (which somehow didn't violate the licensing agreement), including *MechWarrior 2: Ghost Bears Legacy* and *MechWarrior 2: Mercenaries*; the games totaled more than $70 million in sales.

Throughout the late 1990s, Activision started to acquire a number of smaller companies as subsidiaries. In 1997, Activision acquired Raven Software, a small company that had previously been independent. The acquisition was the result of an exclusive publishing deal between the two companies, and games that resulted from it have included *Hexen II, Heretic II,* and *Soldier of Fortune,* among others. In '98, Activision helped to found Pandemic Studios via an equity investment; Pandemic's president and CEO were both former Activision employees. Activision was also able to make deals with Marvel Entertainment, Disney Interactive, and LucasArts, among other notable companies, that same year.

Neversoft, best known for the *Tony Hawk's Pro Skater* line of games, was acquired by Activision in 1999. The *Pro Skater* games began development after Hawk's first appearance at the 1998 X-Games, and ended up being one of the most popular game series of the early aughts. Though the series has certainly seen its ups and downs – with some games having been critical and commercial flops – it maintains a strong fanbase. In total, 15 games in the overall *Tony Hawk* franchise have been made.

In 2001, Activision acquired Treyarch; the next year they made an equity investment in Infinity Ward, a new studio primarily comprised of people who had developed *Medal of Honor: Allied Assault.* In 2003, Infinity Ward developed the first *Call of Duty* title, and was fully acquired by Activision.

*Call of Duty* largely revolutionized the first-person shooter genre at large, and won a number of Game of the Year awards from a variety of publications. It has since spun into one of the largest gaming franchises

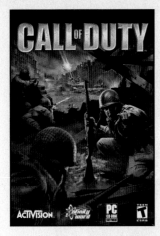
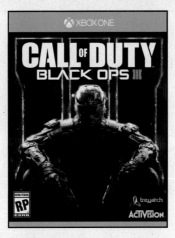

around, with annual releases altering developers between Infinity Ward, Treyarch, and Sledgehammer Games since 2006. The series is now comprised of 13 main console entries, plus a handful of spin-offs and handheld tie-in titles. The *Call of Duty* series at large has sold more than 175 million games, with sales topping $10 billion.

The mid-2000s also saw the music game revolution begin with the release of the first *Guitar Hero* game. The first game in the series released in 2005, developed by Harmonix and published by RedOctane. Gameplay involving a guitar-shaped controller to play popular rock music proved to be an instant hit. Activision acquired the rights to the series when it bought out RedOctane in 2006. The series rapidly expanded – a dozen *Guitar Hero* entries, plus the first *DJ Hero* spinoff, had released by 2010 – and

the bubble popped fairly quickly. Many believe that simple oversaturation (coupled in part by the *Rock Band* games published by competitor EA) led to the swift decline for this series. A reboot was attempted in 2015 with the release *Guitar Hero Live*, but it failed to sell enough to garner further entries. That said, in total, the *Guitar Hero* series has earned more than $2 billion around the world.

## MERGER AND RECENT DEVELOPMENTS

Activision merged with Vivendi Games in the summer of 2008; Vivendi's ownership of Blizzard led the new company to be called Activision Blizzard. Kotick remains the CEO of the merged company, which has continued to produce high-quality titles.

Besides Blizzard's many titles,

the merged company has kicked off several high-dollar franchises, including *Skylanders*, the first of several games to use near-field communication (NFC) technology. *Skylanders* is somewhat of a spinoff of the *Legend of Spyro* series (with the first game bearing the subtitle *Spyro's Adventure*) but is largely its own separate entity. The game uses small figures of the characters that have NFC chips embedded in the base. By placing figures on a "portal," the character appears in-game. By bringing toys to "life" in-game, *Skylanders* was an instant family hit – and the figure sales in addition to the software didn't hurt either. *Skylanders* has since become a large multimedia franchise, with a comic series published by IDW and a Netflix-exclusive cartoon show. The success of *Skylanders* has directly influenced other NFC lines, such as Nintendo's amiibo series.

Activision Blizzard also revived Sierra Entertainment in 2014. Sierra was a popular developer of graphic adventure games for computers in the 1980s, such as *Mystery House, King's Quest* and many others. The company had been somewhat defunct since 2008, and was brought back by Activision to re-publish or otherwise reboot older titles.

With Activision now the largest publisher of video games in the world, it's difficult to imagine an industry in which they didn't exist. What began as just four irate programmers striking out from Atari has become the biggest juggernaut in the business. Though they may not be everyone's favorite, it's very easy to recognize one thing – this industry would not be the same without Activision.

## KEY GAMES:

- ☐ **Pitfall**
- ☐ **MechWarrior**
- ☐ **Guitar Hero series**
- ☐ **Call of Duty series**
- ☐ **Tony Hawk's Pro Skater series**
- ☐ **Skylanders series**

BY CARRIE WOOD

Though perhaps not the largest company in the business, Bethesda Softworks has seen some truly unprecedented success with the likes of the *Elder Scrolls* series as well as with *Fallout*. Over more than 30 years, the company has turned from a small RPG developer into a juggernaut of blockbuster gaming.

Bethesda Softworks was founded in 1986 by Christopher Weaver, under the larger umbrella of Media Technology Limited. The company was named for where it was founded – Bethesda, MD – and was created out of Weaver's desire to develop for personal computers. Weaver, a Massachusetts Institute of Technology graduate, had also worked in the broadcasting industry with NBC and ABC as well as within the U.S. Congress as the Chief Engineer on the Congressional Subcommittee on Communications.

## SPORTS PHYSICS AND A DIFFERENT KIND OF "ARENA"

Bethesda is generally credited with the creation of the first physics engine in gaming, which was used in the 1986 release, *Gridiron!*, a game for the Atari ST and Commodore 64/128. The game wasn't much to look at graphically, but the physics were so impressive to the folks at Electronic Arts that they opted to hire Bethesda to help develop the very first *John Madden Football*, which released in 1988.

EA was actually sued by Bethesda in 1987 for $7.3 million. Bethesda claimed that EA had halted the release of *Gridiron!* on other consoles (something EA had bought the rights to do) after choosing to incorporate several major elements of the game into *John*

*Madden Football*. They believed that EA had bought the *Gridiron!* rights simply to get their hands on the underlying code of the physics engine. The details of how the lawsuit played out have never actually been made public. The *Madden* series continues to see annual releases and maintains its status as one of the best-selling sports series ever.

Bethesda released a number of other sports titles in their early years of game development, including *Wayne Gretzky Hockey, NCAA Basketball: Road to the Final Four,* and *Hockey League Simulator*. They also released a handful of games based on licensed properties such as *Home Alone, Where's Waldo?* and *The Terminator*.

The company took a sharp turn away from what they had previously worked on with the development of *The Elder Scrolls: Arena*, which released in 1994. Many members of Bethesda's staff had become enamored with tabletop role-playing games, and that experience helped influence the creation of the *Elder Scrolls'* world. *Arena* was not originally planned as a role-playing game, instead being developed first as a gladiatorial tournament game that would also feature sidequests. Eventually, the quests – and various other traditional RPG elements – kind of took over and became the game's focus.

The game was still called *Arena,* despite not actually having any arena combat, thanks to how marketing material had already been printed with the title, and Bethesda wasn't interested in spending more money to re-print anything. The company irritated distributors by missing their Christmas 1993 deadline, and the game only shipped 20,000 copies when it was finally finished in March of '94. Fortunately, *Arena* managed to achieve success through positive word-of-mouth, and helped to establish the defining series for Bethesda Softworks.

## THE ELDER SCROLLS UNFOLD

*The Elder Scrolls II: Daggerfall* entered development immediately after the launch of *Arena*. Much more in-depth than its predecessor, *Daggerfall* featured a com-

plex character and class creation system as well as a deeper plot that could result in a variety of different endings. It was developed using the XnGine game engine, one of the earliest 3D game engines, giving it a look most other RPGs of the time did not have yet.

*Daggerfall* released on August 31, 1996 – on time, unlike *Arena* – though it suffered early criticisms due to bugs in the code. The game would eventually be patched to fix many of the bugs, but the experience left the developer with a better sense of how to be cautious with announcing release dates. The game was also a popular choice for modders, who added a variety of additional quests and enhancements.

Spin-off titles were introduced shortly after the release of *Daggerfall*. There were three being worked on all at once – *Battlespire*, *Redguard*, and *Morrowind* – all of which had originally been intended to become expansion packs for *Daggerfall* but took on a life of their own as stand-alone titles. *An Elder Scroll Legend: Battlespire* arrived first, on November 30, 1997. It featured multiplayer for the first time and was more of a survival horror/dungeon-crawling experience than a RPG. *The Elder Scrolls Adventures: Redguard* arrived the following year, on October 31, 1998. It did not allow for character creation and was a very linear experience compared to the previous open-world exploration of the main series titles.

Neither *Battlespire* nor *Redguard* performed particularly well with even the most hardcore *Elder Scrolls* fans. The harsh sales downturn forced Bethesda to file for bankruptcy, and in 1999 they were acquired by ZeniMax Media, another company founded by Christopher Weaver.

*Morrowind* did eventually come out, however. The game's story was conceived during *Daggerfall's* development, but technology limitations of the time prevented Bethesda from being able to put their ideas into action. The company ended up tripling their staff for the development of the game and created *The Elder Scrolls Construction Set* first; it allowed for easier development and modification of the game.

*The Elder Scrolls III: Morrowind* was the third main entry in the series and released on May 1, 2002. It became the first *Elder Scrolls* title on a home console when it released for the Xbox in June of that year, helping to expose the series at large to a wider audience.

*Morrowind* took the player out of the traditionally European-styled main lands of Tamriel and put them on the exotic Dunmer (a race of dark elves) island of Vvardenfell. The story focused on the reincarnation of the Dunmer hero, the Nerevarine, who has been prophesized to defeat the demonic Dagoth Ur. *Morrowind* got two expansion packs – *Tribunal* and *Bloodmoon*.

*Morrowind* received wide critical acclaim upon its release, with the overall richness of the world it contained being its strongest selling point. It won a number of awards, including several Game of the Year nods from the video game press, and sold well enough to get a secondary release, the "Game of the Year Edition," which contained both expansions along with the main game.

Outside of the *Elder Scrolls* series, Bethesda continued to publish a variety of other titles, including the *IHRA Drag*

*Racing* series, *Magic & Mayhem, Zero Critical*, and *Symbiocom*.

## MASS APPEAL WITH OBLIVION AND FALLOUT

Work on a follow-up to *Morrowind*, to be called *The Elder Scrolls IV: Oblivion*, began in 2002 after *Morrowind* proved to be a success. The game was officially announced in 2004, and was released in 2006. *Oblivion*

featured a new game engine – the Havok engine – and also made smart usage of the "Radiant AI" system for better in-game artificial intelligence. Radiant AI was developed in response to criticism from fans regarding the simplistic behavior of non-playable characters in *Morrowind*; it allows for more complex activities for the NPCs, essentially.

*Oblivion* followed the player character as they sought to bring an end to the "Oblivion Crisis" plaguing the province of Cyrodiil. Oblivion gates – portals that connect the mortal realm to the otherworldly – have opened all over, leading to an invasion of demonic Daedra. *Oblivion* received universal acclaim and picked up dozens of awards, though the game was noted to be somewhat buggy and featured a leveling system that was considered unbalanced. Two expansions, *Knights of the Nine* and *Shivering Isles*, were later released.

*Oblivion* did face a small controversy following its release. The PC version of the game could be hacked to find an otherwise locked file that would have allowed people to play through the game with topless female characters. This prompted the Entertainment Software Rating Board (ESRB) to change the rating from T (Teen 13+) to M (Mature 17+). Though Bethesda complied with the ESRB's request to send out stickers for stores to change the rating, there was a large public disagreement about the reasons why.

While Bethesda was working on *Oblivion*, they were also acquiring what would become one of their flagship series: *Fallout*. The *Fallout* games were created and developed by Interplay Entertainment for the PC, but after they went totally out of business, they sold the rights to Bethesda. While early *Fallout* games featured an isometric top-down view, *Fallout 3*, the first Bethesda-developed title in the series, switched gears to become more of a first-person shooter-style experience.

*Fallout 3* takes place in a post-apocalyptic District of Columbia as the player seeks out their missing father. Escaping from a Vault, they must explore the irradiated Capital Wasteland, which is home to dangers of all sorts. The game was a wild success (despite bugs that were slowly becoming an unfortunate trademark of Bethesda titles) both commercially and critically – though many longtime fans of Interplay's *Fallout* games didn't care for the direction the series took. Several expansions were later released.

## RAPID EXPANSION AND NEW IP

The mainstream success of both *Oblivion* and *Fallout 3* helped propel Bethesda forward at an incredible pace. In 2008, ZeniMax and Bethesda expanded into Europe, creating the publisher ZeniMax Europe; further expansions happened into Tokyo, Paris, Hong Kong, Sydney, and elsewhere. ZeniMax also acquired id Software, whose titles have been published by Bethesda ever since.

As far as *The Elder Scrolls* go, *The Elder Scrolls V: Skyrim* released on November 11, 2011 for the PC, Xbox 360

and PS3, to universal critical acclaim. The game focused on the adventures of the "Dragonborn," the player character, who has the soul of a dragon and is thus the only person who can stop the dragon Alduiin, the "World-Eater," from bringing about the end of times. *Skyrim* uses a new game engine created specifically for it as well as takes greater advantage of the Radiant AI system. Two expansions, *Dawnguard* and *Dragonborn*, were added to enhance the story, as well as a smaller add-on, *Hearthfire*. A high-definition enhanced remake for the Xbox One, PS4 and PC, *The Elder Scrolls V: Skyrim – Special Edition*, released in 2016.

The Elder Scrolls Online, an MMORPG set in the game's universe, launched in 2014 for PC and in 2015 for consoles. It received mixed-to-positive reviews and has received a large number of updates since its initial release.

A follow-up to *Fallout 3* was released in 2010, called *Fallout: New Vegas*. The game was not developed by Bethesda, and was instead developed by Obsidian Entertainment. It focuses on a courier in the Mojave Wasteland as they seek revenge after being left for dead, and soon uncover a larger plot to control Hoover Dam. They must choose between factions, leading to a variety of different endings that are possible. Like *Fallout 3*, *New Vegas* featured a variety of expansions that furthered the story. *New Vegas* was not as successful as *Fallout 3*, though it remains a favorite of many longtime *Fallout* fans who appreciated the return to the U.S.'s West Coast for the setting.

In 2012, Bethesda released *Dishonored*, a new intellectual property developed by Arkane Studios. The game combined old-school stealth gameplay with stylish action, which, combined with a compelling storyline, made for a success. *Dishonored* received a number of awards following its

release and was considered one of the best games that year by many. Sales exceeded expectations, and a sequel, *Dishonored 2*, was announced in 2015 and released in late 2016.

The acquisition of id Software proved to be a smart one for Bethesda, as they were able to not just publish ports of older titles like *Doom* but also new releases, such as *Wolfenstein: The New Order*, which released in 2014. A follow-up, *Wolfenstein: The Old Blood*, released the following year. Both were developed by another Bethesda subsidiary, MachineGames, rather than by id Software themselves – who were busy on the new *Doom* title, which arrived on May 13, 2016.

After several years of speculation and rumor, *Fallout 4* was announced at E3 2015 and launched in November of that year. The game returned to the East Coast, taking place in Boston and the surrounding areas, and focusing on the mysteries of "The Institute" and the nature of the "Synths." The game shipped more than 12 million units within the first 24 hours of its release and picked up a number of awards along the way.

Bethesda Softworks has, over a little more than 30 years, gone from a small game developer just looking for better game physics and has become an absolute force to be reckoned with in the gaming industry. Now not just a publisher of in-house titles but also those of Arkane Studios, id Software, MachineGames and many more, Bethesda is clearly a company on the up-and-up.

## KEY GAMES:

☐ Elder Scrolls series
☐ Fallout series (since 3)
☐ Rage
☐ Dishonored series
☐ The Evil Within

# BioWare® CORP

BY RAE CARRA

For 20 years, BioWare has won the hearts of millions, specializing in RPGs that bring the character-driven, multi-thread narrative style of a tabletop roleplaying game to the screen.

BioWare Corp was founded in 1995 by Ray Muzyka, Trent and Brent Oster, Augustine Yip, and Greg and Marcel Zeschuk. Three of the team, Muzyka, Greg Zeschuk, and Yip, met at the University of Alberta and provided funding from their successes in the medical field to develop their first game. This game, released in 1996, was an MS-DOS-based *MechWarrior*-style action game called *Shattered Steel*. The frantic alien-slaying mission was notable in part for deformable terrain that responded to nearby explosions.

## DIGITAL JOURNEYS IN THE FORGOTTEN REALMS

After *Shattered Steel*, the team turned to their love of pen-and-paper roleplaying games for a new project, ultimately developing a demo they called *Battlefield: Infinity*. Under suggestions from publisher Interplay Entertainment, which owned a license for *Dungeons & Dragons* at the time, the so-dubbed Infinity Engine was retooled to reflect the D&D ruleset. This resulted in the hugely successful RPG *Baldur's Gate*, published in 1998. Selling 2 million copies, it was almost as successful as Blizzard's *Diablo*, which seemingly otherwise had a stranglehold on the RPG market.

*Baldur's Gate* featured

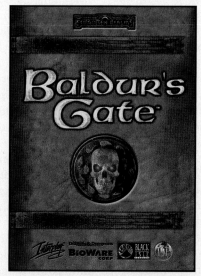

a top-down isometric view and gameplay that closely modeled D&D, including the opportunity to create a character with a distinctive class, race, abilities, and skills. Players selected dialogue options and narrative choices to navigate the story, a sprawling tale of conspiracy and dead gods in the Sword Coast, defeating both sinister monsters and economic crises alike.

BioWare published an expansion pack for *Baldur's Gate* in 1999, *Tales of the Sword Coast*, which added new sidequests and regions without changing the main story of *Baldur's Gate*. The Infinity Engine was also later used for other D&D-licensed games published by Interplay Entertainment, namely Black Isle Studio's *Planescape: Torment* and *Icewind Dale* series.

BioWare then returned to the action genre, and in 2000 released a sequel to Shiny Entertainment's *MDK*, picking up immediately where the original left off with new waves of aliens invading Earth. This return to genre also constituted BioWare's first game developed for consoles, as the third-person shooter *MDK2* released on Windows, Dreamcast, and PlayStation 2.

That same year, BioWare released a sequel to *Baldur's Gate*, the equally successful *Baldur's Gate II: Shadows of Amn*. The new installment picked up shortly after the original game ended, drawing the hero and their companions into further adventures as the party battled for the fate of the hero's very soul. *Baldur's Gate II* introduced several features players of BioWare's most

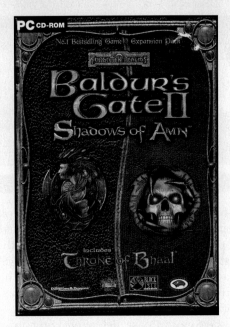

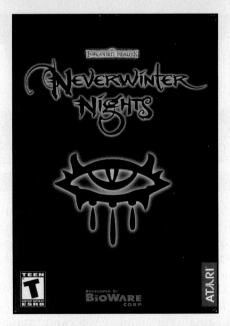

popular franchises will recognize, including banter from party members, their interjections into conversations with non-player characters, and the option to romance a party member. In 2001, BioWare released an expansion pack, *Throne of Bhaal*, which added a new dungeon and tied off the story of *Baldur's Gate*'s hero.

Despite the success of *MDK2* and *Baldur's Gate II*, Interplay Entertainment suffered financially and ultimately crumbled, such that BioWare began working with Infogrames (later rebranding as Atari after acquiring that company from Hasbro). Infogrames, having acquired Interplay's D&D license, worked with BioWare to publish *Neverwinter Nights* in 2002, another well-received D&D product. The story swept players into an intrigue of cults and plagues, and elder entities fighting for dominance.

*Neverwinter Nights* also introduced BioWare's Aurora Engine, a successor to the Infinity Engine, along with a powerful multiplayer platform and the "DM Client," which let players orchestrate servers like a D&D gamemaster. While other RPGs had attempted to include such a feature, *Neverwinter* was largely considered the first game to implement it with real success.

Like its predecessors, *Neverwinter Nights* was followed by two expansion packs in 2003, adding a new campaign and new character specialization options. Atari later went on to release a sequel, *Neverwinter Nights 2*, developed by Obsidian Entertainment.

## A GALAXY MUCH LONGER AGO THAN USUAL

After releasing *Neverwinter*, BioWare sold their D&D license to Atari and worked with LucasArts to release the critically-acclaimed *Star Wars: Knights of the Old Republic* (KotOR) in 2003. *KotOR*, set several thousand years before the original *Star Wars* story, follows a Jedi initiate fighting against the Sith at the height of the Republic's power. The game was well-regarded by critics and fans alike, and all told, won more than 40 Game of the Year awards.

With the help of a solid team of voice actors and a significantly advanced graphics system that allowed for character performance onscreen, *KotOR* continued the trend BioWare had begun with *Baldur's Gate*. The game provided a world full of characters with their own fully realized stories and character arcs. It also introduced features BioWare would later keep as mainstays, including the Light/Dark alignment system that tracks a protagonist's actions and weighs their virtue. The game's turn-based combat system was rooted in computerized dice-rolling, like *Baldur's Gate* and *Neverwinter Nights*, though it was released on their Odyssey Engine, an update from *Neverwinter*'s Aurora.

The following year, under BioWare's suggestion, Obsidian Entertainment released a sequel, *Star Wars: Knights of the Old Republic II – The Sith Lords*, but BioWare wouldn't personally return to the series until 2011, when they released *Star Wars:*

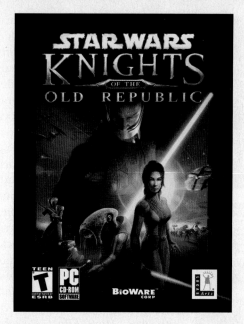

*The Old Republic*, an MMORPG. The game was noted within mere days of its release as the fastest-growing MMO in history, counting more than 1 million registered subscribers in the first three days. The game later successfully adopted a hybrid free-to-play business model.

*The Old Republic* puts players in the middle of a "cold war" between the Sith Empire and the Galactic Republic after a devastating victory on the Sith side cast the Jedi in a decisively negative light. In the ensuing years after its release, BioWare has added three expansions to *The Old Republic*: *Rise of the Hutt Cartel*, *Shadow of Revan*, and *Knights of the Fallen Empire*, with a fourth, *Knights of the Eternal Throne*, announced in July 2016 and slated for release by the end of that year.

After *KotOR*, BioWare took a brief break from sci-fi to work on their first original intellectual property, the action-RPG *Jade Empire*, which follows a chosen hero and their allies through a tale of martial arts, magic, and sickness. *Jade Empire* maintained several of BioWare's favorite game components, including the romanceable party member, conditional dialogue, and an alignment system. This alignment system, along with choices made during the story's climactic final encounters, determined the ending tableau of the game.

From late 2005 to late 2007, BioWare took part in a corporate juggling act. Several months after *Jade Empire*'s release, BioWare announced a partnership with Pandemic Studios. Then, in 2007, EA bought the partnership, making BioWare a unit under EA's structure, although they kept their own branding. Under EA's umbrella, BioWare expanded, opening several new offices and adding additional units, including EA's Mythic Entertainment in 2009, which was later renamed BioWare Mythic.

In 2008, in connection with Sega, BioWare released a game for Nintendo DS: *Sonic Chronicles: The Dark Brotherhood*. The game marked Sonic the Hedgehog's first foray into roleplaying games, and met with surprisingly positive reviews, considering the franchise's flops through most of the 2000s. Despite this experiment with handheld gaming, BioWare never returned to the platform, instead focusing on PC and major consoles.

## THEN, IN A GALAXY MUCH CLOSER...

*Jade Empire*'s commercial success in many ways paved the way for BioWare's next major release, the 2007 science fiction action-RPG *Mass Effect*. Set in a fictional version of our own galaxy less than two centuries after modern day, *Mass Effect* plunged players into a massive original universe populated with diverse alien races and formidable foes. It's snarled in ugly political turmoil that the game's hero, Commander Shepard, would struggle to unravel over the course of three games.

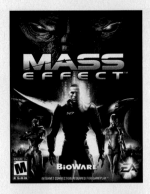

*Mass Effect 2*, released in 2010, followed Shepard through a universe that didn't believe their warnings about the intergalactic evil on their doorstep, bringing even more new characters and refined gameplay to the table. *Mass Effect 3*, the final installment, was released in 2012, wrapping up the story of Shepard with a mass-scale alien invasion threatening to wipe out all of known existence.

The series maintained several key features from prior BioWare games, including the Paragon/Renegade personality track modeled on *KotOR*'s Light Side/Dark Side and *Jade Empire*'s martial path. *Mass Effect* also highlighted party-member romance, and continued BioWare's strong trend toward well-developed characters.

The ending of the trilogy, however, met with considerable controversy. To many, a climax that seemed to have only one acceptable answer, and only one "good" ending under specific circumstances that required playing *Mass Effect 3*'s multiplayer scenarios did no credit to the series' focus on choice. Fans and critics of the series also pointed to strange ambiguity and plot holes in the ending. In response, BioWare's team released a free DLC pack called the "Extended Cut" in June, just three months after the game's release in March 2012, which added several scenes to clarify and elaborate on the ending.

Like BioWare's earlier RPG expansion packs, the *Mass Effect* series added hours of gameplay by way of downloadable content. It included new sidequests and locations for *Mass Effect*, additional gear, party members, and short side-stories for *Mass Effect 2*, and new character customization, story missions, and an additional character for *Mass Effect 3*.

The series also sparked a cascade of derivative work, including four novels, three mobile apps developed by other companies, and 10 comics. These tie-in products spotlighted locations, characters, and events referenced in the main series, and built upon the *Mass Effect* universe and its inhabitants. Of note was *Mass Effect Galaxy*, an EA-developed iOS shooter focusing on Jacob Taylor, a *Mass Effect 2* party member. There was also a single-issue comic released by Dark Horse, *Mass Effect: Blasto: Eternity is Forever*, which focused on a fictional action hero whose popular and comically horrendous movies are referenced frequently in backgrounds and ambient dialogue in the series.

The next entry in the *Mass Effect* universe, *Mass Effect: Andromeda*, was officially announced in June 2015, and is expected to release sometime in 2017.

## A RETURN TO KNIGHTS, MAGIC, AND DRAGONS

Following the success of *Mass Effect*, BioWare released another RPG using original IP – their high fantasy epic, *Dragon Age*. The series began with *Dragon Age: Origins* in 2009, followed by 2010's *Dragon Age: Origins – Awakening*, a story whose scope caused it to straddle the line between DLC expansion and another game in its own right. *Origins* began a trend that has maintained throughout the *Dragon Age* franchise, wherein protagonists are given a title according to the story, not dissimilar to Commander Shepard's rank. *Dragon Age: Origins* specifically follows the Warden, a member of an ancient order devoted to repelling evil creatures festering like a wound in the earth.

*Dragon Age II*, released in 2011, introduced Hawke, later dubbed the "Champion of Kirkwall." *Dragon Age II* was significantly smaller in scope than *Origins*, focusing on key events divided into acts all taking place in a single city-state, rather than the world-hopping, sprawling events of *Origins*. The third installment in the series, *Dragon Age: Inquisition*, was released in 2014 and met with considerable accolades and praise, including Game of the Year awards from 15 different publications. *Inquisition* followed the Inquisitor, a hero marked by fate and tasked seemingly with both stopping an elder evil and saving everyone around them and the world itself from its own horrendous messes.

The *Dragon Age* franchise maintains BioWare's reputation for rich narratives, fully realized characters, engaging romances, and responsive writing and gameplay that reacts to player decisions. Though *Dragon Age* does not use the alignment system distinctive to *KotOR*, *Jade Empire*, and *Mass Effect*, the game tracks the protagonist's choices and attitude, such that some characters and events change slightly based on the hero's personality as it is revealed throughout the story. In keeping with this, *Dragon Age: Origins* and *Dragon Age: Inquisition* track party members' opinion of the protagonist based on the character's choices and behavior. It offers the rare opportunity for characters the hero has particularly angered to leave the team altogether. *Dragon Age II* included a similar mechanic, albeit with departure a much rarer outcome, specifically during the endgame.

Like *Mass Effect*, *Dragon Age* features considerable DLC expansions, including additional party members, campaigns, and side-stories for *Dragon Age: Origins*, three new stories for *Dragon Age II*, and a wealth of gear and two additional storylines for *Dragon Age: Inquisition*. In addition, the *Trespasser* storyline was added to *Inquisition*, in 2015, wrapping up the events and loose ends of the third game and heavily hinting at what would come in a fourth.

Also like *Mass Effect*, *Dragon Age* has sparked a considerable number of tie-ins in other media. The franchise's licensed products include five novels expanding on the series' lore and political sphere in particular, two web series, four comics, two derivative games, and even a tabletop roleplaying game published by Green Ronin – in a way bringing BioWare full circle back to its start.

In 20 years of game development BioWare has dabbled in just about anything and everything, without straying too far from their pen-and-paper roots. They've gone from being computer-exclusive to designing for handheld and consoles, developed for numerous licensed IPs, created several of their own to immense success, and, especially under EA's management, expanded to three different offices in Canada and the U.S. Despite a recent gutting of major BioWare executives and writers, with a handful of major writers and two co-founders leaving the company, BioWare is standing strong. And, if past releases are any indication, it's safe to assume BioWare has only scratched the surface of what they have to offer.

## KEY FRANCHISES:

- Baldur's Gate series
- Star Wars: Knights of the Old Republic series
- Neverwinter Nights series
- Jade Empire
- Mass Effect series
- Dragon Age series

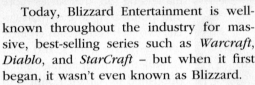

# BLIZZARD ENTERTAINMENT

## By Zanne Nilsson

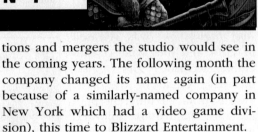

Today, Blizzard Entertainment is well-known throughout the industry for massive, best-selling series such as *Warcraft*, *Diablo*, and *StarCraft* – but when it first began, it wasn't even known as Blizzard.

Blizzard Entertainment was first founded as Silicon & Synapse on February 8, 1991 by three UCLA graduates: Allen Adham, Mike Morhaime, and Frank Pearce. Silicon & Synapse developed and released their first title, a Super Nintendo racing game called *RPM Racing*, just nine months later.

Although Silicon & Synapse developed two more of their own games – a side-scrolling puzzle-platformer called *The Lost Vikings* (1992) and a battle-racing game with a soundtrack of licensed rock songs called *Rock n' Roll Racing* (1993) – they focused much of their energy on making ports of other studios' games for the Windows 3.x, Commodore 64, Macintosh, and Amiga. In 1993, Silicon & Synapse was named "Best Software Developer of the Year" by *VideoGames Magazine*, and at the very end of the year the company decided to change their name to Chaos Studios.

In April 1994, Chaos Studios was acquired by Davidson & Associates for $6.75 million – the first of many acquisi-

tions and mergers the studio would see in the coming years. The following month the company changed its name again (in part because of a similarly-named company in New York which had a video game division), this time to Blizzard Entertainment.

## THE BEGINNINGS OF WARCRAFT, DIABLO, AND STARCRAFT

The very first game released under the new Blizzard Entertainment name also marked the beginning of its biggest hit franchise. *Warcraft: Orcs & Humans*, released for MS-DOS in November of 1994, is a real-time strategy game which pits the Human inhabitants of the planet Azeroth against the invading Orcs. The game – especially its multiplayer mode and innovations in gameplay and mission design – was well-received by gamers and reviewers alike, and went on to win several awards.

In addition to releasing three other games and launching its website the following year, Blizzard continued the *Warcraft* series with *Warcraft II: Tides of Darkness*. This sequel, like its predecessor, highlighted plot and personality. The game was especially praised for allowing players to set up multiplayer games on both local area networks and over the internet using the Kali emulator software, and *Warcraft II: Tides of Darkness* went on to sell 1.2 million copies. An expansion pack called *Warcraft II: Beyond the Dark Portal*, developed by Cyberlore Studios, was released the following year.

In 1996, Blizzard's parent company Davidson & Associates was acquired by CUC International, Inc. However, business continued as usual and at the very end of the year Blizzard released the first installment in another one of its hit franchises: *Diablo*. An action RPG origi-

nally published for Windows and Mac, *Diablo* centers on a lone hero battling through dungeons beneath the town of Tristram in order to defeat the Lord of Terror, Diablo. The game debuted as the #1 top-selling PC title and was critically-acclaimed on its release.

Launched alongside *Diablo* was Blizzard's new online gaming platform, Battle.net, which – unlike other online gaming services of the time – was directly incorporated into the games that used it. Battle.net went on to become popular amongst many gamers and helped drive sales of *Diablo* and the Blizzard games that followed it. In its first month of operation more than 150,000 players used Battle.net, and a little more than a year later the service had 1.5 million users.

March 1998 saw the release of *StarCraft*,

the progenitor of yet another major Blizzard franchise. *StarCraft*, a military sci-fi real-time strategy game set in the 25th century, focuses on three species battling for dominance in the Koprulu Sector: the insectoid alien race Zerg, the Earth-exiled human Terrans, and the humanoid Protoss species. The game, praised for its compelling story and pioneering gameplay, has been called one of the most important and best video games of all time. Though originally released only for Microsoft Windows, *StarCraft* was later ported to Mac OS and the Nintendo 64, and sold three million copies in the first three months following its release. The

game was even considered culturally significant enough that a copy of it was taken aboard the space shuttle Discovery during the first docking mission for the International Space Station in 1999. An expansion pack for the game, *StarCraft: Brood War*, was also well-received and sold more than 1.5 million copies. More than a million copies of the original game and its expansion sold in South Korea, making it the most popular video game ever released in that country at that time.

At the end of 1997, CUC International, Inc. merged with HFS Incorporated to form Blizzard's new parent company, Cendant. However, following an accounting fraud scandal surrounding CUC International, Cendant's stock plummeted and the company sold Blizzard and another one of its video game companies, Sierra On-Line, to French company Havas. Soon after, Havas was bought by Vivendi, and Blizzard officially became part of Vivendi Games.

## INTO THE NEW MILLENNIUM

June 2000 saw the release of *Diablo*'s follow-up, *Diablo II*. It sold a million copies in its first three weeks, making it the fastest-selling computer game in history up to that point. *Diablo II* built on the first game's plot and gameplay, and even included a "hardcore

mode" in which a player's character could be permanently killed, rendering it unplayable. Blizzard thought highly enough of the game's plot and animation that it submitted the game's opening cinematic for Academy Award consideration as a short film titled *Diablo: The Calling*. An expansion pack called *Diablo II: Lord of Destruction* was released the following year.

At the end of 2000, Vivendi acquired Universal Studios, making Blizzard a part of the new Vivendi Universal. In 2002, Blizzard was able to get the rights for three

of the earliest games it developed – *Rock n' Roll Racing*, *The Lost Vikings*, and *Blackthorne* – back from their original publisher, Interplay, and release ports of all of them on the Game Boy Advance.

In 2002 Blizzard released the third installment of its *Warcraft* franchise, *Warcraft III: Reign of Chaos*. This new real time strategy title added two more playable races, the Undead and the Night Elves, to the world of Azeroth and allowed the player to experience the plot from the point of view of every playable race. *Warcraft III* was lauded by critics and won more than fifty awards from several different publications. The game's expansion pack released the following year, *Warcraft III: The Frozen Throne*, met with similar praise and also won its share of awards.

## GOING WORLDWIDE: WORLD OF WARCRAFT, BLIZZCON, AND THE WORLDWIDE INVITATIONAL

Blizzard hosted the first of four Worldwide Invitational events in January of 2004. Taking place in Seoul, South Korea for the first three years and in Paris, France for the final year, the Worldwide Invitational events combined promotion with international eSports competition featuring major Blizzard titles. Although the name seems to have been discontinued after 2008, similar Blizzard-sponsored events have continued to take place in the years since.

But perhaps the best-remembered event of 2004 was the release of the fourth and most well-known title in the *Warcraft*

franchise, *World of Warcraft*, a massively multiplayer online role-playing game (MMORPG) set in the *Warcraft* universe which a player pays a regular subscription fee to play. Although far from being the first MMORPG ever made, it is undoubtedly the biggest and most recognizable; if you asked the average person to name one MMORPG, it's almost certain that *World of Warcraft* would be the first words out of their mouth. The game spread into wider popular culture, referenced everywhere from a question on *Jeopardy* to an entire episode of *South Park*.

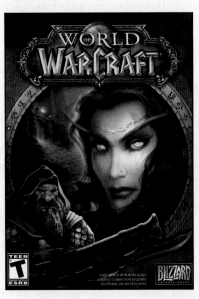

*World of Warcraft* was an instant success, breaking all previous sales records in multiple countries on its first day of release – at least, according to Blizzard itself. In the year following its initial release in North America, Australia, and New Zealand, the game was rolled out in South Korea, Europe, China, Taiwan, Hong Kong, and Macau, and by December of 2005 had five million subscribers. In the years since, Blizzard has released several expansions to *World of Warcraft*.

Although *World of Warcraft* peaked at 12 million subscribers in 2010, 5.5 million subscribers were still playing the game as of 2015 and it is still counted as the world's most-subscribed MMORPG – not bad for a game that's more than 10 years old.

In October 2005, Blizzard hosted its first BlizzCon in Anaheim, California. An event that combines traditional video game convention events such as panels and costume contests with promotional events for Blizzard games, it has proven to be popular amongst gamers and has been held semi-regularly (finally becoming an annual event beginning in 2013) ever since.

## CONTINUING THE LEGACY

In the following years Blizzard spent much of its time hosting its events and releasing new expansions for *World of Warcraft*, which expanded into Latin America and Russia in 2008. The same year, Vivendi merged with Activision to form Activision Blizzard.

In 2010, Blizzard released *StarCraft II: Wings of Liberty*, which became the fastest-selling real-time strategy game of all time when it sold more than three million copies in its first month. It has since been followed by two expansions: *StarCraft II: Heart of the Swarm* (2013) and *StarCraft II: Legacy of the Void* (2015).

Two years later, in 2012, Blizzard released the long-awaited *Diablo III*. The game sold in excess of 3.5 million copies in the first day of its release, breaking the record for fastest-selling PC game – a record which was, at that time, held by the *World of Warcraft: Cataclysm* expansion. In 2013, for the first time in many years, Blizzard moved back into the console market by releasing *Diablo*

*III* for PS3 and Xbox 360. The game was followed by an expansion in 2014, *Diablo III: Reaper of Souls*, which was later sold with the original game in one package for home consoles called the "Ultimate Evil Edition."

However, Blizzard hasn't been content in recent years to coast on its past successes. In 2015 the company released *Heroes of the Storm*, a multiplayer online battle arena game (or "hero brawler," as Blizzard prefers it to be called) featuring heroes from other Blizzard games, including the *Warcraft*, *StarCraft*, and *Diablo* series as well as lesser-known titles like *The Lost Vikings*. And in May of 2016, Blizzard released its latest

success, a multiplayer first-person shooter called *Overwatch*. The game has achieved massive critical and commercial success, possibly positioning it as the progenitor of the company's next hit franchise. Whatever the future holds, it's clear that Blizzard still has a few tricks up its sleeve.

## KEY FRANCHISES:

- ☐ **Warcraft**
- ☐ **Diablo**
- ☐ **StarCraft**
- ☐ **Overwatch**

# BUNGIE

## By Zanne Nilsson

During their more than 25-year history, Bungie has grown from one college grad in a basement apartment assembling 2,500 game boxes by himself to a well-staffed developer whose games make hundreds of millions of dollars at launch. The journey in between has been an unpredictable one, and along the way Bungie has treated both its successes and its setbacks with an irreverent attitude that has set it apart from other developers of its stature.

## FROM ONE-MAN OPERATION TO MAJOR DEVELOPER

In May 1991, Alex Seropian – then a recent graduate of the University of Chicago – founded Bungie Software Products Corporation. The choice of the name Bungie had a "very strange reason" behind it – at least according to the old company history page on Bungie's website, which jokingly treats the story behind the name as a closely-guarded secret. But whatever the reason behind the name, the reason behind the founding itself was simple: Seropian wanted to publish *Operation: Desert Storm*, a top-down tank shooter game he had recently designed for the Macintosh. The game went on to sell about 2,500 copies – a pittance compared to the sale numbers of Bungie's later games. But at the time, it was considered a "minor hit" for what was then a one-man operation. This was not, however, the first game Seropian released; he had previously made a *Pong* clone called *Gnop!* which he distributed for free.

Following this small success, Seropian teamed up with former classmate Jason Jones to publish Jones' dungeon crawler *Minotaur: The Labyrinths of Crete* for the Macintosh in 1992. The top-

down game included a multiplayer mode which relied on networking using either the Point-to-Point Protocol or the AppleTalk protocol. The game, whose tagline ("Kill your enemies. Kill your friends' enemies. Kill your friends.") went on to appear in later Bungie titles, also went on to sell roughly 2,500 copies but gained a cult following. At this point Bungie decided to focus on the Macintosh game market; in a later interview, Jones said this was primarily because it was "easier to compete" in the Macintosh market compared to the PC game market at the time.

According to Jones, the next game the still-tiny company worked on was intended to be a 3D remake of *Minotaur* – indeed, the old Bungie history page humorously referred to the final result as "*Minotaur* in a tube" – but for various reasons the game evolved into its own entity. This game, *Pathways into Darkness*, casts the player as a Special Forces soldier who must keep a sleeping god beneath a Mexican pyramid from waking up and destroying the world. *Pathways into Darkness* was both a critical and commercial success, giving Bungie enough funds to hire more staff and finally move into their own office in Chicago. The game also convinced the company, in their own words, that "without a story a game is a lesser thing."

The company's next project once again began as a sequel and once again became an independent title, this time called *Marathon*. In this game, the player assumes the role of a security guard on a futuristic starship who must fight off aliens trying to invade the ship. If the plot sounds vaguely familiar to fans of Bungie's later games, so will some of *Marathon*'s key features: cutting-edge 3D graphics, an intricate plot, networked multiplayer, and an incorporeal AI who helps the protagonist. Unsurprising, then, that *Marathon* and its two sequels are considered forerunners to the *Halo* games; the *Marathon* games even introduced the concept of AI "rampancy" which later became a plot point in the *Halo* series. After its release in late 1994, *Marathon* won multiple awards and was considered a total triumph which helped elevate Bungie from its status as just another tiny game developer to a major publisher – at least in the world of Macintosh game publishing.

Bungie quickly followed this success by releasing the company's first completed sequel, *Marathon 2: Durandal*, in November 1995. One of the game's notable features, which also reappeared in later Bungie games, was the ability to play the single-player story in co-op mode as well. Though the initial release was for Macintosh only, the game was ported to PC as well, officially turning the rapidly-growing Bungie into a multiplatform publisher. The final game of the trilogy, *Marathon Infinity*, was released in 1996; it included the built-in editing tools Forge and Anvil, which players could use to build their own levels.

The very next year, Bungie published *Myth: The Fallen Lords*, a real-time tactics game set in an unnamed land where the forces of "Light" and "Dark" are battling for control. The title, which was the first Bungie game released simultaneously on Mac and PC, was a critical and commercial success which sold over 350,000 units. In 1998 Bungie released a sequel, *Myth II: Soulblighter*.

After the success of *Myth*, Bungie moved to another Chicago office, and established Bungie West, a studio branch located in San Jose, CA. Bungie West's first and only game was *Oni* (2001), a third-person action game for PC, Mac, and PlayStation 2 set on a dystopic future version of Earth. *Oni* received mixed reviews, partially because it didn't deliver on all of its promised features, such as LAN multiplayer.

In 1999, video game publisher/developer/distributor Take-Two Interactive purchased a 19.9 percent share of Bungie. While the deal gave Bungie a lot of money and better distribution strength, there were bigger deals to come – and a big project in the works.

## HALO AND MICROSOFT

*Halo* – then planned as a real-time strategy game to be simultaneously released on PC and Mac – was first publically announced in 1999, followed by a trailer at E3 2000. A little more than a month later, on June 19, 2000, Microsoft announced that it had acquired Bungie and *Halo* (which had evolved into a third-person action game). Soon after, Bungie moved its offices from Chicago to Redmond, WA. Following the acquisition, a lot of big changes were made to *Halo*: its engine was rewritten, it became a first-person shooter, it turned into an Xbox-exclusive game, its title was changed to *Halo: Combat Evolved*, and its planned online multiplayer feature was removed because the Xbox Live service wouldn't be online when the game launched.

*Halo: Combat Evolved*, released on the same day as the Xbox itself in late 2001, takes place on a massive ring-shaped space station five hundred years in the future, when humanity is at war with a group of aliens known as the Covenant who are trying to wipe out all of mankind. In *Halo: Combat Evolved* and most of the following games the player takes on the role of a "supersoldier"

called Master Chief who must fight against the Covenant, as well as a race of parasitic aliens called the Flood who take over other living organisms.

The game, which brought many groundbreaking mechanics to the FPS genre and included the first LAN multiplayer mode on a console, was a runaway success. A sequel became inevitable, and sure enough work on *Halo 2* began shortly afterward. Although

Bungie had big ambitions for *Halo 2*, many of the elements planned to be included in the game fell by the wayside in order to finish the new online multiplayer modes in time for the game's release date in late 2004. *Halo 2* was also a massive hit both in terms of reviews and sales.

Before development on *Halo 2* was even completed, some of the staff at Bungie began work on *Halo 3*. The move from the Xbox to the Xbox 360 made a lot of improvements to the game possible, including better graphics, sound and AI. *Halo 3*, like the two before it, was a commercial and critical success which helped cement Bungie's place in video game history.

## BACK TO INDEPENDENCE

However, after the release of *Halo 3*, Bungie announced that it would be leaving Microsoft to become a privately-held limited liability company: Bungie, LLC. As part of the arrangement, Microsoft retained the *Halo* IP and a minority stake in Bungie. However, the companies would be working together on two final *Halo*-related projects.

On the development side, Bungie divided its staff into two teams, each working on new spinoffs to the main *Halo* series. In the first, *Halo 3: ODST*, the player fights alongside a group of Orbital Drop Shock Troopers in the ruins of New Mombasa, Kenya during the events of *Halo 2*. Production on the game, which was strongly influenced by film noir, took about 14 months with a team of 75 people. On its release in 2009 the game became the top-selling Xbox 360 title worldwide, and it was generally well-received by critics and gamers.

The second spinoff – and Bungie's final contribution to the *Halo* series – was *Halo: Reach*, a prequel to *Halo: Combat Evolved* which follows a supersoldier called Noble Six during the Covenant's attack on the human colony Reach. Microsoft spared no expense in marketing *Halo: Reach* and their investment paid off, with the critically-praised game set-

ting a new first-day sales record for the franchise at $200 million.

In 2009 Bungie's staff grew to 165 people and the company moved into a new office almost double the size of the old one. The following year Bungie made a 10-year publishing deal with Activision Blizzard; one of the conditions of the new deal was that Bungie would own any new IP they came up with.

The first game created under the Bungie-Activision partnership – and Bungie's first new franchise since the start of *Halo* – was *Destiny*, which released in 2014. The game, described as a "shared-world shooter" and blends aspects of role-playing games, first-person shooters, and massively-multiplayer online games, takes place 700 years in the future when humanity has been almost wiped out. The player becomes one of the Guardians who use the power of "Light" to protect the last safe city on Earth from hostile alien races aided by a power called the "Darkness." Guardians must also revive a protective celestial body called "the Traveler" which saved the humans of Earth from extinction. While critics' opinions on the game were mixed, *Destiny* managed to make $500 million on its first day of release and won awards from GamesRadar and the British Academy Video Games Awards.

Clearly, Bungie isn't a company that dwells on the past; for its entire history it has been constantly moving forward and creating new games to play, characters to inhabit, and worlds to explore. Though the path they take from here on out may be unpredictable, we can certainly count on Bungie to keep surprising us.

### KEY FRANCHISES:

☐ **Marathon**

☐ **Myth**

☐ **Halo**

☐ **Destiny**

# CAPCOM®

BY ZANNE NILSSON

For a company that's been around for more than 30 years, it would be easy to assume that we can expect nothing new from Capcom. But nothing could be further from the truth – over the past three decades Capcom has delivered some of the best-selling, most-beloved franchises in video game history, seemingly producing new hit franchises every year while continuing to release new titles for most of their classic series. But to find out why, we'll have to go back to a time before Capcom was even known as Capcom.

## CAPSULE COMPUTERS

Capcom had its roots in the I.R.M. Corporation, which was founded by Kenzo Tsujimoto in 1979 in the Osaka prefecture of Japan, where it has been headquartered ever since. I.R.M Corporation and its subsidiary Japanese Capsule Computers Co., Ltd. – both of which made arcade machines – changed its name to Sanbi Co., Ltd. in 1981. However, Capcom considers its official start to be June 1983, when Capcom Co., Ltd. itself was founded by Tsujimoto to sell software. The name "Capcom" derived from the phrase "capsule computers," which the company used to distinguish their arcade machines from personal computers.

The company's first official product was the coin-operated *Little League* machine, but its first "real" arcade video game was *Vulgus*, a scrolling shooter game released in 1984. In December of that year Capcom released *1942*, another arcade game which became the first title in a fairly popular series referred to as *19XX*. The next year it released more arcade games, including *Commando* and *Ghosts 'n Goblins*, as well as establishing Capcom U.S.A., Inc. in California to distribute Capcom's products in the USA. At the end of 1985 the company released a port of *1942* for the Nintendo Entertainment System – Capcom's first title on a home console. Ports of *Ghosts 'n Goblins* and *Commando* soon followed.

## STREET FIGHTING AND A MEGA MASCOT

In August of 1987 Capcom released the arcade game *Street Fighter*, a fighting game which sparked one of Capcom's biggest hit franchises. The game's sequel, *Street Fighter II* (1991), was a massive success both in arcades and living rooms, and the series spawned several more games. These have included a total of five numbered entries, though most of those have had enhanced spinoffs (such as *Street Fighter IV: Arcade Edition*, and so on). *Street Fighter* characters

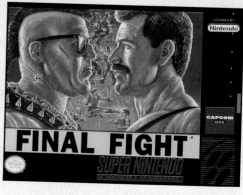

have appeared in a number of other franchises, and in outside media, such as two live-action Hollywood films – *Street Fighter* (1994) and *Street Fighter: The Legend of Chun-Li* (2009), neither of which were received well – and animated adaptations.

A few months later, Capcom went from a fighting game to a game featuring a super fighting robot: *Mega Man*. The NES game (featuring notoriously awful box art) centers on a little blue android who can use the powers of his fallen enemies, and has led to several sequels and spinoff games set in various different timelines. A few animated adaptations of the series have been made, including a 1990s TV show which is perhaps better-remembered for its bad puns than for its faithfulness to the source material. *Mega Man* became one of Capcom's most beloved franchises, maybe more so by gamers than by Capcom itself; the company came under fire for its decision to cancel the 3DS title *Mega Man Legends 3* and has drawn criticism for not releasing any new original titles for the series since.

After Sanbi officially merged with Capcom and changed its name to Capcom Co., Ltd., the company released the arcade game *Final Fight* (1989). The side-scrolling beat'em'up was successfully ported to the Super NES in 1990 and was well-received by critics. It too led to several sequels, and all the titles of the series combined have sold more than 3 million units.

## CONTINUED SUCCESS WITH ROLE-PLAYING AND SURVIVAL HORROR

In April of 1993 Capcom released the role-playing game *Breath of Fire* for the SNES. In *Breath of Fire* the player assumes the role of Ryu, a boy with the ability to shapeshift into a dragon, as he searches for his sister Sara. The game was a success and has been followed by five console sequels to date. A mobile title, *Breath of Fire 6*, was released in Japan in early 2016.

March 1996 saw the release of *Resident Evil* for the PlayStation, a genre-defining survival horror video game about a special law enforcement team who ends up trapped in a supposedly-abandoned mansion with a group of mutated creatures. The game was both a critical and commercial success, leading to a whole host of sequels and spinoffs that are still being released to this day. The games also inspired a successful series of live-action Hollywood films which have made more than $900 million combined,

as well as a series of CG-animated films produced in Japan.

In 1999, the *Resident Evil* team produced *Dino Crisis*, a survival horror game about a spec ops agent named Regina who must investigate an island research facility filled with dinosaurs. The game was well-received and the PlayStation version alone sold more than 2.4 million copies. To date, *Dino Crisis* has been followed by four sequels, with the most recent being the mobile title *Dino Crisis: Dungeon in Chaos* in 2003.

## DIFFERENT GENRES IN THE 21st CENTURY

Capcom continued its winning streak into the new millennium, starting with *Onimusha: Warlords* in January 2001. The action-adventure game, released for the PlayStation 2, was planned around the same basic gameplay as *Resident Evil*, but set in a "ninja house" in Japan during the Sengoku period where the player must battle against demons. The game sold more than 2 million copies worldwide and inspired two direct sequels and two spinoffs.

In August of the same year Capcom released *Devil May Cry* for the PS2, a game initially intended as an entry in the *Resident Evil* series which instead evolved into its own entity. The action-adventure game, which makes multiple allusions to Dante Alighieri's poem *The Divine Comedy*, centers on a demon hunter named Dante who avenges his mother's and brother's deaths by killing demons. The game was a huge success, leading to three sequels and a reboot.

Capcom was clearly on a roll in 2001, since in October of that year they also released the first title in yet another successful franchise: *Phoenix Wright: Ace Attorney*. The visual novel adventure game, originally released for the Game Boy Advance, follows defense attorney Phoenix Wright through investigations and courtroom trials as he tries to prove his clients' innocence. This game, too, was a hit, landing in the west several years later as a DS port of the GBA title and quickly gaining a cult following. It has since inspired several sequels, spinoffs,

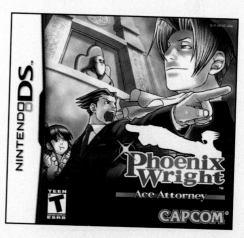

stage productions, manga, a live-action film, and anime.

*Monster Hunter* – an action RPG which is about, well, hunting monsters – was released for the PS2 in 2004. While undoubtedly more popular in Japan, *Monster Hunter* gained a cult following in North America which has helped drive sales of its multiple sequels on various platforms. The company extended its efforts abroad into the mobile games market a couple years later with the establishment of the U.S.-based Capcom Interactive, Inc. to distribute mobile games outside Japan.

In August of 2006 Capcom released *Dead Rising*, a survival horror beat'em'up game for the Xbox 360 about a photojournalist named Frank West who must fight his way through a zombie-infested shopping mall. The game was a commercial success, selling more than 1 million copies, and inspired three sequels as well as a few film adaptations.

The year 2006 also saw the initial release of *Lost Planet: Extreme Condition* in Japan, followed by a worldwide release at the beginning of 2007. The multi-platform third-person shooter game follows "snow pirate" Wayne Holden on the planet of E.D.N. III as he fights both a megacorporation trying to colonize the planet and an alien race called the Akrid who threaten the human colonization efforts. The Xbox 360 version alone sold more than 1.6 million copies and led to two sequels and a spinoff game.

## THE FUTURE IS NOW

Capcom, clearly unafraid to go beyond arcades and consoles, plunged into the smartphone game market with its first iPhone game (*Resident Evil: Degeneration*) in 2009, followed by its first iPad game (*Resident Evil 4: iPad Edition*) the next year. As the company approaches its 35th anniversary, it's natural to wonder what lies ahead for Capcom. But given how well the company has adapted to advances in gaming technology, it's likely they'll be here for another 35 years to come.

## KEY FRANCHISES:

- Street Fighter
- Mega Man
- Resident Evil
- Onimusha
- Devil May Cry
- Ace Attorney
- Monster Hunter

# ELECTRONIC ARTS

## By Zanne Nilsson

EA. Those two letters have long had a tendency to stir a variety of opinions amongst gamers of all ages. But EA was once a small publisher with a noble mission: to give a voice to the artists behind independent games.

## BEGINNINGS AND MADDEN

Founded in 1982 by former Apple employee Trip Hawkins, who initially wanted to name the company Amazin' Software; he ultimately called it Electronic Arts to emphasize the artistic aspect of video games. One of the company's innovations, led by Hawkins, was packaging of computer games by putting them into boxes with custom artwork and highlighting designers' names on the packaging. On May 21, 1983, the company released its first six computer games. Three of them – *Hard Hat Mack*, *Pinball Construction Set*, and *Archon: The Light and the Dark* – were bestsellers, and the other three – *M.U.L.E.*, *Worms?*, and *Murder on the Zinderneuf* – are also fondly remembered.

In 1984 the company began building its distribution network and became the first computer game company to license an individual athlete's – Julius "Dr. J" Irving – name and likeness in a game; they paid Irving $25,000. After licensing Larry Bird's name and likeness as well, EA released *Dr. J*

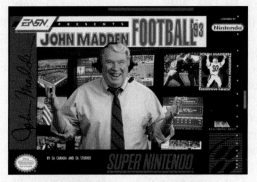

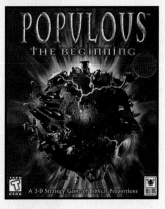

*and Larry Bird Go One-on-One*. The commercial success of the game pushed EA to license football coach and commentator John Madden's name and likeness for *John Madden Football*. The game, released in 1988, inspired a number of *Madden* sequel titles which EA has released annually since 1990. The *Madden NFL* series at large has sold more than 100 million copies worldwide, and has in turn influenced players and coaches in the sport itself in a number of ways. The talk of the "Madden Curse" comes about every year, with featured cover players having a mysterious tendency to get injured that season.

Between 1985 and 1989, EA released three other notable games: fantasy role-playing game *The Bard's Tale* (1985); skateboarding game *Skate or Die!* (1987), the company's first internally-developed title; and *Populous* (1989), which is considered by many to be the first "god game." During the same timeframe, the company also began expanding outside the United States by opening an office in the UK near London and starting to distribute games in Australia. The company went public in 1990 with shares starting at $8 per share; the price rose to $35 per share before the end of the year. The same year, the company began producing home console titles for the Nintendo Entertainment System.

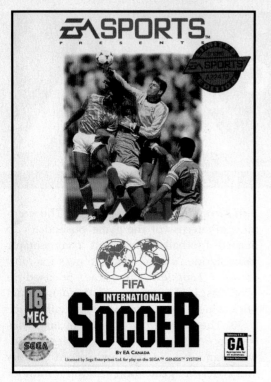

## ESTABLISHING SERIES IN THE '90s

Two monumental things happened to EA in 1991: Trip Hawkins resigned as CEO to form The 3DO Company – though he remained Chairman of the Board until 1994 – and EA created its now-iconic EA Sports brand. In 1992, EA acquired Origin Systems, Inc., creators of the *Wing Commander* franchise; EA became the publisher for the series from then on, and brought the series to the big screen with less-than-stellar results. The same year, EA published *Desert Strike: Return to the Gulf*, a shoot 'em up game which became EA's best-selling title ever at the time.

In 1993, EA released *FIFA International Soccer*, another licensed sports game which became a hit with both players and critics. Like *Madden*, *FIFA* games soon became annually-released staples of the sports game genre.

Later, in 1994, EA released *Road & Track Presents: The Need for Speed*, a racing game which was praised for its realism, commentaries, and gameplay. The game sold well, and has been followed by more than 20 sequels to date. In the next few years EA continued to acquire other companies, including Bullfrog Productions, Ltd. and Vision Software, Ltd. – but they had even bigger plans in the works.

*Ultima Online*, a massively multiplayer online role-playing game set in the universe of Origin's *Ultima* games, was released on September 24, 1997. The game has since been credited with helping to popularize the MMORPG genre and won eight world records, was placed into the Game Developers Choice Online Awards Hall of Fame, and was named one of the 100 best video games of all time by *Time* magazine.

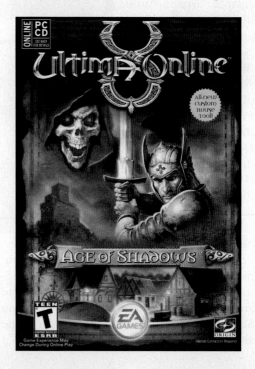

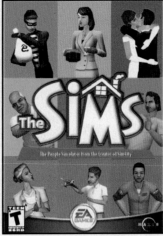

## NOT JUST SIM-ULATED SUCCESS

In June 1997 EA acquired Maxis, the studio which helped make *SimCity* a massive success, as a wholly-owned subsidiary. EA has published all sequels and spinoffs in the series ever since – one of which became a much bigger hit than anyone could have anticipated.

That spinoff, *The Sims*, was released in February 2000. Unlike *SimCity*, *The Sims* simulated life on the personal level, following one or more individual "Sims" as they go through their daily lives. The game, which was inspired by game designer Will Wright's experiences rebuilding his life after he lost his home in a firestorm in 1991, went on to become a big critical and commercial success. The years since have seen the release of several sequels and spinoffs, and *The Sims* has become one of the highest-selling video game series of all time.

In addition to acquiring Dreamworks Interactive and scoring the worldwide interactive rights to the *Harry Potter* book/film series, in 2000 EA also licensed the *Quake III: Arena 3D* engine to be used in several games. One of these games was *American McGee's Alice*, a psychological horror game set as an unofficial, somewhat macabre sequel to Lewis Carroll's books *Alice's Adventures in Wonderland* and *Through the Looking-Glass*. The game – which included a soundtrack by Nine Inch Nails member Chris Vrenna – was lauded by critics especially for its visual design, and has sold more than 1.5 million copies.

In 2002 EA released *Battlefield 1942*, a first-person shooter set in various battle locations during World War Two. It has since spawned 14 sequels set in various different eras both real and imagined and the series shows no signs of stopping.

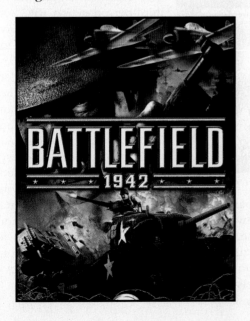

Over the next few years EA continued the studio acquisition binge it had been on since 1991, most notably picking up Mythic Entertainment, who released the fantasy MMORPG *Warhammer Online: Age of Reckoning* a couple years later. During this same time period EA made a number of sport licensing deals, including an exclusive NFL license and a 15-year deal with ESPN. In 2005 EA also got the rights to produce video games based on the hit TV show *The Simpsons*.

*Crysis*, an FPS set in the near-future on the fictional Lingshan Islands, where an ancient alien structure has been discovered, released in 2007. The game was praised by critics especially for its graphics and won a handful of awards from game publications. *Crysis* has since been followed by a few main sequels and several spinoffs.

*Spore*, a single-player title which has been variously described as a life simulator, real-time strategy game, and a god game, was released the following year. In *Spore*, which was designed by *SimCity* and *The Sims* designer Will Wright, the player controls the development of a species from the single-celled stage onwards. The game was generally well-received – though it came under fire for its digital rights management software – and inspired a whole host of spinoffs.

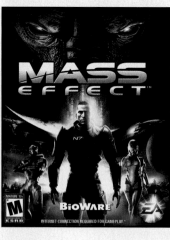

In 2008 EA also released *Army of Two*, a third-person shooter which follows the exploits of two mercenaries. The game has inspired two sequels so far – *Army of Two: The 40th Day* (2010) and *Army of Two: The Devil's Cartel* (2013) – as well as graphic novel and comic book adapta-

tions, with talk of a film adaptation as well.

EA was busy in 2008, and released three more big games that year: *Dead Space*, *Mirror's Edge*, and *Mass Effect*. *Dead Space*, a survival horror third-person shooter set on an interstellar mining ship, pits the player against horrific reanimated human corpses called "Necromorphs." It was a hit with both critics and players, who bought more than 2 million copies of the game, and has been followed by two sequels and three spinoffs.

*Mirror's Edge* is an action-adventure platformer in which the player controls Faith, a "runner" who carries messages across a city's rooftops while dodging the totalitarian government's surveillance. The game got primarily positive reviews, with critics especially lauding the gameplay. It was followed by a prequel, *Mirror's Edge Catalyst*, in 2016.

EA published the PC version of *Mass Effect* in 2008, one year after it had been released to consoles, and has published every installment in the series since. The first game, a single-player third-person action RPG set in the Milky Way galaxy in 2183, puts the player in the role of an elite human soldier called Commander Shepard, who must stop the return of the Reapers, an advanced machine race who are believed to wipe out all organic civilization every 50,000 years. Critics praised the game's storytelling in particular, and *Mass Effect* won several awards. It has been followed by three major sequels and three spinoffs, as well as a stunning number of adaptations and spinoffs in other media, including comics, novels, anime, rides, and fan-created media.

## HIGH FANTASY AND HIGH SUCCESS

In 2009 EA published *Dragon Age: Origins*, a fantasy RPG in which the player's character must unite the fictional kingdom of Ferelden to repel an imminent invasion by the demonic Darkspawn and defeat the Darkspawn's leader, the Archdemon. The game was well-received by critics and has been followed by two sequels and three spinoffs so far.

*Dante's Inferno*, an action-adventure game based on the first part of Dante Alighieri's poem *The Divine Comedy*, was released the following year. The game follows a fictional version of Dante as he goes through Hell to save his love, Beatrice, from Lucifer. Generally praised by critics, *Dante's Inferno* was also adapted as an animated film.

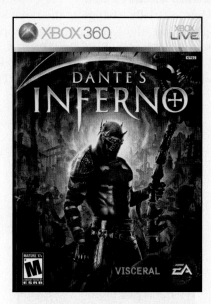

Then in 2011, EA released *Star Wars: The Old Republic*, an MMORPG set in the *Star Wars* universe. While it had some difficulty retaining its initial subscribers, *Star Wars: The Old Republic* received mainly positive reviews and has inspired its own comic book and novel adaptations.

Another *Star Wars* game was soon to follow. *Star Wars Battlefront* (2015), either a first- or third-person shooter depending on which view the player prefers at any given time, lets players control either one of several characters from the original films or a common Rebel Alliance soldier or Imperial Stormtrooper. While the game received mixed reviews it sold exceptionally well, and a sequel is already in the works.

## WHAT COMES NEXT?

Due to the annual nature of many of EA's franchises, their future may seem somewhat predictable, especially with regards to their sports titles. But while some of the future may seem certain, EA's track record proves that new hit franchises emerge all the time. It wouldn't be at all surprising if EA was still going strong 30 years from now.

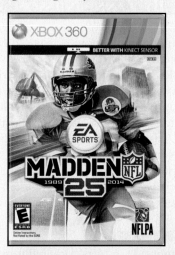

### KEY FRANCHISES:

- Madden NFL
- FIFA Soccer
- Sim City
- The Sims
- Battlefield
- Crysis
- Dead Space
- Mirror's Edge
- Star Wars: Battlefront

# NAUGHTY DOG

BY ZANNE NILSSON

Naughty Dog – now a major developer with multiple hit franchises to its name – downplays the importance of its early days in its website's official history page, saying: "Although we have sometimes claimed to have started in 1984, we were just working on garage titles back then to be honest." Nevertheless, the company's early accomplishments shouldn't be overlooked – especially since it began as a team of two teenagers making games on their own.

## JAM SOFTWARE

Naughty Dog was originally founded as JAM Software by friends Jason Rubin and Andy Gavin in 1984, when they were both only 14 years old. The friends' first original title was an educational game for the Apple II, *Math Jam* (1985). Afterwards they worked on a skiing game, *Ski Crazed* (1986), which was published by the small company Baudville, and sold about 1,500 units.

This modest success led Gavin and Rubin to develop *Dream Zone* (1987), an adventure game set in a dream world. The game was well-received by critics and sold more than

10,000 copies, but afterwards JAM Software ended its publishing deal with Baudville, believing the publisher wasn't big enough to reach the heights Rubin and Gavin aspired to. JAM Software made a deal with Electronic Arts instead.

## BECOMING NAUGHTY DOG

After officially changing their name to Naughty Dog, the first game the company made with EA was *Keef the Thief: A Boy and His Lockpick* (1989), a comedy RPG which went on to sell 50,000 copies. Their

next title was *Rings of Power* (1991) for SEGA Genesis, which sold 100,000 copies in three months.

After *Rings of Power* both Rubin and Gavin wanted to take a break from making games, but they were sucked back into the industry by the chance to develop games for the 3DO. In 1994, the company released its only 3DO game, *Way of the Warrior*. The fighting game was the first title the pair didn't work on by themselves, and they signed a deal with Universal Interactive Studios to release the game and produce three new titles as well.

## CRASH BANDICOOT

The basic concept for their next game was talked out during a road trip as Gavin and Rubin moved from Boston to L.A.; they wanted to use an animal character and settled on a bandicoot who was eventually named Crash. *Crash Bandicoot* (1996) was released for PlayStation, and was well-received by critics. The story centered on Crash, who was subjected to Dr. Neo Cortex's Evolvo-Ray and escapes. He becomes determined to stop Dr. Cortex from experimenting on other animals, including a female bandicoot named Tawna, who Crash bonded with while in captivity. *Crash Bandicoot* became one of the best-selling PlayStation games of all time, and Crash himself became an iconic video game character, quickly becoming one of the mascots for the PlayStation console.

Naughty Dog developed two sequels, *Crash Bandicoot 2: Cortex Strikes Back* (1997) and *Crash Bandicoot: Warped* (1998), as well as a kart racing spinoff, *Crash Team Racing* (1999). Afterwards they split with Universal Interactive Studios – who retained the rights to the *Crash Bandicoot* IP, pushing Naughty Dog to move on to new projects.

## JAK AND DAXTER

Naughty Dog's run as an independent publisher ended in 2001, when it was bought by Sony. *Jak and Daxter: The Precursor Legacy* (2001) for PlayStation 2 released later that year. The game's story follows the silent 15-year-old Jak and his loudmouthed friend Daxter, who is transformed into an otter-weasel hybrid called an "ottsel." The pair leave their home

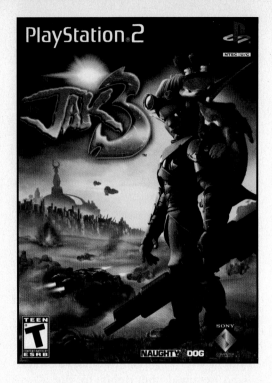

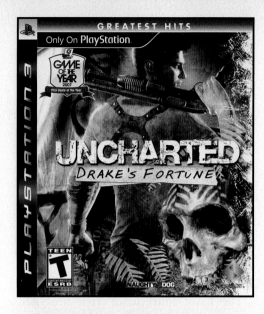

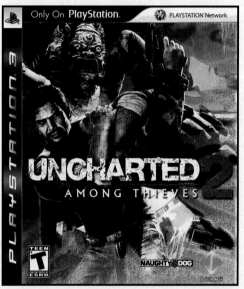

of Sandover Village and travel through the world to find the Dark Sage Gol Acheron, who is the only person who can return Daxter to his previous form; along the way, they discover Gol Acheron's plans to capture the other four sages and transform the world, and must stop him from succeeding.

*Jak and Daxter: The Precursor Legacy* got positive reviews from critics and sold more than two million copies. Naughty Dog developed two sequels, *Jak II* (2003) and *Jak 3* (2004), as well as a vehicular combat spinoff, *Jak X: Combat Racing* (2005). The fourth main game, *Jak and Daxter: The Lost Frontier* (2009), was developed by High Impact Games, a developer partially made up of former members of Naughty Dog.

In 2004, Rubin left the company to work on the comic book *The Iron Saint*. But the company soldiered on, and soon set its sights on the next console generation.

## UNCHARTED

Inspired by the PlayStation 3's new capabilities, Naughty Dog decided to go in a more realistic direction for their next series. They achieved this in their next game, *Uncharted: Drake's Fortune* (2007), an action-adventure platformer for PS3. The game's story follows protagonist Nathan Drake as he travels through South America

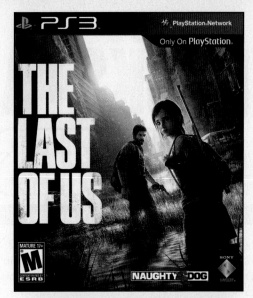

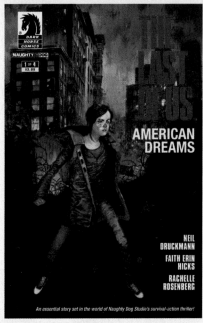

searching for the treasure of El Dorado. Drake is accompanied by his friend Victor "Sully" Sullivan and journalist Elena Fisher – and hounded by pirates and mercenaries. The game received great reviews from critics and sold more than 2.6 million copies.

Naughty Dog developed three sequels to the game: *Uncharted 2: Among Thieves* (2009), *Uncharted 3: Drake's Deception* (2011), and *Uncharted 4: A Thief's End* (2016). Other spin-offs in the series were developed by SIE Bend Studio, One Loop Games, and Playspree.

## THE LAST OF US

Naughty Dog split into two development teams for the first time in 2009, one of which began work on *The Last of Us*. The game, finally released in 2013, is an action-adventure survival horror game which follows teenager Ellie and an adult protecting her, Joel, as they traverse a post-apocalyptic America devastated by the outbreak of a mutant fungus which takes over people's bodies and minds.

*The Last of Us* was universally lauded by critics for its story, design, and characters, and the game won more than 240 "Game of the Year" awards – making it one of the most-awarded video games of all time. It also sold more than 3.4 million copies in the first three weeks after its release, topped the sales charts in ten countries, and

spawned a comic book prequel miniseries.

Whether or not *The Last of Us* becomes Naughty Dog's next hit series remains to be seen – but given Naughty Dog's impressive track record, it certainly wouldn't be a surprise.

## KEY FRANCHISES:

- Crash Bandicoot
- Jak and Daxter
- Uncharted
- The Last of Us

# ROCKSTAR GAMES

## By Zanne Nilsson

Rockstar Games was founded in December 1998 by British video game producers Terry Donovan, Gary Foreman, Dan Houser, Sam Houser and Jamie King – prior BMG employees who moved to NYC after BMG Interactive was bought by Take Two Interactive. In an interview with the Design Museum, Dan Houser said that the group had two main goals: to make games adults like them would want to play, and to expand the game-playing experience.

## CONTROVERSIAL GAMING

While still at BMG, the group had worked with DMA Design to make the first *Grand Theft Auto* game, and brought DMA Design into their new company to continue the series. They released two mission packs for the original game (*Grand Theft Auto: London 1969* and *Grand Theft Auto: London 1961*), followed by *Grand Theft Auto 2* in 1999.

However, the series didn't become the controversial best-seller it's known as today until the release of *Grand Theft Auto III* in 2001. The game – released under DMA's new name, Rockstar North – was lauded by critics, particularly for its 3D open world design, won a few Game of the Year awards, and became the highest-selling game that year. However, *Grand Theft Auto III* also generated more than its share

of controversy for the violent and sexual content present in the gameplay, and was even briefly banned in Australia, forcing the company to release a censored version there.

Controversy didn't deter sales, and the series has continued ever since, now encompassing 15 games and expansions. The series as a whole has sold more than 235 million units so far and doesn't show any signs of stopping.

## EXPANDING THE CATALOG AND STARTING NEW SERIES

In 2000, Rockstar released *Smuggler's Run*, a racing game in which the player takes on the role of a smuggler trying to move cargo through large, open levels while evading the border patrol, CIA, and rival smuggling gangs. The game received generally positive reviews and was followed by a sequel, *Smuggler's Run 2*, in 2001.

That year also saw the release of *Midnight Club: Street Racing*, a racing game in an urban setting which stars a cab driver who joins a mysterious group of street racers known as the Midnight Club. This game, too, got mostly good reviews and sold more than 1.9 million units. It was followed by three sequels: *Midnight Club II*, *Midnight Club 3: DUB Edition*, and *Midnight Club: Los Angeles* which were also favorably reviewed.

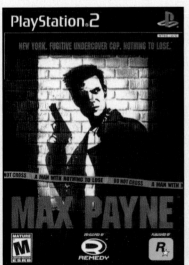

In 2001, Rockstar published the PlayStation 2, Xbox, and Game Boy Advance ports of *Max Payne*, a third-person shooter in which the titular character – a DEA agent and former NYPD officer – goes rogue to find and get revenge on the people who killed his wife and newborn daughter as well as framing him for murdering Alex Balder, his partner. Rockstar published *Max Payne 2: The Fall of Max Payne* in 2003 and developed a second sequel, *Max Payne 3*, in 2012. The first game of the series also got a film adaptation starring Mark Wahlberg in 2008 called simply *Max Payne*, though it was met with mostly negative reviews.

Rockstar also published VIS Entertainment's beat 'em up video game *State of Emergency* in 2002, but the game received mixed reviews and its sequel was published by SouthPeak Interactive.

The company released *Manhunt* – a survival horror game which had been in development at the Rockstar North studio since the early 1990s – in 2003. The game focuses on the supposedly-executed inmate James Earl Cash, who is forced to make a series of snuff films in exchange for his freedom. In spite of its generally good reviews, *Manhunt*'s graphic violence again sparked controversy for the company and the game was banned in several coun-

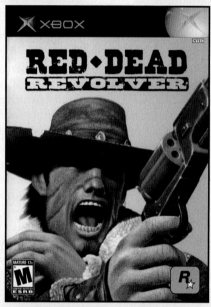

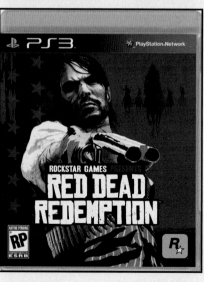

tries. Nevertheless, it was followed by a sequel, *Manhunt 2*, in 2007, and the games' combined sales are in excess of 1.7 million copies.

The Rockstar San Diego studio (formerly Angel Studios) developed and eventually released *Red Dead Revolver* (2004), a third-person shooter action-adventure game set in the Wild West. *Red Dead Revolver*, which was heavily influenced by Spaghetti Western films such as *A Fistful of Dollars* and *Once Upon a Time in the West*, follows the adventures of a bounty hunter named Red who tries to avenge his parents' murder many years before. The game received mostly positive reviews and was followed by a sequel, *Red Dead Redemption* (2010), which also maintains a strong fanbase.

## THE WARRIORS, BULLY, L.A. NOIRE, AND MORE

In 2005, Rockstar released Rockstar Toronto's beat 'em up *The Warriors* for PS2 and Xbox. *The Warriors*, based on the cult 1979 film of the same name, is about a Coney Island-based street gang known as the Warriors, who are framed for a murder they didn't commit while stranded in rival gangs' turf and must travel across New York City to return to Coney Island. The game received positive reviews, but a planned "spiritual sequel" called *We Are the Mods* was ultimately cancelled.

The next year, Rockstar released *Bully* for the PlayStation 2. The open-world action-adventure game centers on 15-year-old Jimmy Hopkins, who is sent to a private boarding school in New England

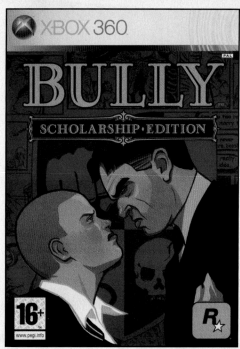

after being expelled from seven other schools. Jimmy becomes determined to bring peace to the school, which is divided into cliques and dominated by bullies. Although there was some controversy surrounding the game before its release, likely because of Rockstar's reputation for creating games with violent or sexual content, the game got very good reviews and won awards from IGN and GameSpot.

Though Rockstar also released a couple lesser-known titles at this time – *Rockstar Games Presents Table Tennis* (2006) and *Beaterator* (2009) – its next new hit release came in 2011: *L.A. Noire*. The game was an action-adventure title which was heavily influenced by the film noir genre in which the player, as LAPD officer Cole Phelps, must solve a number of crimes which occur in Los Angeles in 1947. *L.A. Noire* received acclaim for its advanced facial animations and storytelling and sold well.

With rumors swirling of a possible *L.A. Noire* sequel, one may wonder what lies ahead for Rockstar Games. But if their motto – "Killing good taste wherever we find it" – is any indication, it will certainly be quite the ride.

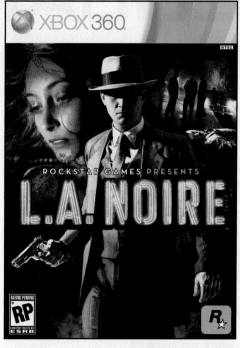

## KEY FRANCHISES:

- ☐ **Grand Theft Auto**
- ☐ **Midnight Club**
- ☐ **Max Payne**
- ☐ **Manhunt**
- ☐ **Red Dead**

# SQUARE ENIX™

## BY CARRIE WOOD

Two of the largest role-playing series in the world both make their home at one company: Square Enix. Though now a single company, its beginnings were in two very separate companies that were for many years close rivals: Squaresoft and Enix.

Square Enix is now a publisher of not just home console video games, but also arcade titles, films, manga, and much more; the company is considered a major powerhouse in the video game industry, particularly when it comes to the Japanese market. But it's taken a long time to get to that point.

## ENIX'S BEGINNINGS

Enix was first founded in September 1975 and didn't while they weren't publishing video games, they were still a publisher – just of tabloid magazines. After a few years, they opted to get into the gaming market by holding a game programming contest for computers; the winner included *Love Match Tennis* created by Yuji Horii, and *Door Door* by Koichi Nakamura.

As they worked to find their foothold in the market, Enix published a number of different games for various Japanese computer systems. Their greatest success came along in 1986, when they released the first *Dragon Quest* title for the Nintendo Entertainment System – a game written by Yuji Horii, and directed by Koichi Nakamura. *Dragon Quest* sold more than 1.5 million copies in Japan and established the series not just as Enix's most profitable property, but as one of the RPG franchises to beat.

By the early 1990s, Enix had started to publish manga in a shonen magazine, *Monthly Shonen Gangan*; they had also established ties with a number of other game developers, such as tri-Ace, the studio behind the successful *Star Ocean* series.

## SQUARE GETS STARTED

Square began as a computer game division of Den-Yu-Sha, a powerline construction company, in 1983. The founder, Masashi Miyamoto, believed that – despite how other companies relied on single programmers to get a game finished – a team of people would be more efficient. The first two titles released by the company were *The Death Trap* in 1984, and the sequel *Will: The Death Trap II* in 1985, both developed by Hironobu Sakaguchi. As text-adventure titles went, they weren't particularly popular, though they proved to be successful enough for Square as a company to continue to develop games.

By 1986, Square was an independent company, and Sakaguchi was named the Director of Planning and Development. However, around this time, Square was releasing a number of unsuccessful video games. Sakaguchi was inspired by Enix's *Dragon Quest* as well as other titles such as *Ultima* and *Wizardry* and sought to make a similar RPG title. The original title of the game he went to work on was *Fighting Fantasy*, but mid-development, it was changed to *Final Fantasy*. It's been said that the game was re-titled as such because Square itself was dealing with the threat of bankruptcy if it wasn't successful; Sakaguchi has also said himself that if the game failed, he'd quit the industry and go back to school.

Fortunately for all involved, *Final Fantasy* was a big hit when it arrived at the tail end of 1987. The original release moved 400,000 copies in Japan – and many more hundreds of thousands when an English version released in America – and along with the critically positive reviews, gave Square renewed life.

Though *Final Fantasy* very quickly

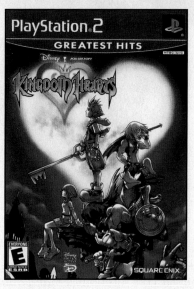

became the main franchise for Square, they published a number of other role-playing titles, such as *Chrono Trigger, Secret of Mana, Romancing SaGa,* and *Kingdom Hearts.* They also notably worked with Nintendo on *Super Mario RPG.* Square quickly gained a reputation throughout the 1990s as one of the main publishers for high-quality RPGs.

## THE MERGER

Talks about a merger between Squaresoft and Enix had been discussed since 2000, but Square's financial woes in the Y2K era – especially with the total flop of their film,

*Final Fantasy: The Spirits Within* – Enix was reluctant to proceed. However, thanks to the success of both *Final Fantasy X* and *Kingdom Hearts* on the gaming front, Square's finances got back on track, and on November 25, 2002, the merger between the companies was officially announced.

Square Enix, as a new company, came into existence on April 1, 2003. Square president Yoichi Wada became president of Square Enix, with Enix president Keiji Honda becoming vice president of the new corporation.

Following the merger itself, Square Enix immediately got to work on acquiring new development studios. The first major studio acquired was Taito, known best for their arcade lineup such as *Bubble Bobble, Space Invaders* and *Arkanoid*. Taito became part of Square Enix in 2005. By 2009, the company had acquired Eidos Interactive, the publisher responsible for such series as *Tomb Raider, Hitman, Deus Ex,* and *Thief,* as well as all of Eidos' subsidiary development studios. Eidos was quickly merged with the company's European publishing arm to create Square Enix Europe.

Since the merger, Square Enix has proved to be wildly successful. Besides the continuing and seemingly never-ending popularity of the *Final Fantasy, Dragon Quest* and *Kingdom Hearts* series, the company has also released a variety of other titles, including *Sleeping Dogs, Kane & Lynch, Life is Strange,* and *Just Cause,* among dozens of others.

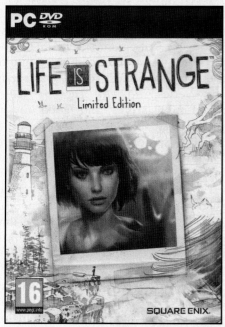

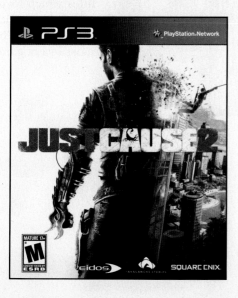

## BEYOND GAMING

Enix didn't just bring *Dragon Quest* to the merger with them, they also brought their manga publishing division. Square Enix's manga branch, called Gangan Comics, has published a number of hugely successful series, including *Fullmetal Alchemist, Soul Eater, Durarara!!, Space Dandy*, and *Black Butler*, just to name a few. Though these series are all licensed in English by a variety of different publishers, Square Enix launched a digital manga store in 2010 that's available for American audiences.

Square Enix has also produced a handful of films; the first of these was *Final Fantasy: The Spirits Within*, produced by Square Pictures in 2001, prior to the merger. Since then, a few other *Final Fantasy*-related pictures have been made. These have included *Final Fantasy VII Advent Children*, released in 2005, and, more recently, *Kingsglaive: Final Fantasy XV*, released in 2016. A web series, *Brotherhood: Final Fantasy XV*, was also released online in 2016.

Though it started as two smaller rival companies, Square Enix has become an absolute role-playing powerhouse in the years since it formed. Thanks to the acquisition of Eidos and a number of other companies, they have diversified into genres beyond the sword-and-sorcery seen in their RPGs, and are likely going to be sticking around for quite some time.

## KEY FRANCHISES:
- [ ] **Dragon Quest**
- [ ] **Final Fantasy**
- [ ] **Kingdom Hearts**
- [ ] **SaGa**
- [ ] **Star Ocean**
- [ ] **Mana**
- [ ] **Hitman**
- [ ] **Just Cause**
- [ ] **Deus Ex**
- [ ] **Tomb Raider**

# UBISOFT

BY ZANNE NILSSON

Although today it is one of the biggest independent game publishers in the world – known for such hit franchises as *Far Cry*, *Assassin's Creed*, *Rayman*, and *Prince of Persia* – Ubisoft Entertainment SA had humble beginnings.

Officially founded in March of 1986 as Ubi Soft Entertainment Software in the small village of Carentoir in the Brittany region of France, Ubisoft had its roots in the partnership between Yves Guillemot and his four brothers; they first began programming games for the Commodore 64 and MSX computers in the early 1980s. The Guillemots soon expanded into distribution as a small mail-order business.

Ubisoft continued to grow after their first game, *Zombi*, was released in 1987 for the Amstrad CPC. *Zombi*, a first-person arcade adventure centered on four protagonists fighting zombies in a shopping mall, was praised for its immersive atmosphere and saw a re-release on the ZX Spectrum, Amiga, Commodore 64, DOS, and Atari ST in 1990. After making deals with such companies as MicroProse, Electronic Arts, and Sierra On-Line to distribute their games in France, Ubisoft began branching out into wholesale and foreign markets. In-house game development began at Ubisoft in the early 1990s, and in 1994 the company opened a studio in Montreuil, France, which has become the company's unofficial headquarters.

## RAYMAN

In 1995, *Rayman*, one of Ubisoft's most beloved series, saw its first release. Originally developed for the SNES but ultimately released for the Atari Jaguar, Sony PlayStation, PC, and Sega Saturn, *Rayman* is a cartoony side-scrolling platformer in which the titular character must restore balance to his world by freeing the six Electoons and recovering the Great Protoon from the evil Mr. Dark. The game was well-received and especially praised for its vibrant art, beautiful animation, cheerful atmosphere, and unique soundtrack. *Rayman* has since seen several re-releases and sequels which have continued into the present day. The most recent major game in the series, *Rayman Legends* (2013), received high scores and good reviews from critics.

A 2006 spinoff in the Rayman series called *Rayman Raving Rabbids*, which centered on Rayman completing minigame trials to escape his imprisonment by the Rabbids, has led to several sequels of its own. While the first three games in the *Raving Rabbids* series featured or included Rayman, the rest have been standalone titles which focus on the Rabbids themselves. The most recent game

in the Rabbids series is *Rabbids Land*, released for the Wii U in 2012.

Through the late 1990s and early 2000s, Ubisoft branched out into online gaming with such games as *The Matrix Online* and *Uru: Ages Beyond Myst* and went on to establish an online division, though later they backed out of publishing *The Matrix Online* and cancelled the online portion of *Uru: Ages Beyond Myst*.

## TOM CLANCY'S SPLINTER CELL

In 2002, following their acquisition of Red Storm Entertainment, Ubisoft published *Tom Clancy's Splinter Cell* to great success.

The stealth game, starring NSA Black Ops agent Sam Fisher, was extremely well-received and won multiple awards. Unsurprisingly, it's spawned five sequels so far, the most recent of which is *Tom Clancy's Splinter Cell: Blacklist*.

The series has also formed the basis of seven novels written by three different authors; all three authors used the pseudonym David Michaels for the first six novels. Peter Telep, the most recent author to write for the series, chose to write *Tom Clancy's Splinter Cell Blacklist: Aftermath* under his own name instead. Interestingly, the late Tom Clancy had very little to do with developing any of the games in the *Splinter Cell* series – or any of the other Clancy-branded titles by Ubisoft, such as *Rainbow Six* – in spite of the fact that they all bear his name.

A film based on the series – one of many film adaptations Ubisoft is planning to make of its hit franchises – is currently in development as well.

## PRINCE OF PERSIA

After acquiring the rights to the *Prince of Persia* series with the rest of the intellectual properties in The Learning Company's games division in 2001, Ubisoft rebooted the franchise with *Prince of Persia: The Sands of Time* in 2003. The action-adventure puzzle-platformer game, which is widely considered to be one of the greatest video games of all time, incorporated acrobatic abilities and the power to rewind or manipulate time into its

gameplay and narrative. Well-received by both reviewers and players, *Prince of Persia: The Sands of Time* is credited with renewing interest in the series and making it into the massive franchise it is today.

Three more games set in the same continuity as *Prince of Persia: The Sands of Time* were released over the next several years: *Prince of Persia: Warrior Within* (2004); *Prince of Persia: The Two Thrones* (2005); and *Prince of Persia: The Forgotten Sands* (2010). Another game in an alternate continuity, simply titled *Prince of Persia*, was released in 2008 as well.

A film adaptation of *Prince of Persia: The Sands of Time* was released in 2010 and, in spite of receiving mixed reviews, became the highest-grossing film based on a video game of all time – at least until 2016, when *Warcraft* took the top spot.

## ASSASSIN'S CREED

Ubisoft's best-selling (and perhaps best-known) series originated in an attempted sequel to *Prince of Persia: The Sands of Time*. When creative director Patrice Désilets began work on the sequel – then titled *Prince of Persia: Assassin* – he decided that a prince was not a fitting protagonist for the concept he had in mind, and instead made the player character an assassin who must rescue the prince. However, Ubisoft decided that a *Prince of Persia* game that didn't star the prince himself wouldn't be the best idea, but instead of scrapping the idea entirely, they took out the prince character and made the game into a standalone title.

The game's framing device, which takes place in 2012, centers on a bartender named Desmond Miles who is kidnapped and forced to view and control the genetic memories of one of his ancestors using a machine known as the "Animus." This ancestor, Altaïr Ibn-La'Ahad, is an Assassin living in the time of the Third Crusade who is tasked with assassinating nine members of a rival secret faction known as the Knights Templar. The Templars, who seek peace via control, are searching for ancient artifacts known as "Pieces of Eden," objects which can control other people's minds; the Assassins, who fight for free will, are trying to stop them. The other games in the series primarily revolve around Desmond's other Assassin ancestors and the struggle between the two factions over these artifacts, a conflict which continues throughout the centuries into the modern day.

The majority of the gameplay in the series relies on synchronization between the Assassins' memories and the player's actions; actions or events which break the synchronization (such as deaths or actions which go against the Assassins' way) force the player to restart from a previous checkpoint. The memories also limit which areas the player can explore in the open-world environment. Gameplay in the Assassin segments emphasizes free-running and stealth; certain actions can draw the attention of guards, forcing the

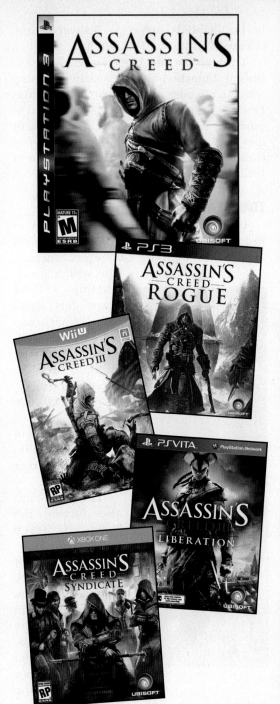

player to hide until the guards' alertness is reduced. There are also sections in which the player can directly control Desmond, who has learned Assassin techniques through use of the Animus device.

The original *Assassin's Creed* has led to the release of eight "major" sequels in the series, the most recent of which is *Assassin's Creed Syndicate* (2015), and eight "supporting" games, with the latest being *Assassin's Creed Chronicles: Russia* (2016).

The series has also expanded to include comics, novels, animated short films, and a 2016 theatrical film simply titled *Assassin's Creed*.

## FAR CRY

In 2004, Ubisoft published Crytek Studios' *Far Cry*, a first-person shooter originally released for Windows then later remade for the Xbox and Xbox 360 as *Far Cry Instincts*. The first *Far Cry* focuses on Jack Carver, an ex-special forces soldier searching for a female journalist – Val Cortez, who hired Carver to secretly escort her to an uncharted island – after their boat was destroyed by mercenaries, leaving them both stranded on a mysterious tropical archipelago. The game was lauded for its visuals, freedom of exploration, and gameplay, and proved to be a commercial hit. Its success prompted Ubisoft to develop three standalone sequels: *Far Cry 2* (2008), *Far Cry 3* (2012), and *Far Cry 4* (2014); the company has also developed seven spin-off games so far, most recently releasing *Far Cry Primal* in 2016.

The series has also led to two films: the first, directed by Uwe Boll and released direct-to-video in 2008, was poorly received by both fans and critics; the second film, which will most likely be unrelated to the first in any way, is currently being developed by Ubisoft Motion Pictures.

## JUST DANCE, WATCH DOGS, AND BEYOND

Ubisoft attempted to extend its reach in online gaming once again in 2009, when it acquired fellow French developer Nadeo, best known for its series of *TrackMania* racing games. The same year also saw the release of *Just Dance*, a dance video game for the Wii, whose easily-accessible gameplay made it a massive commercial

(though not critical) success. More than two dozen sequels, specials, and spin-off games have since been released in the Just Dance series, which has become Ubisoft's second-biggest franchise. In the following years Ubisoft continued to expand, creating mobile-exclusive games and its film/television production division, Ubisoft Motion Pictures.

In 2014, Ubisoft released the highly-anticipated open world third-person shooter *Watch Dogs*, which received mixed reviews but had the biggest first-day sales numbers of any Ubisoft game ever made. The game will be followed by a sequel, *Watch Dogs 2*, in 2016, but whether this becomes Ubisoft's next hot franchise remains to be seen.

It's uncertain exactly what lies ahead for Ubisoft, but it's certainly impressive how many beloved and recognizable series have come from a French company started by five brothers 30 years ago.

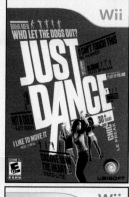

## KEY FRANCHISES:
- ☐ Rayman
- ☐ Raving Rabbids
- ☐ Tom Clancy's Splinter Cell
- ☐ Prince of Persia
- ☐ Assassin's Creed
- ☐ Far Cry
- ☐ Just Dance

# VALVE

By Zanne Nilsson

Today known for hit series such as *Half-Life*, *Portal*, *Team Fortress*, and *Left 4 Dead*, Valve may have had some not-so-humble beginnings, considering it was founded by two former Microsoft employees who had become millionaires. But like all new game companies, it too had to prove itself before it became the giant it is today.

## EARLY SUCCESS WITH HALF-LIFE AND TEAM FORTRESS

On August 24, 1996, former Microsoft employees Gabe Newell and Mike Harrington founded Valve, LLC in Kirkland, Washington. The pair secured the rights to use the *Quake* engine from their friend Mike Abrash, another former Microsoft employee who was then working for id Software. After significantly modifying the engine and renaming it GoldSrc, they

quickly went to work on the company's first game, *Half-Life*. However, they initially had trouble finding a publisher willing to take a chance on a new developer. Finally Sierra On-Line stepped in and agreed to a publishing deal with Valve, releasing the game on November 19, 1998.

*Half-Life*, a first-person shooter which also incorporates puzzles, tells its immersive story completely without cutscenes, instead using scripted sequences which are integrated into the gameplay. The game takes place in the fictional Black Mesa Research Facility in New Mexico. There, Dr. Gordon Freeman (the player character) participates in a lab experiment which goes horribly wrong and opens a portal to another dimension called Xen, releasing hostile alien creatures into the facility. Freeman must battle both the Xenian

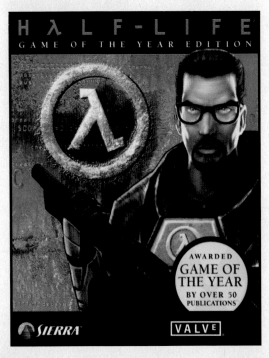

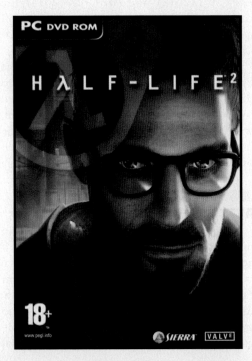

creatures and a special government unit sent to cover up the incident by eliminating the aliens as well as all of the surviving lab employees.

The game was an overwhelming success credited with revolutionizing the FPS genre, and it was named the all-time best-selling FPS for PC by Guinness World Records in 2008 – at which point it had sold 9.3 million copies. It was followed with two expansion packs developed by Gearbox Software as well as three sequels: *Half Life 2*, *Half-Life 2: Episode One*, and *Half-Life 2: Episode Two*. Another sequel, *Half Life 2: Episode Three* has been announced, but a large number of delays combined with company silence on the game's development have made confirmation of the game's release into a bitter running joke in the gaming community.

In 1998, Valve acquired TF Software PTY – the team behind the *Quake* mod *Team Fortress* – to develop and release a port of *Team Fortress* on GoldSrc. The resulting game, *Team Fortress Classic*, was released in 1999. *Team Fortress Classic* is an online team multiplayer FPS where each player is assigned to either the red or blue team in a match and can choose from nine character classes with unique weapons and abilities: Spy, Sniper, Medic, Engineer, Heavy, Demoman, Pyro, Soldier, and Scout. There are a variety of game modes to choose from, each with a different objective.

*Team Fortress Classic* was well-received and work soon began on *Team Fortress 2* but, in a move that would become characteristic of the company, Valve delayed *Team Fortress 2* and made little mention of it until 2004. The game was finally released in 2007 as part of *The Orange Box* game compilation with *Half Life 2*, *Half-Life 2: Episode One*, *Half Life 2: Episode Two* and *Portal*. *Team Fortress 2* was widely praised, especially for its humor, multiplayer gameplay, and art style.

## COUNTER-STRIKE AND COMPANY CHANGES

Valve encouraged and supported independent mods to *Half-Life*, sometimes to the point of acquiring and re-releasing them as official Valve titles. One of these was *Counter-Strike*, which was initially

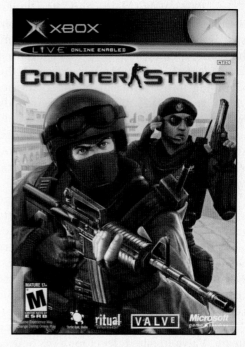

developed and released in 1999 as a *Half-Life* mod by Jess Cliffe and Minh Le. Valve noticed the mod's success, hired Cliffe and Le, acquired the mod's IP, and officially released *Counter-Strike* as its own title in 2000. The game was very well-received and led to a remake as well as multiple sequels; the series as a whole has sold more than 25 million units.

That same year, Harrington left Valve. More changes were to come: in 2003 the company changed its name to Valve Corporation and moved its headquarters to Bellevue, WA. 2003 also saw the retail release of *Day of Defeat*, another *Half-Life* mod which Valve purchased the rights to. *Day of Defeat*, a multiplayer FPS set on the western front of the European theatre in World War Two, was also generally praised by critics.

## STEAM RISES

In 2003 Valve launched its digital distribution platform, Steam. While Steam was initially implemented to streamline the game update process, it was somewhat controversial among gamers in the beginning. Most criticism of the platform, which at first was buggy and frequently crashed under stress, was leveled at its online authentication and DRM requirements, especially when Valve required installation of Steam to play any of its games starting with *Half-Life 2* – even retail copies.

However, opinions started to change when Steam began offering third-party games in 2005 and rolled out new features over the next few years. The Steam Store has since become one of the biggest distributors of PC games, and has become known and loved for its seasonal game sales.

Around the same time it launched Steam, Valve finished developing its Source engine, which was created as a successor to GoldSrc. The new engine first debuted in the remake *Counter-Strike: Source*, as well as Source remakes of *Half-Life* and *Day of Defeat*. Source is free to the public and has been used to make games such as *Dear Esther*, *The Stanley Parable*, and *Titanfall*.

## THINKING WITH PORTALS

Valve's next game, *Portal*, was created as a successor to the puzzle game *Narbacular Drop*, made by DigiPen Institute of Technology students. After seeing *Narbacular Drop*, Gabe Newell

hired the entire team behind it to work for Valve and further develop the game, which was released as part of *The Orange Box* compilation in 2007.

*Portal* is a first-person puzzle platformer set in the *Half-Life* universe – partly as an excuse to reuse some art assets from *Half-Life* games – in the fictional Aperture Science research facility. The player takes on the role of Chell, a test subject selected by the Aperture Science computer AI GLaDOS to complete a series of test chambers designed to examine the capabilities of Aperture Science's portal gun, which can create portals on certain surfaces.

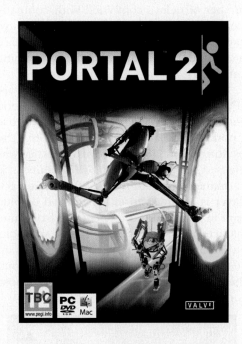

The attention *Portal* received is especially impressive considering the other two highly-anticipated titles which were first released as part of that compilation: *Half Life 2: Episode Two* and *Team Fortress 2*. *Portal* was praised by critics, especially for its unique gameplay and dark humor, most of which is delivered through GLaDOS's voiceover. The game won multiple awards and sold more than 4 million copies by 2011 – when it was followed by a sequel, *Portal 2*, which was similarly acclaimed.

## LEFT 4 DEAD AND OTHER RECENT MOVES

In November 2008, Valve published *Left 4 Dead*, developed by Turtle Rock Studios – which Valve acquired in January 2008 and turned into Valve South. *Left 4 Dead* is a co-operative FPS set in a post-apocalyptic world where four survivors of a "Green Flu" pandemic – which effectively turns people into zombies – must fight their way through hordes of people infected with the dangerous disease to find a place where they will be safe from the infected.

The game got a very positive reception from critics and sold exceptionally well. A sequel, *Left 4 Dead 2*, was released the following year; combined, the two games have sold more than 11 million copies.

In addition to publishing other titles over the years – including *Ricochet*, *Deathmatch*, *Alien Swarm*, *Dota 2*, and

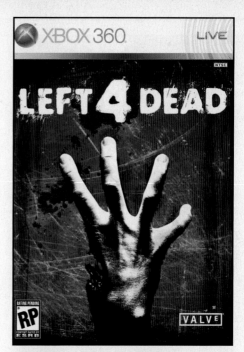

*Dota 2 Reborn* – Valve released its own Linux-based operating system, SteamOS, in 2013. In November 2015 they also released a SteamOS-running PC-console hybrid called the Steam Machine, along with the customizable Steam Controller.

The Steam Controller

It may not be certain what lies ahead for Valve – except perhaps a few more game delays – but from where they stand now, the future looks bright.

**KEY FRANCHISES:**

☐ **Half-Life**

☐ **Team Fortress**

☐ **Counter-Strike**

☐ **Portal**

☐ **Left 4 Dead**

☐ **Dota**

# MEMORABILIA

## Interview with Brett Martin

**Overstreet:** Please introduce yourself!

**Brett Martin (BM):** I'm Brett Martin, owner of the Guinness World Record for the largest video game memorabilia collection, and also creator of the Video Game Memorabilia Museum at videogamemm.com. I also write for *Nintendo Force Magazine*.

**Overstreet:** How did you get involved in video game collecting - and did your interest in game memorabilia spin out of that? What kind of things do you favor in your own collection?

**BM:** My parents bought me a little Mario with mushroom figure, and I noticed there were more in the set. Once eBay started, I started finding the rest of the set, and through that searching I found other sets. Before I knew it I had a shelf full, then a bookcase full, then several bookcases, and now a full room.

**Overstreet:** Tell us a little bit about your website, VideoGameMM.com. How did you get started?

**BM:** I started the site late in 2005 as just a gallery of the things I had. I was starting to catalog. When I added forums, people started coming to ask me questions about the collection and specific items. We started to get a great crew of people who knew a lot about video game merchandise, and whatever I didn't know about was filled in by someone else. We've always been a small, tight-knit group, and we've helped each other with our respective collections many times over. I've built several tutorials on how to import items from Japan, how to avoid fakes, and how to store collections. When I revamped the website in 2010, I added the ability for anyone registered to add photos of items and help build a database of video game memorabilia. It's tough work, and eventually I need to spend some more time to make that process easier, but we have a ton of stuff to sift through right now.

**Overstreet:** The website has a whole section dedicated to identifying and exposing fake merchandise. How serious is the bootleg memorabilia problem?

**BM:** It's ridiculous. Our group has literally tried everything to petition eBay to take fakes down, but when they make a ton of money off of them, there's no motivation for them to remove them. Now, eBay mostly consists of fakes. Several other marketplaces that allow people to add items, like Amazon, Rakuten, and even Wal-Mart.com are also inundated with counterfeit merchandise. When I see collections full of these counterfeit items, it makes me die a little, having worked so hard to keep my collection counterfeit-free.

Counterfeit example

**Overstreet:** Is there a franchise that sees a particularly high amount of fakes?

**BM:** *Super Mario*, and plushes specifically. Plushes are cheap to make and sell well. They are also less obvious because even if the pattern is a little off it's still easily recognizable. Most of the plushes are made in China, so sometimes a pattern will leak and more precise counterfeits will hit the market. There are also a ton of fakes for *Kirby*, *Sonic* and Square Enix properties.

Counterfeit example

**Overstreet:** Are there any common signs of forgery with fake merch that people can watch out for?

**BM:** Tags are where I look first. A while back, the *Mario Party 5* tag was attached to everything fake, then the *New Super Mario Bros.* tag, and now the generic *Super Mario* tag. If you see a Yoshi plush with a *NSMB* tag, it's fake because Yoshi never appeared in that game.

Tags are super-easy to counterfeit, but oftentimes the tag looks poorly printed, but you have to be able to hold the item to see it. Any online auction or marketplace seller that originates from out of the country and uses stock imagery of the item is most likely fake. Any Luigi item that looks like Mario but is painted to be Luigi is fake. They've gotten better and better, but in most cases I can still tell. Sometimes with figures they'll make a mold of the licensed product, so it's more exact, but the copyright info on the feet will be unreadable, tipping me off. If a seller will not give you pictures of the actual item in-hand, avoid that seller. It's that bad out there.

**Overstreet:** How has video game memorabilia evolved over the years?

**BM:** It's funny. There have been waves of large amounts of merchandise and then large gaps of nothing. There was a huge push of Nintendo merchandise in the late 80s and early 90s, then a big gap, and then in the early 2000s there was another large push of Nintendo merchandise, along with a lot of other franchises like *Halo*, *Assassin's Creed*, Capcom licenses, Konami licenses, etc.

We are currently in the largest boon of video game merchandise I've ever seen, with most retailers carrying something related to gaming, and most stores have a section for the goods now. Most major games have a lot of merchandise as well. *Fallout, Destiny, Call of Duty*, Valve properties and many others are well-represented. If you really like a game, it's likely you can find merchandise for it, and this is the first time in history that's true more often than not. My poor wallet...

We're also seeing the quality of the merchandise becoming much better and more durable. Past items could be quite fragile, whereas now we are seeing high-end polystone statues, much more expensive apparel and more articulate figures.

**Overstreet:** Do you have a favorite piece of memorabilia that you've come across since you've been collecting?

**BM:** I always jump to the prototype figures I own for my favorite pieces because they are literally one-of-a-kind items that were never released, but these high-end statues coming out of First 4 Figures, Gaming Heads, Sideshow Collectibles and more are simply amazing. They sure pack a punch to your wallet, but they are the best representations of the characters money can buy. Highly articulated figures, like Figmas, S.H. Figuarts and Medicom figures are amazing as well, and I love all the accessories that come with them.

**Overstreet:** What's the strangest piece of gaming memorabilia that you've seen?

**BM:** I have a whole playlist dedicated to this stuff on my YouTube channel (Nightram56). A *Super Mario Bros.* shower head or ceiling fan? Bowser air freshener? Donkey Kong figure toothbrush? We've got all of that stuff.

**Overstreet:** Where do you go most often to purchase gaming memorabilia?

**BM:** Yahoo Japan Auctions for the rare stuff, AmiAmi.com for the retail import stuff, and brick-and-mortar stores for the new stuff released here in the states. I have a list of other stores that are good for each type on my website, as several online retailers have started to specialize in it, like Gamerabilia.com.

**Overstreet:** What advice do you have for people looking to get into game or game memorabilia collecting?

**BM:** Now's a great time for all the new stuff coming out, and having a lot of the overseas stuff getting globally distributed is nice to see. However, the vintage stuff now costs a really pretty penny, so if you're going for the old stuff, you'll need some deep pockets.

Photo provided by Brett Martin

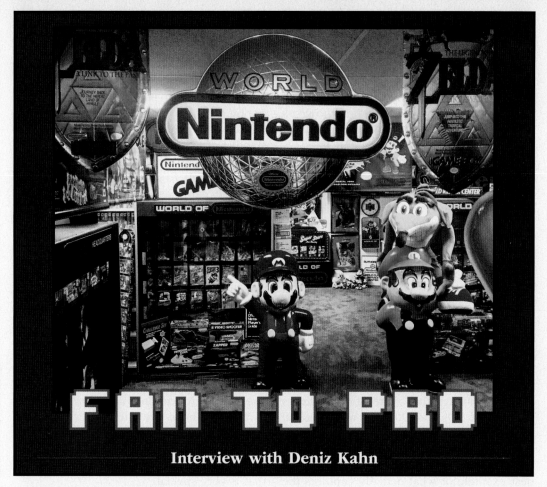

# FAN TO PRO

### Interview with Deniz Kahn

**Overstreet:** What was it that first got you into video gaming in the first place?

**Deniz Kahn (DK):** Well I grew up with video games. My uncle had brought over a Super Nintendo to my brother, who's three years older than me. So we're talking the early '90s, and I was probably one or so when this happened. So I grew up around the Super Nintendo watching my brother. I was just enamored by it. I started playing *Mario Paint* on the Super Nintendo and some other games, like *Fun with Letters* and whatnot.

**Overstreet:** Oh, those edu-tainment Mario titles?

**DK:** Yeah, people are always like 'who ever bought those?' Me, I was the kid who was learning how to spell with those games. I was the target demographic. So those were the games I started with. Now, my parents weren't really aware of the games that we were actually playing. My uncle had just brought over things that were popular, and those included like *Mortal Kombat* and

whatnot. But it all started there, that was where the interest started.

**Overstreet:** So did collecting video games evolve naturally out of playing them or was it a more conscious decision to start a collection?

**DK:** It was sort of a combination. Another huge contributing factor was that my dad was a collector – he collected comic books. So as a kid I'd go around to comic book shows with him and I was exposed to the whole collecting world through that. Before I was even aware of video game collecting I was very aware of collecting as an industry through comics and toys.

**Overstreet:** As far as your personal collection, what is it that you choose to focus on?

**DK:** I started kind of tying together the games that I had into franchises and trying to complete sets of those franchises. I had to educate myself on that, and that opened me up to a larger world. When I started collecting, I didn't even know about the original NES. I thought the Super Nintendo was it – because that's what I started with. So that blew my mind, and I started going after those games. It's funny, today when I reflect back, the system that I've had the most fun collecting for was the original NES. And even though online I'm known as Super NES Man, the Super Nintendo is actually the weakest aspect of my collection.

I completed my NES complete in-box collection, and I did the same with the N64, and I'm pretty far along with Game Boy stuff. But I'm pretty far behind on Super Nintendo. But it's all fun to me. Obviously, the most fun for me would definitely be the games that I grew up with – *Super Mario World* is a big one, the *Zelda* games. *Ocarina of Time* was huge for me. And *Final Fantasy* was also big for me, especially *Final Fantasy VII* on the PlayStation. Those games for me are probably the pinnacle for me in terms of nostalgia.

What I love to really collect, my kind of niche, is the memorabilia. The displays, the original displays that were sent to stores back in the '80s and '90s that were trashed – and in most cases the employees were instructed to destroy them. So very few of them have survived. Those, I feel, are the best example of what actually captures the nostalgia. When you see something like that, it takes you back to the time when you walked into a store and were surrounded by all those games. That's what I'm trying to capture.

**Overstreet:** Have you encountered any difficulty in finding the things you like to collect? I imagine the standees from 20-plus years ago are hard to come by.

**DK:** Oh, absolutely. As collectors, we like to talk about certain kinds of displays – how many of these exist, how many of those were even made. It's sometimes almost seemingly impossible to get your hands on some of those things, because so few of them have surfaced. Some of them are kind of like a pipe dream. You can't expect that you're going to find some of these things. It's kind of like anthropology – you're trying to find what you can and then preserve it.

With the games, it's a little different. Usually, for a collector, if you have deep enough pockets, you can find anything you

want. But with displays, we're still finding new things all the time.

**Overstreet:** Do you have a favorite part of your collection?

**DK:** There are a handful of displays that are by far the most meaningful to me. One of them is a standee that's a *Mortal Kombat* standee of Goro. There's five or six of them that have been discovered so far, and I'm lucky enough to have two of them. One of those came with a hand-written note from John Tobias, who worked on *Mortal Kombat* and played a lot of the bald characters. The letter was written to whoever was supposed to keep this thing, and it's a long thing explaining how this specific standee was in the creators' room all throughout the creation process. So that's a really cool thing – I'm surprised that guy ever let that thing go.

I just love unique things like that. Anyone can get games at the end of the day, even if it's a sealed copy of *Stadium Events* or a *Nintendo World Championship* cartridge. Those are out there. It's these one-of-a-kind things that mean the most to me. Even if they're not monetarily worth a lot of money, they have an intrinsic value that is very special.

**Overstreet:** Is there a "holy grail" kind of item that you'd want to have in your collection?

**DK:** That's a tough question. Regarding games, I'm always in the hunt. I'm never putting anything past me. There's nothing that I've been dying to get game-wise.

*Stadium Events* complete in-box for a long time was something that I wanted because I never would've been able to complete my NES collection without that. Fortunately, things played out that allowed that to happen, and I did eventually get a copy of that. But the search never ends. I know that there's always going to be something I'm going to want. I've limited things more to displays, and when it comes to those, there isn't any one display that I want like crazy. The ones that I'm really just dying to have one day are these interactive displays. There's a video on YouTube that's like a training video from the late '80s, early '90s, of this guy going through an old Nintendo store and showing how all of their interactive displays work. And those machines – I don't even know if they've survived – if I could ever get my hands on something like that, that would probably be it.

**Overstreet:** What advice do you have as far as preserving and storing a game collection?

**DK:** Everyone's different. There's a guy I buy from who's so obsessive that when I go over there he puts on gloves to handle his stuff. And there's some people who don't even understand factory-sealed games – if you can't play it, what's the point? My advice is to do what you feel is right. I think that as collectors, we need to decide for ourselves how we want to treat our items. It's important to treat them with care, but there's a fine line between being careful and being obsessive. Obviously if you look

at something like comics, with condition, every scuff for a key book can mean hundreds, thousands, if not tens of thousands of dollars. So it's important to take care of your items, but also consider why you're collecting in the first place. For me, I try to find a balance. If I buy brand-new old-stock displays, they come in cardboard boxes – you can't even display them. But I want to display them. So I'll take them out of the box and find a way to display them without damaging it. But some people would say even that's wrong.

That's just the way I like to collect – I like to be able to see the things I'm collecting. A lot of my fellow collectors have their collections stored away in a closet, essentially. They're fulfilling something just by the act of collecting. But for me, I want to be able to see it and share it with other people. I guess I might say I'm not the best person to give advice if you want to maintain high monetary value. But I'd just say to do what feels right to you.

**Overstreet:** You've been able to turn your collecting hobby into a successful business alongside your father's store. How did you go about doing that?

**DK:** I started young, and I had a lot of time on my hands. Other than schoolwork, I did this – I actually did this during school. Whenever there was a computer available in school I'd be online in chatrooms and on eBay looking for deals. Then I'd go home and resell. That's the only way to really make money, to buy huge lots, to clean

everything, and then to resell them online. I did that all the time, setting up deals while in school, go getting the lots after school and then taking them home and working on them.

So then, pause that. Towards the end of my schooling, my dad's getting ready to retire and he's got all these comics and toys and whatnot. We were talking about it and he was paying a lot of money just to store his stuff. He had, I think, three storage rooms' worth of stuff. So we decided that enough was enough, closed those down and bought this place in Kenosha, Wisconsin, and he'd sell his comics and toys and I'd sell my video games. Of course, my section is dwarfed by his – three storage rooms is a lot, and my inventory doesn't even pale in comparison. But it evolved from there. The store serves as a space for me to sell so that I don't have to deal with eBay all the time. From there, it became more my dad's thing, and now he runs the store four days a week, and my games are still there. But that's a limited audience. It's just a small town in Wisconsin. So a lot of the

more premium stuff I want to sell, I still do that online or through private deals with people I know. It's definitely a fun thing for me, and for him, it's become his life – and it's something we can share together, which is the most important part.

**Overstreet:** Anything else you'd like to add about your game collecting experience?
**DK:** It's just exploding now. There's a lot of people getting into the hobby now that don't realize what it used to be, and then there's people who were involved a long time ago who have become really disillusioned with where it's going. And I think that's the wrong attitude to have. The hobby is evolving, and that's just what happens. Prices are oftentimes what people get so angry about – and I understand that, because it's getting much harder to get these games at "reasonable" prices. When I started collecting, *Contra* was maybe a $15 game. And now it's at least $60 for just the cartridge. So everything's increased at least three or four times since I've started. That turns a lot of people off.

Collecting is whatever you want it to be. Too often people will let others in the community dictate what collecting should be for them. I think people get too caught up in that, and there's so much drama you see on forums about it. It's nonsense. Why let other people tell you anything about your collecting habits? You collect for your own personal reasons and you should let it be that way. Everyone's collections, whether they're 10 games or 10,000 games, everyone has the right to be proud of whatever they have.

My biggest advice to any collector is just to collect for whatever reason makes you happy. At the end of the day, that's why we collect – to make us happy.

# PRESERVATION AND STORAGE

By Carrie Wood

Unlike paper products such as comic books or posters, video games have such a variety of different parts (not to mention the fact that they are electronic) that it can be a challenge to protect, restore and preserve them. Consoles are a challenge in their own right, and are a totally separate monster from the games themselves; of course, games can largely be broken down into cartridge-based or disc-based varieties.

Here, we take a brief look at how you can keep your video game collection looking in the best shape it possibly can be. While every different system and its respective games will have its own unique set of challenges, we hope that the following advice proves to be useful on your collecting quest.

## PREVENTING CONSOLE YELLOWING

Consoles that were once bright sparkling white out of a box have a tendency to slowly yellow over the course of time; we see this fairly often in the older Nintendo systems. So, why does this happen? It's because the console manufacturers have added bromine to the plastic that the systems are housed in as a flame retardant. Over the course of time, the chemicals react together and start to turn yellow, and heat and sunlight can accelerate the process.

The best thing to do to prevent yellowing from happening in the first place is to keep your consoles out of direct sunlight, and in a temperature-controlled area. For example, even though attics are likely dark, if your SNES sits in a hot room for too long it'll go yellow very quickly!

For consoles that have already experienced a degree of yellowing, there are two main methods for reversing the process. For cases where the yellowing is only on the surface of the plastic itself, people have taken to using very fine sandpaper to essentially sand down the surface of the plastic and remove the yellowed part, exposing the natural color of the plastic that remains underneath. Of course, this is physically removing part of the body – if the yellowing has gone too deep into the

THE OVERSTREET GUIDE TO COLLECTING VIDEO GAMES 137

plastic, there's a significant risk of damaging the shell permanently in your effort to restore it.

The other method of removing yellowed plastic is a chemical process that involves the use of hydrogen peroxide to essentially bleach the plastic back to its original color. A risk here is the potential to accidentally bleach it *lighter* than it originally was. There are a number of online resources and tutorials for this process, which should be followed closely and carefully; working with chemicals is always something to be done with extreme caution.

## CLEANING AND RESTORING CARTRIDGES

While each family of cartridge will have its own set of particulars, there are methods of cleaning an old cartridge to bring it to working order that can be applied essentially across the board. This being said, some carts do end up just too far gone after years of neglect.

Sometimes all a cart needs in order to be back in functional condition is a little bit of rubbing alcohol. When using rubbing alcohol, you want to get the highest percentage concentration that you can get; higher concentrations have less water, and you want as little water on the metal contacts as humanly possible. Using a cotton swab (which should be wet but not dripping with the rubbing alcohol), gently scrub both sides of the conductive contacts that connect the cart to the system. Once you've done this, use the dry side of the swab to get any excess moisture or dirt off of the contacts.

Do not use Windex or any other kind of standard cleaner in lieu of rubbing alcohol. These products have ammonia in them, as well as dyes and perfumes, which can cause a lot of damage to the contacts.

There are some people who prefer a more thorough cleaning and want to crack open a cart to clean out the entire inside. Simply opening up a cart requires that you have a special set of screwdrivers for the specialized screws that Nintendo, Sega and similar companies used in their production – they didn't want just anyone to be able to open them up, so you will have to find the correct screwdriver for your cartridge online. Some people like to use a brass cleaner of some sort to clean off the contacts at this point, though it should be noted that these polishes are not designed with electronics in mind.

A number of different techniques have been developed over the years for cleaning out an old cartridge; those looking to go more in-depth than the most basic cleaning should seek out additional information or tutorials online.

## CLEANING AND RESTORING DISCS

Discs are a little more straightforward than carts and a little less high-maintenance in most cases. Discs should really only be cleaned when necessary, if you've noticed that it's accumulated dirt or dust on it. For most discs, a cloth dampened with water is good enough for the job – you want to be sure, however, that you're using a lint-free material like cotton or microfiber. Rougher materials like paper towels increase the chance that you'll scratch the disc in the process. Simply using water and gently wiping off any dirt from the disc usually gets the job done.

Obviously, never insert a wet disc into a system. Let it dry on its own or gently dry it off yourself. Do not use any household cleaners on discs, either, as these can damage the disc's surface. Discs that have endured a lifetime of fingerprints or some minor staining can usually be fixed up with rubbing alcohol instead of water, or a disc-specific cleaner spray.

For minor, light scratching, there are a variety of seemingly bizarre ways to getting the disc to function again. Perhaps the most notorious is the toothpaste method, but people have also used petroleum jelly and bananas among other household products to fill in small scratches. There are online tutorials for all of these, which should be undertaken only while knowing the risk involved in potentially damaging the disc further. There are plenty of products on the market designed specifically for fixing minor disc scratches, such as scratch remover machines that will buff the disc to remove the scratch. Deep scratches may not be fixable at all.

## REMOVING STICKY RESIDUE

Thanks to how many children would distinguish their cartridge or system from their siblings' or friends' things by decorating them with stickers, we now have a glut of gaming items on the market that are coated in stickiness. Fortunately, thanks to how almost all major gaming items have an all-plastic surface, Goo Gone and similar formulas are a wonderful way of eliminating any residue.

Now, if you have a sticker on top of a cartridge label, it's important to be careful. Rushing through the process may lead you to accidentally tearing off the game label as well. Putting some of your stick-removal formula on the sticker and letting it soak for a few minutes should allow you to remove the top sticker without damaging the cart label.

## CLEANING CONTROLLERS

Because of how controllers sit in our hands the entire time that we're playing, they have the greatest tendency to get grody in a hurry. People will log hundreds of hours of game time over the course of many years – which means that there's usually many years' worth of dead skin and sweat and grime all built up in the crevices of a controller.

Many people like to use baby wipes or other similarly gentle cleaning pads to actually wipe down the surface of a controller, which is a good basic thing to do on a regular basis. But all the little nooks and crannies are more problematic. Shoulder buttons and under the thumbsticks are the grimiest areas on a controller usually because they're getting the most consistent use. You want to get at these with smaller

things, like cotton swabs soaked in rubbing alcohol; some people use toothpicks or similarly tiny tools to dig out dirt. Be aware of any seams your controller might have, as these get gunked up and are most often forgotten about.

## OTHER GENERAL TIPS

*Stay out of direct sunlight*: Not only will UV rays cause older systems to go yellow in a hurry, but sunlight will also fade all of the labels on cartridges and all of the box art of your games. In order to keep a collection looking as good as possible for as long as possible, it's important to keep that collection in an area where it's not in any direct sunlight.

*Avoid DVD folders*: Though a popular space-saving measure, the fabrics used in many of these folders are too rough for many game discs and have a tendency to cause scratching. Keeping disc-based games in their original cases not only looks better but will be better for the disc itself in the long run.

*Give your games room to breathe*: Cramming cases on a shelf to the point where you can't pull one game out without pulling at least two more out with it is not good. Pressure caused by slamming too many games together can cause damage to the game case, which runs a much higher risk of cracking, and by extension to the disc itself.

*Keep it cool:* As discussed earlier, heat can be a problem in terms of things breaking down. Avoid storing things directly next to a television or any other heat source, and they'll stay in better condition for much longer.

*Get creative:* Video game collectors have long had a wild artistic flair for their actual collections' displays. Whether you've got every color of the Game Boy Color or a *Pokémon* collection that dates to the original 151, the most important thing is to have fun with how you show that fandom off. Video games are *games*, and collections of those games should be just as fun to explore as the worlds of the games themselves.

# The Most Valuable Games on Every System

By Kurt Kalata

## Why do these games get so expensive?

It's usually due to one or a combination of these reasons:

### It was a late release for the system

Companies often supported older consoles in the twilight years of the system - publishing games on the NES after the SNES released in particular - but they were usually printed in small quantities and often sold in very small numbers.

### It's a niche genre

Both shooter and RPG fan bases are quite avid, collecting all available titles on a given platform. In many of these cases, games may have had poor sales or low print runs when initially released, but become popular years later due to positive word of mouth, driving up prices. This is particularly true with 2D shooters in the 32-bit area, since the genre was becoming more niche to the prevalence of 3D games, as well as JRPGs in the 32-bit era, due to the increasing popularity amongst English speakers with the success of the *Final Fantasy* games.

### It could only be obtained from certain places for a limited time

For the rarest of rare, they tend to be titles that were only available directly through mail order, or as promotional releases, by grocery products, through game shows, and so forth.

Also, if a game you want looks too expensive, consider importing a game from another territory if it's cheaper. Many of the expensive NES titles have substantially cheaper Famicom counterparts. Ditto with Saturn games. The language barrier can be an issue with text-heavy games - since RPGs were produced in huge quantities in Japan, titles like *Mother 2* (*Earthbound*) and *Chrono Trigger* are incredibly cheap, while their American counterparts remain highly priced.

*\*\*Prices listed for games have been gleaned from GameValueNow, a site that aggregates completed online auctions for video games, and by compiling other auction data. We have also gathered data from Video Game Price Charts for North American releases, and from Amazon JP and Surugaya for Japanese releases. Price range largely represents what a loose cartridge would be versus what a complete or in-box copy would cost. The prices here only represent what our research has turned up; your own results may vary.*

***This should not be your only guide for prices, and should only serve as a starting point for the games discussed.***

Also excluded: tournament cartridges, though some limited edition games are included. We are also not counting "deluxe" or "limited" editions of games that already have releases. There are a few cases where a limited release non-game product is published for a platform.

If you plan to purchase these games, make sure to watch out for "reproductions," which is an optimistic way of saying "bootlegs."

Some of these titles do get expensive, so it's somewhat understandable that people want something that looks nice on their shelves or can be played on a real system. Just beware that these are technically not legal, and also know that the going price for these are typically about $30-$50, so don't pay anything more unless you want to get ripped off. They also hold no real value amongst collectors.

## ATARI 2600

Back in the early days of console games, there was no central licensing – anyone could develop anything they wanted for the platform, without approval of the console developer. This caused a glut of poor products to flood the market. But it also meant that any old company could make and publish their own games. Most of the rarest games only sold through mail order to extremely limited markets, with their existence only acknowledged through magazine advertisements.

**See also:** *Mangia, Springer, Out of Control, Cakewalk, Malagai, Berenstain Bears, River Patrol, Quadrun, Sword of Saros, Bugs Bunny, Spider Maze, Swordquest Waterworld, X-Man, Texas Chainsaw Massacre, Q\*Bert Qubes,* anything from the publisher Xante

### Air Raid - *$30,000-$32,000*

The only game released by a company called Men-a-Vision, it's a fairly standard shooting game. There is only one complete copy known in existence and it sold for over $32,000 at auction in 2012. Earlier auctions of the game that included the box (though were otherwise incomplete) also passed the $30,000 mark.

### Pepsi Invaders - *$1,800-$2,100*

There were a handful of food-and-drink product based games for the Atari 2600, including Chase the Chuckwagon (for Purina dog food) and Kool-Aid Man. Pepsi Invaders was actually commissioned by their competitor, Coca-Cola, and only sold at their 1983 sales convention. It's basically a ROM hack of the platform's *Space Invaders* game, but with the alien replaced with the letters "PEPSI" (plus one more alien since there are six spaces in a row). It also turns it into a time-attack game by giving unlimited lives but keeping to a three-minute time limit. Sales via eBay have ranged from about $1,800 back in 2005 to more than $2,100 in 2010.

### Gamma-Attack - *???*

*Gamma-Attack* is a shooter developed by Gammation, a company that had put out a rapid fire joystick attachment for the Atari 2600. They were supposedly developing a game too, but it was never actually released. Its existence was only discovered 30 years later at a lucky garage sale purchase. This is the only known copy in existence, and it was listed on eBay for $500,000 in 2008 but went unsold.

### Birthday Mania - *???*

A publisher called Personal Games Company had an interesting idea to sell customized games to be given as presents. Their only title was *Birthday Mania*, which opens with the personalized name displayed, then you blow out falling candles. Only approximately 10 copies were sold, and copies have not yet hit public auction, so it's difficult to tell how much it would really be worth.

### Red Sea Crossing - *$10,000-$14,000*

Developed in 1983, there were about 100 copies of this game produced for sale through mail order. A pair of copies popped up in 2012, where one sold at auction for nearly $14,000, and another for about $10,000. As the title suggests, it's a religious themed game where you control Moses' crossing of the Red Sea.

## NINTENDO ENTERTAINMENT SYSTEM

Almost all of the rare and valuable NES games released at the end of the system's life, well after the Genesis and SNES were introduced. This is especially true for games released by Taito. There are also a handful of unlicensed carts, like any of the Panesian adult games.

**See also:** *Moon Crystal, Bonk's Adventure, Snow Bros., Zombie Nation, Chip & Dale Rescue Rangers 2, Dragon Fighter, Ducktales 2, Cowboy Kid, Gun\*Nac, Mighty Final Fight, Hammerin' Harry (PAL), Bubble Bobble 2, Recca, Power Blade 2*

### Panic Restaurant - *$700-$1,100*

A good number of games on this list are late NES releases from Taito, who supported the system long after the Genesis and Super NES were on the marketplace. Reviews lambasted their dated graphics, kids wouldn't buy them, and as such, they became incredibly rare. Panic Restaurant is one such game, a fairly decent food-oriented action platformer. The Japanese version, known as *Wanpaku Kokkun no Gourmet World*, is far cheaper.

## Little Samson - $1,000-$2,500
Another late-era NES release, *Little Samson* stars a young kid who can switch into various animal forms with different skills, feeling a bit like a variation on *Mega Man*. The Japanese version, known as *Seirei Densetsu Lickle*, is also on the pricey side, though not as much as the American NES release.

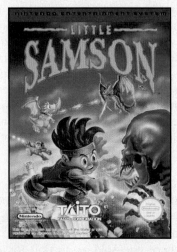

## Flintstones: The Surprise at Dinosaur Peak - $700-$1,900
The first *Flintstones* game is barely worth anything. This one though, like so many other late Taito releases, is a small gold mine. There is no Japanese release at all either.

## Cheetahmen II - $800-$1,200
What started off as a hilariously bad *Teenage Mutant Ninja Turtles* rip-off in the *Action 52* cartridge ended up becoming a minor cultural

phenomenon with the sequel, a standalone release. It's terrible, but the soundtrack is surprisingly catchy. Someone actually succeeded in running a Kickstarter to fix the programming and do another (very small) print run.

## Hot Slots - $800-$1,300
Nintendo had a very strict hold on the content for the NES, ensuring that they were safe for children. But that didn't stop some unlicensed publishers from creating some adult titles for the system. These all were published under the label Panesian, which was actually part of the Japanese company Hacker International. Three games were released in America: *Peek-A-Boo Poker*, *Hot Slots*, and *Bubble Bath Babes*. All three of Panesian's titles are extremely expensive, due to both their scant distribution and their notoriety.

## Stadium Events - $8,000-$43,000
Probably the most famous rare video game cartridge known by the mainstream audience, this title was originally published by Bandai for their fitness pad. It only made it out into stores in extremely small quantities before Nintendo bought the rights to both the accessory and the game and rebranded them.

Other than the name, the game is identical, but due to the rarity of the original game, especially in box, its value has propelled to astronomical heights. A full in-box copy of *Stadium Events* sold on eBay in early 2016 for more than $43,000. There is a European version of the game which isn't worth nearly the amount as the American version, but is still much higher than a typical NES game.

## SEGA MASTER SYSTEM

While Sega's 8-bit console died an early death in America and Japan, it lived on in several other territories, including Europe, Brazil, and Australia. Most of the in-demand SMS games are from popular franchises released in these territories, though there are some special cases.

**See also**: *Ninja Gaiden, OutRun 3D, Ghouls n' Ghosts*

### Golden Axe Warrior - $100-$250

Sega's famous beat-em-up was somehow turned into a *Zelda*-clone in this rare Master System release. The thing is, it's actually a good one, and in some ways bests Nintendo's classic, despite obviously not being original. Information about SMS distribution is scant and it may have dribbled out in America in small numbers, but is largely seen as a European exclusive.

### Power Strike - $70-$200

Also known as *Aleste,* in North America this only sold through mail order in the back of Sega's promotional magazine. It was more widely released in Europe, so that version is less in demand. The American version has a distinct monochromatic color, while the European version uses the same art as the Japanese release, but otherwise they're identical.

### James Buster Douglas Knockout Boxing - $115-$750

Like *Sonic the Hedgehog,* this was one of the last North American releases for the Master System. It's a little closer to the older SMS game *Rocky* than the Genesis version, which itself was a licensed port of a Taito arcade game called *Final Blow*. The game was released in PAL territories without Douglas' endorsement under the name *Heavyweight Champ*.

## GENESIS

Genesis games never quite received the same price spike as the SNES, though select titles have been creeping up in recent years. However, the situation is different in Japan – while the SNES and Genesis were neck-and-neck through most of their lives, the Mega Drive came in third place in the "Japanese Console Wars." As a result, its late releases were aimed at the remaining hardcore audience.

**See also**: *Pepenga Pengo, Contra: The Hard Corps (JP), Vampire Killer, Snow Bros., Slap Fight, Undeadline, Crusader of Centy, The Punisher, Beggar Prince, Pier Solar, Gleylancer, Battlemania Daiginjou, Eliminate Down, Twinkle Tale*

### Panorama Cotton - $450-$750

The first two *Cotton* games (the arcade release, simply titled *Cotton*, and the SFC release, *Cotton 100%*) were standard side-scrolling shooters. *Panorama Cotton*, however, is much closer to *Space Harrier*, utilizing a behind-the-back perspective. Since the Mega Drive doesn't support hardware scrolling, most of these titles end up suffering from choppy visuals, but Panorama Cotton ranks up there as evidence of what the system could do if placed in the right hands. Certain editions of *Panorama Cotton* came with a tea cup. Adding this together with a boxed copy of the game increases its value substantially.

### Rock Man Mega World / Mega Man: The Wily Wars - $170-$350

A *Super Mario All Stars*-style compilation, this includes the first three *Rock Man* (*Mega Man*) games with updated visuals and music, along with a few extra bonus bosses. It received cartridge releases in Japan and Europe, but ended up as a Sega Channel exclusive in North America. It's very expensive in both of these territories. The European version is known as *The Wily Wars*, and is priced just as high, but despite being region protected, will work in NA consoles.

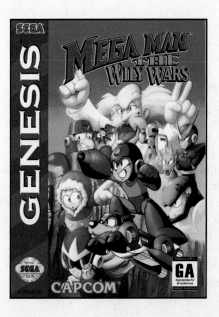

**Alien Soldier - *$300-$600***

Treasure's follow-up to *Gunstar Heroes* is a super difficult boss rush, and while it's a magnificently crafted title, it has a high learning curve, particularly due to the large size of the player character. But like the rest of Treasure's titles, it's a fantastic showcase for the Mega Drive. It was released in Japan and Europe, with the latter version cleaning up the silly Engrish in the introduction scroll. It was reprogrammed for PAL, so it's not really playable on U.S. consoles. It was rereleased on the *Gunstar Heroes Treasure Box*, as part of the Sega Ages 2500 line for the PS2, and includes both the JP and EU versions.

**MUSHA - *$175-$350***

An offshoot of *Compile's Aleste* (AKA *Power Strike*) series, this game features mechas in Sengoku-era Japan, and an amazing hard rock soundtrack. It was published by Toaplan in Japan and Seismic in America. Both versions command a premium due to its reputation, though the American version is more expensive due to its low distribution. It has been released worldwide on the Wii Virtual Console. Its sequel, *Robo Aleste* for the Sega/Mega CD, is a little cheaper in comparison, though not quite as good of a game.

**Pulseman - *$100-$400***

Developed by Game Freak, who would later develop Nintendo's *Pokémon* series, *Pulseman* is a solid action-platformer. Like *Mega Man: The Wily Wars*, it was scheduled to be released in North America, but instead ended up as a Sega Channel exclusive, so the only option for a physical release is the Japanese version.

## SUPER NINTENDO

The SNES has seen tremendous price spikes over the past several years, with even the most popular, common titles being sought after. However, most of the priciest titles generally have one thing in common: they're all games that were generally ignored by either the press or gamers at the time they released, and only caught fame after being recognized by the retro community.

**See also:** *E.V.O.: The Search for Eden, Ninja Gaiden Trilogy, Majyuuou, Final Fight Guy, Mega Man X3, Mega Man 7, R-Type III, Ghoul Patrol, Chrono Trigger, Super 3D Noah's*

*Ark, Super Copa, Ninja Warriors, Harvest Moon, Space Megaforce, Castlevania: Dracula X, Gourmet Sentai Barayarou, Undercover Cops, Whirlo (EU), Iron Commando: Koutetsu no Senshi, Yoshi Cookie Kuruppon Oven de Cookie, Exertainment Mountain Bike Rally/ Speed Racer (combo release)*

**Earthbound - *$200-$1,000***

Earthbound is probably one of the most well-known games on this list. Known as *Mother 2* in Japan, it released in 1994. It was fairly popular in its own territory, with the game (and its predecessor) having been written and conceived by pseudo-celebrity Shigesato Itoi. When Nintendo released it in America though, RPG fans stuck their noses up at the childish graphics, and Nintendo fans were baffled at how uncharacteristically bizarre it was. Its incredibly lame advertising campaign proclaimed "This game stinks!" with a tie-in with scratch n' sniff stickers, which did little to help.

Over the years word spread quickly, and soon that weird game no one understood became appreciated as a remarkably progressive, well-written gem, filled with weird pop culture attachments and RPG meta-references. With that, the game shot up in value.

It only became worse over time. *Mother 1 & 2* was ported to the GBA, but Nintendo refused to translate it. A sequel was made for the GBA, but Nintendo also refused to bother with it. Furthermore, the company danced around any attempt to get it rereleased, citing copyright reasons, assumed to be due to unauthorized use of samples in its soundtrack. This perceived indifference to its fans only brought more attention to the series and increased demand even more.

In 2015, Nintendo released *Earthbound* on

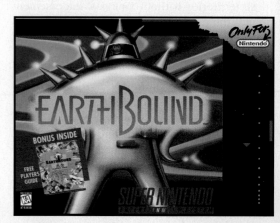

the Wii U Virtual Console, worldwide, without any changes. However, the SNES version has still maintained most of its value. This is especially true for complete copies, as the game was released in gigantic boxes that included an incredibly detailed strategy guide, featuring clay models of the assorted characters. Complete versions of the came frequently hit four figures in online auctions.

### Super Turrican 2 - $200-$1,200
An SNES exclusive entry in the series that began on the Commodore 64 and Amiga, the last true entry in the *Turrican* series has some remarkable graphics, and linear level design that puts it closer to the levels of the *Contra* games, as opposed to the sprawling levels of the original games. It was only released in North America and Europe in the twilight years of the console.

### Hagane: The Final Conflict - $475-$1,200
This is an unusual title. Published by Hudson late in the SNES' life and developed by the same team as *Lords of Thunder* and *Sapphire*, *Hagane* is an action title similar to *Strider* and *Shinobi*. While unpolished in parts, it's still a pretty decent game. The game is so uncommon that people have speculated that it was a Blockbuster exclusive release. No one has verified this though, as people have found copies in the wild without any traces of those Blockbuster stickers.

### Wild Guns - $200-$700
*Wild Guns* is a cool Cabal-type game that ostensibly takes place in the Wild West, but adds in assorted anachronistic elements like robots. The situation to *Wild Guns* is similar to *Hagane* - it was an uncommon SNES title that, while not particularly cheap, was also not that expensive for the longest time. Then again, around 2012 - possibly due to its release on the Wii Virtual Console - more people discovered it, and prices climbed immediately.

### Pocky & Rocky 2 - $300-$1,100
Originating in the arcades under the name *Kiki Kaikai,* this Taito game is an overhead run-and-gun similar to *Commando,* but with a light hearted Japanese mythological theme. The West first saw this game as its sequel, *Pocky & Rocky,* published by Natsume. A third game was released as *Pocky & Rocky 2* later

in the SNES' life. Both of these have seen huge price spikes recently, though *Pocky and Rocky 2* is rarer than the original. The SFC releases of both games are cheaper, though not by much.

### Terranigma - $90-$150
The third in Quintet's "Heaven and Earth" trilogy, which also consists of *Soul Blazer* and *Illusion of Gaia*, this game was translated into English for the European market, but left unreleased in America. Which is tragic, because it's a fantastic action-RPG, and the music is remarkable. It is sought worldwide, but due to region locking and TV display issues, the cartridge only works on PAL SNESes with PAL TVs.

## PLAYSTATION
Among American PS1 games, the expensive games fall mostly into two categories: RPGs and *Mega Man Legends* games, both titles that had decent sales and later went on to cult popularity years after the fact. In Japan, most of the rarer games are small 2D titles or arcade ports, focused solely on a niche audience.
**See also:** *Serial Experiments Lain, Tales of Destiny 2, Klonoa, Adventures of Lomax, Vanark, Tail Concerto, Waku Puyo Dungeon, Rakugaki Showtime, Gaia Seed, Yuuyami Douri Tankentai, Zanac x Zanac, Harmful Park*

### Suikoden II - $70-$300
In 1999, Square released *Final Fantasy VIII*, a follow-up to one of the most popular games on the PlayStation. A few months later, Konami released *Suikoden II*, a follow-up to a well-regarded but ultimately rather plain 2D RPG in the early days of the system. While *Final Fantasy VIII* was more popular, *Suikoden II* was more critically acclaimed, and helped create a small-but-devoted fan base.

*Suikoden I & II* were ported to the PSP, and unlike Square's lazy ports, Konami went the extra mile to actually reprogram the game to properly expand the visuals to a widescreen view. Unfortunately, perhaps due to SCEA's contempt towards straight ports in the early days of the PSP, the game was never localized. The first *Suikoden* released on the PSN eventually, but the second - the one everyone wanted - was not.

## Valkyrie Profile - $50-$280

Similar to *Suikoden II*, *Valkyrie Profile* released within weeks of another Square game, *Chrono Cross*, which massively overshadowed it. While the game has some weird balancing issues, and it's pretty much impossible to get the good ending without following a guide, the innovative battle system and concept have given the game a cult reputation.

The PSP rerelease made a small dent in the price of the PSOne version for a while, but didn't affect the overall price drastically. Why? The port suffers from the same issue as other PSOne-to-PSP ports like *Final Fantasy Tactics*, where instead of properly reprogramming the game to support the system's widescreen graphics, they just stretch and filter them, ruining the pixel artwork and turning the whole thing into a blurry mess. It's not unplayable, but definitely inferior, and the extra rendered cutscenes add nothing of value. The PSP version is available on the PSN, but the PSOne version is not.

## The Misadventures of Tron Bonne - $100-$550

Outside of Nintendo properties, the track record for classic 2D to 3D sequels was not particularly great. Capcom's attempt at this with *Mega Man Legends* defied expectations, largely because it had almost nothing to do with the classic series, but nonetheless remained charming, competent games, with a bright anime-style that looked good even using low-res PlayStation 3D. The *first Mega Man Legends* game was popular enough to be ported to the Nintendo 64 (under the name *Mega Man 64*) as well as the PC.

After that came the spinoff, *The Adventures of Tron Bonne*, a series of smaller games - not quite small enough to be "mini" games but not

big enough to be standalone either - starring the adorably maniacal antagonist Tron Bonne and her army of cutesy Servbots. The actual sequel continued the story of the first, though was a far darker game, and ended up on a strange cliffhanger. Both games have shot up in price, for the same reasons the SNES games have. Furthermore, *Mega Man Legends* has its own brand of notoriety, thanks to the unveiling, and infamous cancellation, of *Mega Man Legends 3* for the 3DS.

## LSD - $250-300

A unique "dream simulator" which was really just an excuse for graphic designs to go crazy with bizarre visuals. It was created by artist Hiroko Nishikawa, and was based off a dream journal she kept for over 10 years. It was also produced and designed by Osamu Sato, who created a number of similarly bizarre, artistic games like *Eastern Mind: The Lost Souls of Tong-Nou*, for home computers. *LSD* isn't really a game, per say, as you just wander around and get tossed into various bits of bizarre scenery, but it is an experience unlike any other. It's been rereleased on the Japanese PSN.

## Captain Commando - $100-$500

One of Capcom's many arcade beat-em-ups, this one saw a scarce release on the SNES (which is also fairly expensive) along with this nearly arcade perfect port to the PS1.

## DREAMCAST

Sega really only supported the Dreamcast for about two years, but that didn't stop numerous third party publishers (and many hobbyists) from supporting the platform well past its due date. Most of the expensive U.S. games were late releases from Capcom.

**Border Down - $80-$200**
The Dreamcast was the system that wouldn't die. Despite being officially discontinued by Sega after just two years, it still received consistent support, mostly in the form of arcade shooters. Most of these were eventually ported to other platforms. G.Rev's *Border Down*, however, was not. The gameplay could be very disorienting, but it's a solid game with cool sci-fi aesthetics and suitably Zuntata-esque weird soundtrack.

**Cleopatra Fortune - $100-$150**
Both the Japanese PlayStation and Dreamcast versions of this Taito-developed puzzler are strangely expensive! The game is included on the *Taito Legends 2* for the PlayStation 2, and even got a cheapo budget release (with abhorrent cover artwork) in North America. The Dreamcast version has redone, higher-res graphics, along with a completely voiced story mode.

**Cannon Spike - $50-$200**
Developed by Psikyo, this shooter/beat-em-up features numerous characters from assorted Capcom games, including Mega Man, and Cammy from *Street Fighter*.

**Mars Matrix - $60-$215**
Near the end of the Dreamcast's lifespan, Capcom released a handful of games for the low retail price of $20, including two shooters – *Mars Matrix* and *Giga Wing 2* – and a 2.5D fighter, *Project Justice*. They're all quite valuable, and all quite good.

# GAME BOY
In general, Game Boy games are not very expensive, at least if you're collecting cart-only. However, since the games were for portable platforms aimed at kids, many boxes were thrown away, so some more desirable titles are substantially more expensive if they include a box and manual.
**See also**: *Castlevania Legends, Magical Chase, Mega Man V*

**Trip World - $200-$400**
Developed by Sunsoft, this incredibly cute platformer starring an adorable little bunny shows an astounding amount of detail for a Game Boy title, even though the game itself is rather short and simplistic. The game also received an extremely limited European release. Both versions are exceedingly rare and expensive, though essentially identical, since there's not really any text.

**Shantae - $275-$1,500**
Developed by the small company Wayforward, Shantae is a GBC game published by Capcom, who bumbled its release and put it on store shelves well after the advent of the Game Boy Advance. Due to its technical inferiority, and the fact that it was priced at $30 where better-looking games were on the shelves around the same price, it was ignored at the places that bothered to stock it and soon disappeared. For a while used copies could be found lumped together with the usual licensed Game Boy junk for a measly $5, but somewhere around 2007 it was discovered by gamers, and the price ballooned into the triple digits, where its stayed for years. The eventual resurgence in popularity allowed Wayforward to publish a sequel on DSiware. *Shantae* was finally released on the 3DS eShop in 2013, making it more widely available – though this hasn't stopped the demand for physical copies.

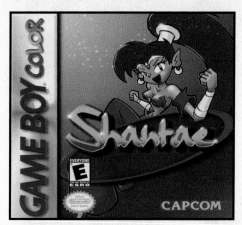

**Amazing Tater - $180-$400**
Developed by Atlus, this game is the sequel to *Kwirk,* and part of a larger series known in Japan as *Puzzle Boy*. It's a puzzle game, roughly similar to *Sokobon*, but with a potato. For reasons unclear, it's insanely expensive, particularly in box.

**Spud's Adventure - $200-$2,400**
The Game Boy is home to not one but two incredibly rare potato-based games. In fact, it's also by Atlus and is considered a spinoff of the *Puzzle Boy* games, though its focus is on action-roleplaying rather than puzzle solving.

## SEGA CD

The Sega CD was a flop more or less everywhere, but some late titles either saw little distribution or caught more popularity with the advent of emulation.

### Snatcher - $200-$1,000

Initially released as a home computer game in the late 1980s, then ported to the PC Engine with a bunch of multimedia enhancements (as well as a completed story), Hideo Kojima's *Blade Runner*-inspired detective story is one of the most well-regarded Japanese adventure games ever made. Konami decided to localize it for English speaking audiences, but since the PCE was long dead overseas by this point, they instead put a ton of resources into porting it to the Sega/Mega CD for North American and European release. Unfortunately, it was released at the time when the Sega CD was pretty much already dead. The game quickly disappeared, but sprang back in the spotlight after Kojima came to worldwide fame with the *Metal Gear Solid* series in 1998.

### Keio Flying Squadron - $300-$1,000

*Keio Flying Squadron* is the kind of game that rarely left Japan - a cute-em-up featuring a female character, with a Japanese sense of humor. Yet somehow, it ended up releasing in North America and Europe, and both are very expensive. As far as shooters go, it's decent but not amazing. The Japanese release is one of the pricier Mega CD titles, but only relatively since there aren't any really expensive titles in that territory, and it's still a fraction of the cost of the English versions.

### Popful Mail - $150-$550

Originating as a PC game in Japan, Falcom's action-RPG received three different conversions for the PC Engine, Super Famicom and Sega CD. Only the Sega CD one made it into English, which was the best choice, since the game was improved to make it feel like one of the later *Wonder Boy* titles. It was localized courtesy of Working Designs, whose overtly goofy script makes the original writing far more colorful. This release is the most expensive of the four Working Designs released Sega CD games - the *Lunar* games are popular but were rereleased on subsequent platforms, bringing down the value a bit.

The Japanese version is extremely cheap, and despite the language barrier, might actually be preferable - Working Designs had a tendency to tinker with the games' difficulty, so they went from making the game a little too easy to a little too hard.

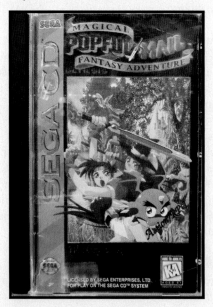

### Lords of Thunder - $75-$200

A conversion of the TurboGrafx-16 shooter, the Sega CD version was developed specifically for American and European territories. It's a fine port too, with only slightly reduced graphics, and a rearranged soundtrack.

## PC ENGINE

The TurboGrafx-16 and its CD-ROM attachment came in distant third in the console wars, with NEC and TTI essentially bowing out in the later days of the 16-bit era. However, in Japan it was successful, less so than the Super Famicom but better performing than the Mega Drive. As for American releases, nearly all of its CD-ROM titles are incredibly expensive. There are also a few insanely rare releases like *Life Active Network* (not really a game) and *Cosmic Yakyuuken Kazenban*, which may be prototypes and only have an extremely limited number of copies in existence, but little information is available on them.

**See also**: *Dungeon Explorer II, Exile: Wicked Phenomenon, Might & Magic III, Super Air Zonk, Syd Mead's Terraforming, Godzilla, Bonk 3, Dynastic Hero, Cotton, (all U.S. releases), Nexzr, Ninja Action Kaze Kiri, Bazaru De Gozaru No Game De Gozaru, Crazy Hospital, Hi-Leg Fantasy, Akiyama Jin no Suugaku Mystery, Beyond Shadowgate, Darius AlphaBazaru De Gozaru No Game De Gozaru:*

**Akumajou Dracula X: Rondo of Blood -** *$150-$300*
Perhaps the most famous PC Engine title, *Akumajou Dracula X* maintained a certain allure for many, many years, due to it being one of the only *Castlevania* games not released outside of Japan, as well as a substantial amount of hype from magazines at the time. For these reasons, it used to command quite the premium. The game was never rare, just heavily in demand. However, due to several rereleases - a remake on the PSP was bundled with a port, as well as a worldwide Wii Virtual Console release - has reduced the price a bit.

**Sapphire -** *$700-$1,500*
The situation surrounding *Sapphire*'s release is a little unclear. Despite being a well designed, visually and aurally impressive shooter, designed by the same team as *Lords of Thunder*, it snuck out in an extremely low print run. It's also the most expensive shooter on a system known for expensive shooters. Just beware of bootlegs - some group probably thought they were doing the world a favor by issuing a small "unofficial reprint" of the game, which has flooded the market with illegitimate copies. Don't go dumping $300+ into something that's not an authentic product. In general, if the sale price is too low, it's almost definitely a reproduction.

**Magical Chase -** *$500-700*
One of the first games from Quest, this is a cute-em-up featuring a little witch. This one did get the benefit of releasing in America, though this version is insanely expensive. Make no mistake, the Japanese version's price is incredibly high too. There were two released in Japan, a standard one and a version released by PC Engine Fan Magazine. Other than a small marking on the packaging, they are identical, and are worth the same amount.

**Dead of the Brain -** *$400-$700*
The last PC Engine game officially released in Japan, *Dead of the Brain* is a port of a collection of sci-fi/horror PC-based adventure games. Given the language barrier, there's probably not much of a reason for an English-speaking collector to grab this one.

## SATURN
Like the TurboGrafx-16, the Saturn was relatively successful in Japan but more or less a flop in America. A handful of late English language RPGs have become expensive, but there are a number of Japanese titles that command a high sum, primarily shoot-em-ups. The rarest releases aren't actually games though: both *Eyeful Home* and *Heim Waltz* are limited promotional releases for housing companies, but both command insane prices from collectors.
See also: *Shining Force III, Burning Rangers, Albert Odyssey, The House of the Dead, Dragon Force, Image Fight & X-Multiply, Street Fighter Zero 3, Crows: The Battle Action, Cotton Boomerang, Kyuukyoku Tiger II Plus, Stellar Assault SS*

**Panzer Dragoon Saga -** *$350-$900*
By 1998, Sega had pretty much given up on the Saturn in North America and Europe. Nevertheless, they still localized two fan-favorite RPGs - the first entry (of three) of *Shining Force III*, and *Panzer Dragoon Saga*. Various auctions like to quote small print-runs but the actual number is not known. Nevertheless, they are both rare titles.

*Panzer Dragoon Saga* is the priciest of these, being an RPG rendition of one of the system's most beloved franchises. The game immediately developed a great reputation and was snatched up by fans, leaving the price to balloon within a year or so, where it's stayed ever since. Unfortunately, Sega revealed that the source code of the game was lost (reported to have been maliciously sabotaged by an irate manager), so chances of a remake are slim to none. The game is far cheaper in Japan, but being an RPG, it's obviously more difficult to play in Japanese (though it's not quite as text-heavy as other games in the genre).

**Radiant Silvergun - *$150-400***
Developed by fan-favorite Treasure, they of *Alien Soldier* and *Gunstar Heroes*, *Radiant Silvergun* began as an arcade, and was later fleshed out for a Saturn release. Unlike their other games, *Radiant Silvergun* was published through ESP, giving it a lesser range of distribution. The Saturn was also dead in North America and Europe at the time and did not find a publisher. The popularity of the company, both at home and overseas, led the game to near-legendary status amongst shooter fans in the late '90s.

The game's follow-up, *Ikaruga*, had popularity that led to more interest in its predecessor, eventually convincing Treasure to port the game to the Xbox 360. The XBLA port has slightly brought down the price of the Saturn version, but not by much.

**Magic Knight Rayearth - *$150-$450***
This Saturn action-RPG, based on the magical girl manga/anime by CLAMP, was one of the first titles released in Japan, and the last released in North America. This is mostly the fault of the publisher, Working Designs, who ran into a huge number of licensing issues. Being the last game on the system already makes a game rather rare, but the fact that it tied into the '90s anime boom made it even more desirable. Compared to most anime tie-ins, it's excellent, with some incredibly attractive 2D visuals and writing that ended up better than the anime/manga localizations.

**Battle Garegga - *$200-$500***
*Battle Garegga* is something of a legend. While unassuming at the forefront, seemingly not much different than any other shooter at the time, it has an astounding amount of depth. It's the only port of the game, and is essentially arcade perfect.

While technically *Battle Garegga* did not have any sequels, there are a number of follow-ups developed by Yagawa, for both Raizing/Eighting and Cave. These include *Battle Bakraid* and *Armed Police Batrider*

(unported), *Ibara* (ported badly to the PS2), and *Muchi Muchi Pork* and *Pink Sweets* (both bundled together for the Xbox 360 and are excellent ports). All are, of course, quite in demand and pricey, though none demand the same respect as *Battle Garegga*. The Xbox 360 pack, initially released in 2011, quickly grew price-wise, though it's leveled out substantially due to the 2013 "Best" release.

**Final Fight Revenge - *$300-$650***
The last game released for the Saturn in Japan, *Final Fight Revenge* is a port of an obscure 3D fighter, developed by Capcom's USA branch and based off the series of beat-em-ups. It's a terrible game (though it's got an amusing sense of humor), which means pretty much no one bought it outside of notoriety. No one's ever going to port this game again either so this will be the only way to play it, if you dare.

## GAMECUBE
The Gamecube played second fiddle to the PlayStation 2 (and Xbox in America), and only really survived thanks to the strong support of Nintendo. Most third parties went with the PlayStation 2, but a handful of quirky titles made it to the Gamecube.

**Cubivore - *$100-$400***
A strange title published by Atlus where you control cuboid animals eating other cuboid animals, this was destined to be a cult classic when it released, as nobody could make anything out of the premise. But games with bizarre premises and unique visuals often obtain cult popularity, and *Cubivore* has both.

**Gotcha Force** - *$100-$450*
This mecha action game from Capcom based on gashapon is essentially a kid friendly version of Sega's *Virtual On*. The name and cover made it easily confusable with a generic *Pokémon* clone though, and it flopped.

**Fire Emblem: Path of Radiance** - *$75-$200*
Nintendo's *Fire Emblem* series had been around since the Famicom days, but didn't leave Japan due to the company's concern that they were too complicated for English-speaking audiences. After *Fire Emblem* characters arrived in *Smash Bros.*, Nintendo finally started releasing them in English, starting with two games for the Game Boy. *Path of Radiance* marked the first console release of a *Fire Emblem* game since the Super Famicom, and while it did okay, it never quite resonated with the target audience. It wasn't until the 2013 3DS game *Fire Emblem Awakening* that the series became a mainstream hit, causing fans to hunt down earlier English releases. The Wii sequel to *Path of Radiance*, *Radiant Dawn*, is also in demand, and one of the more expensive titles on the platform.

**Skies of Arcadia Legends** - *$50-$175*
*Skies of Arcadia* released on the Dreamcast in 2000, and was one of the best RPGs on the system. It didn't reach a wide audience thanks to the failure of the platform, so Sega ported it to the Gamecube, where it was also disregarded as just a port of an old game.

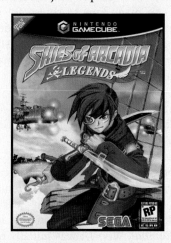

Eventually its reputation caught up with itself, especially considering it's considered the definitive version of the game, with additional content and some tweaks that fix its biggest problems, like reducing the random counter rate. *Skies of Arcadia Legends* has started to

inch into triple-digits in online auctions, as the game has yet to receive any further ports to contemporary systems.

## NINTENDO 64
The Nintendo 64 doesn't have much of a collector's market, with its two most expensive titles being rental-only. Some titles though, like the later Mario Party games, have been creeping up in value, probably due to them not being released on any Virtual Console platforms.
**See also:** *Bomberman 64 Second Attack, Bangai-O, Turok Wars (Grey cartridge), Super Bowling, Stunt Racer 64*

**Clay Fighters Sculptor's Cut** - *$400-$1,700*
*ClayFighter 63 1/3* was the third in Interplay's *Clay Fighter* series, a 2D fighter featuring digitized clay models, which must have seemed amazing at the time. A special edition was released with several extra characters and modes, but was a rental exclusive at Blockbuster. Interestingly, *Indiana Jones and the Infernal Machine*, an N64 port of the PC game, was also a Blockbuster exclusive, however, it does not have nearly the same value as other exclusives.

**Conker's Bad Fur Day** - *$75-$200*
This game is an M-rated parody of all of the other cutesy 3D platformers that released on the Nintendo 64. Nintendo seemed to want to distance itself from this game due to its content, plus it was released in the waning days of the system in 2001. Older gamers had moved onto the PS2 at this point, and kids were too young to play it, so it festered on the shelves. When Microsoft bought Rare, they released a port for the Xbox, which was graphically enhanced but, for some reason, censored much of the swearing. As a result, the N64 game is still highly prized.

**Worms Armageddon** - *$180-$580*
The third game in Team17's explosive multiplayer action game released on numerous platforms, but the Nintendo 64 version is now easily the rarest one, while you can find the PlayStation and Dreamcast version for a few dollars.

## PLAYSTATION 2
The PlayStation 2 is still too "new" to be really considered a collector's console just yet, but there are a handful of titles that have become extremely expensive since its sailed into the sunset.

**Ibara** - *$175-$350*
*Ibara* was the first game developed for Cave by Shinobu Yagawa, formerly of Raizing. As a result, it's the spiritual successor to many of his previous titles, like *Battle Garegga* and *Battle Bakraid*, and feels a little less like Cave's other titles.

Of the four Cave shooters published for the PS2, two were published by Cave (*Dodonpachi Daioujou* and *Epsgaluda*) and two were published by Taito (*Mushihime-sama* and *Ibara*). The first two saw reasonable distribution and while not cheap, aren't quite rare (yet), but the latter two were, for quite awhile, rather expensive. *Mushihime-sama* had wider distribution due to a reprint, plus its price went down after a substantially better port was released for the Xbox 360 and on Windows. However, *Ibara* did not receive any reprint nor future ports, so the only option is this PS2 version.

**Rule of Rose** - *$110-$300*
This survival horror game was published by Atlus and received routinely scathing reviews,

praising the atmosphere but lambasting the actual gameplay, which was subpar in a genre already known for clunky controls. Nevertheless, its pure creepiness and plainly messed up storyline has earned it a considerable cult following over the years, more so than any of Atlus' other titles, and never received any reprints.

**.Hack Part 4: Quarantine** - *$80-$175*
*.Hack* was a multimedia series produced by Bandai, spanning several manga, anime, and video game products. The PS2 games were early examples of episodic releases, consisting of two series, each with four games, released a few months apart. Though the first games in each series were widely developed, later entries were much rarer, as interest dropped off. The fourth entry of the first series, *Quarantine*, is the priciest of these.

**Kuon** - *$65-$200*
As with *Haunting Ground* and *Rule of Rose*, this is another PS2 horror game that was ignored at release but later found popularity among genre fans. It was also developed by From Software, who eventually received larger popularity thanks to their *Dark Souls* series.

**Yakuza 2** - *$70-$120*
A longtime favorite in Japan, Sega tried valiantly to get the American audience to accept its Japanese mafia-themed RPG/beat-em-up. They didn't succeed until well into the PS3 era, causing many fans to return to find the earlier games. The first game was widely produced but the second was quietly shoveled onto the shelves in small numbers, making it much harder to find.

## OTHER PLATFORMS:
**Samurai Shodown V Special (Neo Geo)**
*$1,000-$4,000*
This revised version of the fifth *Samurai Shodown* game was the last AES release. It's also a weird one, because it's remarkably bloody, filled with fatalities in a series that wasn't known to be quite on the level of *Mortal Kombat*. When it was initially released on AES, it was actually heavily censored, which also introduced some severe bugs. SNK issued a recall and resent fixed versions to the customers which restored much of the content and fixed the bugs. However, the few unfixed versions are extremely expensive.

## Metal Wolf Chaos (Xbox)
*$200-$350*

There's not much of a market for Xbox games... except *Metal Wolf Chaos*, one of the few worthwhile games for the system that was only released in Japan. Here, you take control of the President of the United States, as he hops in a gigantic mecha to protect the country from a military coup. It's incredibly ridiculous, compounded by some extremely bad English language voice acting. American fans have been petitioning From Software, the developer, for a PC port, but until then, the Japanese Xbox original is the only way to go.

## Ultima (Apple II)
*$100-$400*

Richard Garriott's *Ultima* is one of the most influential video games of all time, with its roots evident in hundreds upon hundreds of RPGs. The original game was released in 1981 for the Apple II, when home computers were still a huge luxury, meaning very few people owned the game, and especially kept the box. This, along with its place in history, make it one of the most sought after games amongst computer game collectors. *Ultima II* is similarly pricey, though not quite on the same level. *Ultima III* and subsequent games are much more common, though still very much in demand.

## Spider-Man Web of Fire (32X)
*$300-$450*

A follow-up to the Genesis and Sega CD *Spider-Man* titles, this was developed solely for the 32X. It's an okay game but hardly demonstrates why it couldn't have been a regular Genesis release. It was also published right as Sega had dropped the platform, so it was roundly ignored.

## Metal Gear 2 (MSX2)
*$200-$450*

*Metal Gear 2* is in the same situation as the original *Metal Gear* - interest in the series skyrocketed after *Metal Gear Solid*, especially since the game made even more explicit references to it, which most players had never even heard of. Unlike the original *Metal Gear*, no version had ever previously been translated into English, at least officially, leaving everyone who wanted to play it to rely on a fan-translated hack on emulators.

Again, like *Metal Gear*, *Metal Gear* finally released in English on the *Metal Gear Solid 3 Subsistence* pack. However, they changed all of the character portraits. Part of this was to make the visuals more consistent with artist Yoji Shinkawa's artwork for the *Solid* series, but part of this was also due to the fact that almost everyone was obviously ripped off from assorted Hollywood actors. The initial MSX2 release is the only way to experience it in its vaguely copyright-infringing form.

## Ninja Five-O (Game Boy Advance)
*$120-$500*

Developed by Hudson but published under Konami's label, *Ninja Five-O* is a brilliant mixture of *Shinobi* and *Bionic Commando,* and is easily one of the best action games on the Game Boy Advance. But while it was released worldwide - the EU version is known as *Ninja Cop* - for some baffling reason it barely saw any distribution, often only appearing at online retailers.

## Lucienne's Quest (3DO)
*$200-$450*

The 3DO doesn't have a large collector's scene, because much of its library was the kind of junk that was impressive back in the mid-'90s but looks terrible today. One of the few exceptions is *Lucienne's Quest*, the only Japanese RPG on the system, from Micro Cabin. The fact that it was even localized is surprising, but it was ignored by the audience and saw little distribution. A remake was developed for the Saturn called *Sword & Sorcery*, though this was only released in Japan.

## Wizard of Id's Wiz Math (Colecovision)
*$160-$1,100*

Some of the Xonox "Double Ender" cartridges for the Colecovision are extremely rare, like *Motocross Racer/Tomac the Barbarian* and *Sir Lancelot/Robin Hood*. However, the rarest standalone game is *Wizard of Id's Wiz Math* by Sierra Online, an educational game featuring characters from the comic strip.

## Spiker! Super Pro Volleyball (Intellivision)
*$1,000-$1,900*

Few Intellivision games are worth too much except for this one, along with *Stadium Mud Buggies*. These were two of the last games release for the system in 1989, and were only released so late because the publisher didn't have the money to put them out otherwise.

# ARCADE CABINETS

## Interview with Eric Holniker of Save Point

**Overstreet:** Please tell us a little bit about yourself.

**Eric Holniker (EH):** I'm Eric Holniker. I own Save Point, an arcade that is also a game store, and also a couple hundred arcade and pinball [machines] that we take around the country to different events. And I work on development and design for a few different arcade things.

**Overstreet:** How did you first get into video gaming, and more specifically, arcade gaming?

**EH:** I was always lured to it as a child because I grew up around arcade machines. I'm sure a lot of people have memories or stories about their parents taking them to work at some point... I was usually plopped down in front of an arcade cabinet at my dad's work. I guess that's what started the terrible, terrible can of worms.

**Overstreet:** Your store, Save Point, serves as both a console retailer and an arcade. A lot of people tend to choose one or the other, so what drove you to want to do both?

**EH:** So the initial vision for Save Point was to primarily focus on retro stuff. I still feel like we do that, although we're constantly finding ways to expand the retail portion of the store. Over the last couple years [we've] expanded into imports and strange pieces of gaming history that a lot of retail stores overlook.

But arcade games have always been what I'm most passionate about, and today you can't really have an arcade succeed on its own,

and we weren't really sure if a retail store was going to succeed in the [Westminster] area on its own. I mean, Save Point turned into this, it wasn't initially this, it was just a game store with a few arcade machines. And we're just constantly figuring out ways as a team to expand the place.

**Overstreet:** The arcade scene saw its biggest boom in the '80s, so what is it like today?

**EH:** It's pretty dead. There's an active community still in Japan and the UK, Indonesia has a pretty big boom, Brazil, but as far as in the continental United States – other than California, specifically – there's two major chains, and they're really the last thriving arcade chains, and those are Round1 and Dave & Buster's. There's another one that's surfacing called Main Event, but all of these places are giant entertainment centers, they usually offer bowling or karaoke, definitely alcohol [and] food in addition to arcade games and possibly pinball machines.

Most arcades have about 80 percent redemption machines these days, and 20 percent actual classic video arcade machines, or the newer Japanese machines. That's just because that's what makes money, that's what keeps them surviving. The definition of what younger generations think an arcade is, is vastly different than it used to be.

**Overstreet:** What kind of maintenance goes into keeping your arcade cabinets in working order?

**EH:** An insane amount. So, most people might think like, "Oh, well, I have an arcade machine. I have a *Pac-Man*, and it was my dad's, and we put a new power supply in it and it's fine." That's cool. That's in your house, it's not really going anywhere, you might use it 20 minutes to an hour every week, maybe put it on when you have a party or something. But we're talking about machines being on constantly, 100 percent of the time, 24/7. And then when they're taken to events, they are run probably 24/7 during the event on continuous play, and it's quite the challenge to maintain them at events.

So easily more money than the initial cost of the machine goes into maintaining the machine. And it's all random; if I were to say, "We don't need any maintenance," that's when everything breaks. And when you plan on something breaking, it probably won't, unless it's a design flaw. I spend a lot of my time making sure these things work, and going back and fixing them again.

**Overstreet:** Do you find that having arcade machines in your store helps to drive business?

**EH:** I think every piece of this store is not focused around the general definition of business, which is to make money. Honestly, every ounce of money we get either goes straight to our employees or into the arcade machines. It doesn't really go into a profit pool. We're constantly striving to make this store a better place and make sure we can pull off bigger and better events. So I think that we're a really cool thing, and I think that gamers and arcade enthusiasts think the same. But as far as actually making money, there's no way.

**Overstreet:** You have both American and Japanese cabinets. What are (if any) the major differences between them?

**EH:** The biggest difference is [that] machines made on this side of the world tend to be made of wood. It's cheaper to produce a wooden cabinet and there's more facilities in the United States to manufacture wooden cabinets. So by default, unless you're getting into some of the larger Japanese music games, American machines are heavier than Japanese machines.

Something people don't really get is there's specific cultures for arcade machines depend-ing on where you're locale is. In Japan – and, again, it exists in California a lot, but people on the East Coast, people in the Midwest, they don't really see it ever – most upright arcade machines that we're used to, games like *Street Fighter II*, *Tekken*, even puzzle games like *Tetris* or a fighting game like *Marvel vs. Capcom 2*, those are all played in sit-down cabinets. And some of those cabinets do exist [in the U.S.], they're scattered across the country, but they were never officially released here. Those are called "candy cabinets," and they're pretty much universal.

So in the United States, they would crank out one dedicated cabinet made of wood for a particular game, and while you can change the boards and upgrade them, it's not as easy as just swapping a board and a marquee out, it's a little more work. But candy cabinets are completely universal, and that makes them really, really neat. There's a height difference, you're supposed to sit at the candy cabinets, and it feels like a more communal experience. And over here, your average U.S. citizen – even if they grew up playing arcade machines – if they see a candy cabinet, they think, "Oh, that's a children's arcade machine." No, it's not.

So that's the major difference. Most games that are made overseas are, obviously, primarily in different languages. Most games that come out in Japan are in Japanese and most games that come out in Korea are in Korean. In China, it's the same deal. And most of these games have sprinkles of English in them, enough to where – even if you have no idea how to play the game – you can figure it out over time, as long as you have a few bucks to lose.

There's a difference in the types of games, too. If you want to take what is manufactured today in the United States versus what is manufactured in Japan, pinball is a good place to start. Pinball has almost never been a large thing overseas – except for in the U.K. [where] it is a big thing. Currently, there's one pinball manufacturer overseas that I'm aware of making commercial games. And over here in the United States, there's a handful of them left. That's a neat side of it. So pinball is still an active thing in the United States, and it's never really been a thing overseas.

Whereas traditional arcade machines, now you can only really find clones in China, like clones of classic games are still being produced in China. But in Japan, Taito still releases fighting games and puzzle games and other classic genres, but we mostly only see music games from Japan and Korea nowadays. As far as classic arcades in the United States, they've been dead for 10 or 15 years.

I think the last classic arcade machine that I saw at a trade show – and I don't even know if this counts – was Sega Europe [which] was in the United States with the new *Virtua Tennis*, and it was basically in a stand-up candy cabinet. And I asked a Sega representative – and again, this is Sega UK – if they were selling to the United States, and they forwarded me around to a few other people at the Sega booth and I never really got an answer. So it sounds like if you're in the United States and you want a new classic arcade [game] that was being produced, you'd have to have it imported specifically and pay a lot of money.

But most [arcade] operators would agree that it's very hard to make your money back. If you're shelling out $10,000 for an upright arcade machine that does not give tickets or any kind of prize, you're basically burning your money unless it's a thing that you're direly passionate about. There are a lot of novelty games still being made in the United States, and when I say "novelty" it kind of groups together shooting and racing games, based off of movies primarily. I don't mean to throw Raw Thrills under the bus, but anything you find by Raw Thrills lately has felt like a cash grab. They revived *Cruis'n* – the Nintendo series *Cruis'n* is coming back, I believe just as an arcade game. That could go very well or very poorly.

**Overstreet:** You also have a full lineup of pinball machines. Why was it important for you to include pinball in your arcade lineup?
**EH:** I think pinball is not only a staple of the American arcade industry, but it's a frequently overlooked staple in American history. And I think it's very important to preserve the older generation of pinball machines, and to make sure that machines that are currently being manufactured see the light of day and stay maintained. A lot of people forget that pinball's a thing, and people will be like, "Oh, yeah, my dad had one in his basement and it has been dead for 20 years, and we use it as a table." That's what the majority of people think about pinball.

We're trying to make it more accessible for people. We're including pinball in our roster of games to take to conventions. I think we're the first major arcade rental company that has offered totally restored pinballs as part of our lineup, and the response has been amazing.

**Overstreet:** Do you find that people are either pinball customers or video game customers? Or is there a lot of crossover there?
**EH:** There's a lot of crossover. But usually if you're passionate about a specific thing, that's what you're gonna zone in on. And some people are really passionate about pinball, some people are really passionate about music games, other people are really passionate about fighting games. And we'll see retail customers that come in here and they'll just grab handfuls of PlayStation 2 games, and it might be because they can't afford anything else and they thought the $5 rack is really awesome, but on the other hand it might be because they really, really like that system.

**Overstreet:** Are there any really unique or oddball arcade cabinets out there?
**EH:** Oh, extremely. There's a ton of really dumb stuff. You don't have to dig very far into the arcade industry or the video game industry to find a story, and a lot of these stories have been covered on the internet... I guess this very strange side of the video game industry, if you hang around it in any capacity, you are bound to learn way more than you cared to know. And you're absolutely bound to start hearing crazy stories about people that have been doing this for longer than you've been alive. There are crazy tales.

**Overstreet:** What would you consider your favorite cabinet, and why?
**EH:** Well, there's a difference between a game and a cabinet. If I had to pick a specific video arcade cabinet that I considered my favorite, it would probably be based on the design of said cabinet. It would have to be Konami's six-player *X-Men* machine.

A little bit of backstory there: I think Konami had already released *Teenage Mutant Ninja Turtles* and *The Simpsons*, and *X-Men* was their next project. And the previous beat-'em-up games you could get in a two-player variant board or a four-player variant board, and they thought it would be really cool to make a dedicated six-player showcase machine for their new *X-Men* game.

This was before widescreen monitors or LCD TVs existed, and they had the brilliant idea to project a second CRT off of a mirror that was mounted at a 45-degree angle to simulate a widescreen. It's a really crazy thing if you look at it, it's real easy to find images of it. But we're talking about a machine that was released in the 1990s and it's a theoretical widescreen – until you look in the middle where the two screens meet. CRTs are infamous for having warped edges and weird convergence issues, and you have to dial in the colors manually on these arcade CRTs. So you could very easily tell, "Wait a minute, this is two TVs mounted together." But for weight distribution reasons one is mounted in the bottom of the cabinet, and the CRT's yoke connector is flipped, so it displays an inverted image that then bounces off a mirror that will display the correct image. And the second monitor is just flat mounted into the back of the machine. It's a nightmare to move and it's a nightmare to set up, but it's a pretty amazing design.

But yeah, I'd have to say that's my favorite cabinet. Definitely not my favorite arcade game – it's in the top 10 but it's not my favorite game.

**Overstreet:** In that case, what is your favorite arcade game?
**EH:** *Space Harrier. Space Harrier* is incredible and the arcade machine is the best way to play it.

Sega was known for going above and beyond, really shelling out a lot of money when it came to designing their boards. Most people don't realize, but when Nintendo and Sega and other companies used to make these games in the late '80s and early '90s, every single board was proprietary, which meant that every single board was its own unique project. So engineers worked on specific boards for specific games. It wasn't until later in the arcade industry's life – usually you see these board in the late '90s to the early 2000s, before they switched over to computers – [when] the boards became universal systems much like you'd see with the Sega Genesis. There were many arcade-specific game systems that people aren't aware of. The Neo Geo AES is sort of a byproduct of the MVS, which was the arcade version.

A lot of people don't realize that the Dreamcast was kind of a front for something that Sega's arcade division was working on called the NAOMI, where Sega went to different publishers and said, "Here's our concept for this NAOMI system, we're going to make a home version of it too. It's going to be great!" And they were definitely right on track – other than Sony releasing the PlayStation 2. That's why *Marvel vs. Capcom 2* has held its value on the Dreamcast, because it's actually a direct port of the NAOMI game which is theoretically the same hardware that the Dreamcast is.

Getting back to *Space Harrier*, it was a very expensive game to produce. It's very immersive, it's very strange, [and] it feels like an otherworldly experience – which was the kind of thing that people really sought after back in the day when your options were *Centipede* or *Missile Command* or *Space Invaders. Space Harrier* was almost like a dream compared to these other games.

**Overstreet:** What do people need to keep in mind if they plan to include arcade cabinets in a collection?
**EH:** Expect failure. Expect failure and an extreme loss of money. And if you're getting into pinball, multiply that times ten. Don't try to tell yourself that it's all going to stay contained in that wooden box, because it's not. And before you know it, your kitchen is going to be full of arcade machines. Maybe not arcade machines, but boards, cartridges, wiring harnesses, all sorts of crazy stuff. There's always hidden expenses with this stuff. And if you get more than one machine, you're going to find yourself either shelling out a lot of money to get CRTs repaired or you're going to find yourself able to repair CRTs – and that alone is not for the faint of heart.

I shouldn't be trying to steer people away from it, but do your research and know what you're getting into before you make a purchase like that, because they are expensive and they are extremely hard to maintain on occasion. You could get lucky. You could get a newer machine and not have to deal with a monitor, because it's got an LCD in it.

Arcade machines are amazing to have around. But do your research before you make a purchase, and make sure that, worst case scenario, there's people in the area – or you have people lined up on the internet – to do repairs.

# THE JAPANESE VIDEO GAME MARKET

BY KURT KALATA

Japanese video games have seen somewhat of an exodus from their home country. The *Famicomblog* website compared the trend to woodblock prints, which were exported in great numbers in the 19th century after Japan opened their borders. The Japanese did not place great value on these at the time, with no real local marketplace, but they were able to sell to the foreign buyers who found them unique and desirable.

Over an extended period of time, so many of these had left the country that any Japanese collectors needed to re-import them back, often at hugely inflated costs. It's entirely possible something similar may happen to video games. As of 2016, that hasn't quite happened to those lengths, but the trends in the market show that that may become the future, as the Japanese and non-Japanese markets have become intertwined.

The biggest, most obvious reason is the increased ease of importing. There are many native sellers in Japan who specifically cater to overseas buyers via well-respected eBay stores that have been around for a decade or more. However, with these sellers typically comes either a markup, or competition with other bidders that drive up prices. There have always been games that have been expensive in Japan, but due to these factors, they are even more expensive in foreign markets.

However, while Japan has been slow to adopt the internet in the same way that other countries have, they have finally caught up to the online marketplace. Amazon Japan has just as many retro games as other Amazon sites around globe, plus there's Japan's own online marketplace, Rakuten. Other sites focused on video game and anime goods have also expanded and proliferated over the years. Some of these actively court overseas buyers, while others only ship within Japan. The reasons for this are varied and complex, ranging from simply not wanting to deal with the extra paperwork that comes with inter-national shipping, to just not wanting to deal with foreigners.

With this, another industry has stepped in - package forwarding services, which act as an intermediary. For a small fee, they'll give you a Japanese address, then forward any packages to overseas buyers. One service, Buyee, has even become more easily integrated with Yahoo Auctions (the Japanese equivalent to eBay), making it much easier to navigate the arcane landscape of payment and shipping.

Other technological advancements have been made over the past few years. The biggest one being the advancement of online translators, like Google Translate, that allow one to navigate the language well enough to order packages, as well as Japanese banks' greater acceptance of non-Japanese credit cards (though many are still wary of services like PayPal).

The end result of this is that you have many more non-Japanese buyers that can obtain Japanese video games straight from the source. This is great for collectors, but also allowed resellers to build up their stock and add their own markup.

It's also hard to pin down exactly when the retro game boom happened, but it also coincided with the weakening of the Japanese yen. In July of 2011, the conversion rate was approximately 78 yen to $1 US, which is abysmal. However by mid-2013 it has risen to 100 yen, then up to 120 by 2015. The huge strengthening of the dollar made it that

much cheaper to import games, and especially for re-sellers, make the profit even larger. With these, even more games have left Japan.

So far we've just been talking in broad terms, but there have been specific cases of rare games causing a spillover of demand for Japanese titles. Much of it comes from the fact that specific games, especially SNES games, have become so expensive on the American marketplace that some collectors have chosen to import their Super Famicom counterparts instead. This is not desirable in the case of text-heavy games like RPGs, so games like *Chrono Trigger* and *Final Fantasy VI* remain unaffected, but for action games and shoot-em-ups, it remains a viable alternative. For example, Japanese cartridges of *Rockman X2* and *X3* are a fraction of the cost of the American *Megaman X2* and *X3*. This remains doubly so for anyone who collects CIB copies, as the Super Famicom artwork is typically superior to their Super Nintendo counterparts.

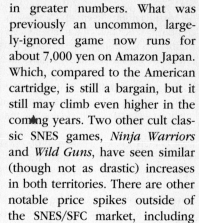

On the low end this generally only has a minor effect, as *Rockman X2* and *X3* can currently still be found for between 1,500-2,000 yen. Which is to say, slightly more expensive than they used to be a few years ago, but still cheap. However, it definitely affects the high end. Mega Drive games like *Alien Soldier, Battlemania Daiginjou* and *Panorama Cotton* have been in the triple digit range for a very long time even in Japan, but their prices have climbed even more in recent years. This has also caused much inflated prices for arcade boards, which is a far smaller market, but with wealthier buyers.

The reasons for this range from the broadening of information, as foreign audiences become more aware of Japan-only titles, to collectors, who simply want to complete their collection. There is little functional value in owning *Vampire Killer* for the Mega Drive, since it's almost identical to the American counterpart, *Castlevania Bloodlines*, but it is a matter of pride for *Castlevania* collectors.

There is at least one specific example of an in-demand game causing price spikes on the Japanese side - the late generation SNES title *Hagane*. According to Video Game Price Charts, as of 2008, the value was about $15 for a loose cartridge. In 2011, the value suddenly spiked to about $100, and it's been rising slowly ever since, which, in 2016, is currently pegged at around $400.

In Japan, as of 2013, this game could also be found cheaply, around 1,000 yen for a bare cart from online sources. But eventually overseas gamers, unable to afford an American cartridge, began importing copies of the game in greater numbers. What was previously an uncommon, largely-ignored game now runs for about 7,000 yen on Amazon Japan. Which, compared to the American cartridge, is still a bargain, but it still may climb even higher in the coming years. Two other cult classic SNES games, *Ninja Warriors* and *Wild Guns*, have seen similar (though not as drastic) increases in both territories. There are other notable price spikes outside of the SNES/SFC market, including *Elevator Action Returns* for the Saturn, which was a 3,000 yen title in 2013 that has dectupled in price to 30,000 yen as of 2016.

Altogether, how much of this is precisely due to influence from overseas is debatable, but the wider market and dwindling supply definitely allows for fiercer competition between both native and foreign buyers.

Incidentally, this is mostly a one way street when it comes to markets affecting each other – foreign markets only really affect Japan. Though some Japanese collectors do import American or European titles, their numbers are currently very small, not enough to have noticeable effect on their home market. There are scattered cases of Western games that are in-demand in Japan, particularly Sega Master System titles like *Sagaia, Power Strike II, OutRun 3D* and *Ninja Gaiden*. These are Japanese-developed titles in popular series that were only released in Europe and Australia, and they are some of the pricier games on the platform. However, these are also desired by collectors within Europe and Australia, and to a lesser extent North America, so it doesn't appear as if Japan is specifically the cause for these cases.

Overall, it's simply important for collectors to keep in mind that overseas buyers are having a significant impact on many titles within the Japanese market – and that buying a Japanese cartridge just in order to have any copy in your possession might not be as good of a deal anymore as you might have once thought.

# VIDEO GAME GLOSSARY

**AI (Artificial Intelligence):** A level of how smart computer-controlled characters behave in-game.

**Anime:** A style of Japanese cartoon; many Japanese-produced games are said to have an "anime aesthetic"

**Backwards compatible**: A term used to describe a gaming system that supports games made for the previous generation or version of that company's system.

**Beat'Em'Up:** Generally used to describe 2D fighters (such as *Streets of Rage*) where the goal is simply to beat up and knock out all enemies on the screen in order to move forward.

**Boss:** Term generally used to describe the final and toughest enemy character of a given area.

**Bullet Hell**: A type of shoot'em'up where the goal is more about dodging the immense numbers of enemy projectiles rather than about defeating the enemy itself. Games in this genre include *Radiant Silvergun* and *Ikaruga*; other terms used here include "maniac shooters" and "danmaku."

**Cel-Shaded:** A graphic style aimed at looking like classic cartoons, where things are brightly colored and often feature a thick black outline.

**Console:** A dedicated video game system. Generally this term does not apply to PCs or handheld systems.

**Cute'Em'Up:** A style of shoot'em'up that features cutesy, bright graphics and often features anime-styled characters.

**Cut Scene:** A narrative intermission that helps to move the story forward. Generally these are not interactive and are simply meant to be observed.

**E3**: Shorthand for Electronic Entertainment Expo, a large video game industry gathering and convention.

**ESRB:** The Entertainment Software Ratings Board, an organization dedicated to rating games for appropriate audiences.

**FPS:** Shorthand for first-person shooter.

**First-Person:** Point of view in which you see the action directly through the eyes of the character. First-person games do not let you see your own body save for maybe your hands.

**Isometric view:** Looking at the game action in a diagonal overhead view rather than purely viewing things at the side or straight overhead.

**JRPG:** Japanese Role-Playing Game. The term is often used to describe RPGs that feature anime-style art and turn-based combat, compared to western RPGs which do not.

**Mod/Modding:** Files (or the process of creating those files) to change or add to a game, written by people who do not work for the company that developed that game.

**MMORPG:** Massively Multiplayer Online Role-Playing Game. Common shorthand is using just "MMO." Games in this genre allow players around the world to come together to role-play characters in an online environment. Examples include *World of Warcraft* and *Everquest*.

**NPC:** Non-player character; any character that the player does not control, usually under the control of the computer AI system.

**Pack-in game**: A game that comes packaged with a system purchase.

**Platforming game:** A game that requires jumping on and navigating platforms in order to reach the end. Can be either 2D or 3D. Major examples of this genre include *Super Mario Bros.*, *Sonic the Hedgehog*, and *Spyro the Dragon*.

**Pre-rendered**: A term used to describe graphics that are static and unmoving and only viewed from a certain angle. Many environments in games throughout the 1990s used pre-rendered areas, such as in the *Final Fantasy* games for the PlayStation.

**Real-Time:** A game where the action does not stop to allow the player to enter specific commands. This is the opposite of "turn-based."

**RPG:** Role-Playing Game. Generally lengthy adventures with in-depth narratives and lots of character development.

**Shmup:** Slang for shoot'em'up.

**Shoulder buttons**: Most controllers since the 1990s have featured buttons located on either side of the controller, facing away from the player. These are also called "triggers" and are generally used as action-focused buttons in a variety of games.

**Third-person:** The opposite of first-person; this perspective puts the player perspective outside of the character they control, usually with the camera above or behind the shoulder of the character.

**Turn-based**: Games where the action pauses to allow players to enter specific commands. The opposite of "real-time."

**Twin-stick control:** A game that uses two analog sticks in order to control the character. Generally one stick will dictate the character's movement while the other dictates the specific direction they're looking at.